ANY QUESTIONS?

ANY QUESTIONS?

Michael Bowen

with

David Jacobs

Robson Books

FIRST PUBLISHED IN GREAT BRITAIN IN 1981 BY ROBSON BOOKS LTD., BOLSOVER HOUSE, 5-6 CLIPSTONE STREET, LONDON W1P 7EB.

British Library Cataloguing in Publication Data
Jacobs, David
Any questions.
1. Any questions (Radio program)
I. Title II. Bowen, Michael
791.44'72 PN1991.77.A/

ISBN 0-86051-156-1

Phototypesetting by Strewlight Ltd., London W1

Printed by The Garden City Press Limited
Letchworth, Hertfordshire SG6 1JS

AUTHOR'S NOTE

My thanks are due to the panellists, and the next of kin of panellists who have died, for saying they were happy for me to quote from their contributions to the programme. I hope that any next of kin I was unable to trace will share my belief that their relative would have liked to be included. In return, I would ask the reader to remember that these are remarks made off the cuff without any specific preparation, some of them many years ago; also, that they are only extracts from longer discussions – to print them in full would have required a book of inordinate length. Freed from the BBC's need for balance, I have picked on what seems to me now particularly worth recalling, individual contributions no less than team discussions. It is bound to be an arbitrary selection as there is so much good material. I regret that so many valued contributors had to be omitted solely through the limitations of space and I hope to include them in a future volume.

I am also grateful to Frank Gillard, inventor of *Any Questions?*, for checking the manuscript and for much help and advice; and to Nicholas Crocker, the first producer, for telling me about his experiences.

Any Questions? people have a habit of being knighted and, in due course, ennobled. I am calling them by the name by which they were known at the time of the particular broadcast. When referring to them at other times, as this is an informal sort of book, I call them what I would call them in conversation.

Okehampton, Devon. July 1981 MICHAEL BOWEN

INTRODUCTION

If you walk through the impressive main doors of Broadcasting House in Portland Place, the headquarters of the BBC in London, and take one of the two front lifts to the third floor, you will be greeted on your arrival by the bust of that most formidable of past Director-Generals, Lord Reith. It's a daunting sight, his eyes seem to follow you as you pass, and you pass only to visit the Director-General or the Governor's Board Room. I made my first appearance on radio in 1944 and I've experienced the rarefied atmosphere of the third floor less than a dozen times, and those only in the last few years. The faded patterned carpet softens your tread as you acknowledge Lord Reith's gaze.

It's very different in Broadcasting House in Whiteladies Road, Bristol. Several Georgian houses are joined together to form the headquarters of the BBC's West Region. On the mantelpiece in its Board Room is the bust of Freddy Grisewood, a contemporary of the great Lord Reith. Freddy's likeness is so welcoming that one feels like going up to it and having a chat and that, I think, is one of the secrets of the success not only of *Any Questions?* but of the West Region itself. Freddy was what I believe radio broadcasting is all about; he was the friend who talked to you when you were often alone and kept you company. He was the man who introduced you to people you might otherwise never have met. He was your host and at certain times your guide to places beyond your reach. It's a friendly place, B.H. in Bristol. It's large enough to produce some of the best television and radio programmes for the national networks and yet small enough for the commissionaire to know everybody by first name. It's that bust of Freddy that does it. Our masters wouldn't have put it there in the first place if they didn't think so, too; and why move it now when it's doing such a good job?

It was the voice of Freddy Grisewood that I heard one evening in 1948 as I drove through the Devon lanes on a journey to Plymouth. He was chairing a new discussion programme on the West of England Home Service. Little did I think then that the programme would still be running over thirty years later and that I would be its chairman, sitting in Freddy's seat. I've been occupying it for nearly fourteen years and they still think of me as the new boy.

The rules of the game really haven't changed much over the years. We invite people we want to meet in the hope and belief that our listeners will want to meet them, too. We try to entertain our teams in a way that will be conducive to good discussion and make their sometimes tedious and wearisome journeys worth while. If we can give them an enjoyable time, then we hope they will return the compliment and give us one, in turn. That doesn't always happen. As in most things, even the best of speakers can be in a dull mood and make what looks on paper to be a team of first XI proportions little better than a group of third division reserves. Mind you, the audiences can just as easily make or break a programme. If they are unfriendly and unwelcoming – a rare occurrence – even four of the biggest stars would fail to move them. I can usually tell the mood of the audience within a minute of going on stage. I have a little joke – I use the same one every week, it's like a mother putting her elbow into the baby's bath water to test the temperature. Whenever it fails, I know that either the microphones aren't working properly or we are in for a difficult time.

I'm often asked if I ever get bored with the programme and I have to admit that I don't – how could I, when each week it's a different location with four different people on the stage and a different group in the audience? Just think of the people I meet and the stories I hear. The mixture – that's what I like about it. I like to hear what a famous actress has to say about solving the problem of inflation or Northern Ireland, just as much as I like to hear with whom a former Cabinet Minister would like to be shipwrecked on a desert island. The programme is very revealing and I have a sneaking suspicion it's here to stay.

August 1981 DAVID JACOBS

1948–1953

When Frank Gillard, Head of Programmes at the BBC, Bristol, rang Freddy Grisewood in the summer of 1948 to invite him to become the travelling questionmaster of a new discussion programme, he assured him that it couldn't possibly last for more than six editions. It was a stopgap, to fill an empty space in the West of England Home Service. When I joined that programme as producer in April 1953, it had clocked up 168 performances. It is still going strong, after thirty-three years. *Any Questions?* is surely the longest-running stopgap in radio history.

Why has it lasted so long? Freddy himself thought it was like a lucky dip – you never knew what was coming up. The two men who alternated for several years to give each programme a solid foundation of West Country rural common sense, Ralph Wightman and Arthur Street, both thought its success demonstrated the streak of cruelty in human beings, who were hoping the team would make asses of themselves. Mary Stocks, undoubtedly the most popular woman to appear on the programme, said its charm lay in the fact that one's indiscretions cannot be suppressed because it is broadcast live.

(DJ: *I think it's because it is a perfect format. And unlike the flour that never varies,* Any Questions? *is different each week, and it's because of those different places we go to and the completely different personnel each week that it has such an infinite variety.*)

The first programme on 12 October 1948, came from Winchester, with a team consisting of Naomi Royde-Smith, the novelist, who lived in the city, Honor Croome of *The Economist*, Jack Longland, then Chief Education Officer for Dorset, and John Arlott at that time a BBC talks producer and, of course, a Hampshire man. It was to be a long time before there were again two women on the team.

In the wartime *Brains Trust* (originally called *Any Questions?*) the team had sat in the cosy isolation of a studio. That evening at Winchester the presence of the audience and the fact that the team was confronted by the questioners revitalized the formula in precisely the way Frank Gillard had hoped, and he was sure they were on to a winner. At the end of the half-hour, while the members of the team were thankfully sipping drinks in the Mayor's Parlour, he was on the phone to the *Radio Times* printers, where the presses were already rolling, to extend the next programme, a fortnight later, to forty-five minutes.

There was soon no more thought of a limit of six editions. Frank's aim became more ambitious – to attract a mass audience and, by making the programme as entertaining as possible, to set up a wave of conversation in millions of homes where perhaps they wouldn't listen to conventional talks programmes. The first producer was Nicholas Crocker, and he and Frank had eighteen months to develop and mould the programme in the comparative obscurity of Regional broadcasting. It gradually became more topical – hints to the audience that questions on current affairs were more likely to be selected than purely general ones had their effect – and this became an important factor in the programme's longevity. The number of politicians on the panel increased. Teams were gradually persuaded to *discuss* issues rather than deliver four separate monologues. John Arlott appeared every week at this formative time, and with his producer's instinct was able to help shape the discussion by his own example. Jack Longland was also helpful.

In June 1950, the Friday evening broadcast moved on to the Basic Home Service, heard all over the country. But the real breakthrough came three months later on 22 September when *Any Questions?* moved to the Light

Programme, with a repeat on the Basic Home Service on Tuesdays. Within quite a short time, sixteen million people were regularly listening to the programme. Frank Gillard had got his mass audience.

Then followed the golden years of *Any Questions?* when it made front-page news and made or marred reputations overnight. It created its own stars – MPs, journalists and, above all, the duo of Street and Wightman. MPs who were seldom or never invited became very jealous of those who appeared frequently.

At that time, there was virtually no other discussion of current affairs for a mass audience on the air, and whenever a news story broke during the week, millions of people asked themselves: 'I wonder what the *Any Questions?* team will have to say about it on Friday?'

By the time I came on the scene, the golden years were numbered, as television's increasing domination steadily eroded the radio audience. It became more and more difficult to make our own stars, until the time came when we had to cash in on those who were already well known, and that often meant those who appeared on television. If *Any Questions?* was to survive it needed to feature Top People, and in the Sixties and Seventies a lot of people were Top People because of television. ('Famous for being famous,' as a later Controller of Radio 4, Ian McIntyre, was to say witheringly about our television personalities.)

I have always thought that once you had to explain in detail who the members of the *Any Questions?* team were, the programme would be doomed. Frank Gillard once told me that he liked to feel that the team knew more about what was going on in the world than he as a listener did. I was more delighted to secure people in positions of power and influence for the team, almost irrespective of their broadcasting ability, than an unknown who happened to be able to speak well. Occasionally, one has an instinct that someone relatively unknown will do well (not always justified in the event), but the less well known a person is, the better he needs to be. I have never regretted inviting someone with real star quality who has turned out to be a flop. The mere fact that he is a flop is not without interest – there is a curiosity value in learning what views he has (or whether he has any views at all), whether he has a sense of humour, and so on. Whereas if obscure Professor Joe Bloggs, recommended by an earnest colleague, turns out to be a dead loss, there is no curiosity value and it is an unmitigated disaster.

I used to get letters from listeners saying they knew of people who needed the money more than the people we used and why didn't we use them instead? The whole point about the *Any Questions?* people is that ideally they don't need the money and they don't need the publicity. The people we most want are the busiest and most sought after. Their glamour and personality keep *Any Questions?* going. But we cannot rely exclusively on established reputations. For one thing, the average age of the teams mustn't be too high. One wants, as well, people not yet old enough to be in *Who's Who*, but with the prospect of making it before long. I feel some pride in having spotted early such future notables as Shirley Williams, Sir Geoffrey Howe and Jeremy Thorpe, who all appeared on *Any Questions?* quite some time before they were MPs.

The organization of the programme has changed remarkably little over the years. A dinner-party beforehand – much to the fury of our more economy-minded listeners – but how are you to produce an after-dinner conversation, which is what *Any Questions?* really is, if you don't have dinner first? It is over dinner, under the chairman's benign influence, that four individuals gradually merge into a team. I am all for saving the licence-payers' money, but money spent on giving the listeners a better programme is never wasted.

About half-way through the dinner-party, the producer, secretary and a statutory BBC official reluctantly abandon all thought of pudding and go to the hall. The audience hand in their questions at the entrance. The producer reads through all of them and chooses twelve for the broadcast. While the question sorting is going on, the BBC official goes on to the stage and does his (or her) best to answer any question about the BBC which the audience care to ask. Then the producer comes on stage, reads out the names of the questioners and they come and sit in the front row in the likely order in which they will go on the air. The chairman and the team make their appearance, there is a rehearsal question to play the team in and provide a voice balance test for the engineers (in the early days, the team merely expressed their rapture at finding themselves in that particular place), and then a flashing red light indicates that the broadcast is about to begin.

(DJ: *I'm often infuriated by the fact that the rehearsal question, chosen because it wasn't a particularly good one, turns out to be answered so fruitfully that one wishes one had got it in the programme. Perhaps it is the mere fact of it not being on the air that makes the team slightly more loose tongued.*)

Do the members of the team see the questions beforehand? No, they do not. And when one considers some of the answers, I find it quite extraordinary that anyone should doubt this. Perhaps they didn't hear John Arlott speaking about the effect of the fluoridization of water on tea, having misheard the questioner who had asked about its effect on teeth.

Mind you, there is nothing to stop the team trying to guess what the questions are going to be and the conversation over drinks before dinner often consists of this sort of speculation. (Tony Benn traditionally comes armed with a list of about fifty possibles.) Wise team members guard against telling their best stories over dinner in case an unscrupulous colleague gets in first with it on the air.

Any Questions? is not an authoritative programme – how could it be when the team members are chosen long before the producer has any idea what subjects they will be called upon to discuss? Therefore, it is better that they should not know the questions in advance, because this gives a genuine spontaneity to the replies, and I use the word 'genuine' deliberately. Tempting though it might be to plant a question which the team had all agreed beforehand would stimulate an excellent discussion, nevertheless, if nobody in the audience submitted it then we just had to do without.

When sorting out the questions each week I tried to choose those which would give each member of the team a chance to contribute something. In the early days, one of them quite often opted out of the discussion – Dr Bronowski never hesitated to remain silent on any question which failed to capture his interest and Anthony Crosland and Trevor Huddlestone both tended to dismiss with disdain any frivolous question. If someone passed, I had an uneasy feeling that either I'd chosen the wrong question or the wrong chap. People often remarked, 'I have nothing to add to what's already been said,' and then spent three minutes proving it, but it seemed to me that everyone we considered worth inviting should be capable of having a go at everything in a reasonably entertaining and stimulating way. I always used to tell the team, semi-facetiously, not to be inhibited by facts. I regarded it as an opportunity for the airing of prejudices.

Even the dreaded 'funnies' – dreaded, that is, by the team; the listeners rightly regarded them as an essential ingredient for the sake of contrast – were of a kind which gave the team a chance to make a relatively serious point if they couldn't think of anything witty.

(DJ: *It's rather fun to hear, say, a former Chancellor of the Exchequer having to discuss mini skirts, for example. Their answers can be almost as revealing as the skirts!*)

Someone who was never at a loss, whatever the question, was Bob Boothby. If I were forced to name one person above all others as the star of *Any Questions?* it would have to be Bob. In his book *Recollections of a Rebel* (Hutchinson), he quoted a letter from me in which I said it was no coincidence that in most of the outstanding editions in my memory the name of Boothby was to be found in the team. He also wrote that Freddy Grisewood ensured that he was regularly in the team. Not so. The producer, not the chairman, selects the team.

(DJ: *Very often I've suggested several people to Michael but they never saw the light of day – or the red light of the programme! But I certainly would agree about Bob. Something extraordinary happened when one heard his first words in that remarkable voice – you knew you were in for a good time. His voice is often imitated – I've imitated it myself – and people start laughing right away.*)

Bob Boothby was so successful because he genuinely relished the occasion and he particularly enjoyed playing up to the audience. Appearing on *Any Questions?* you need to cultivate the audience, make them laugh, shape your sentences and build up to a climax so that they will applaud. You must allow them to inspire you – as Frank Gillard had hoped they would.

This is not to say that many successful members of the team are not nervous. Frank Byers, later to be the Liberal leader in the House of Lords, was so nervous before each programme that he couldn't eat any dinner.

By the beginning of its fifth year, in September 1952, *Any Questions?* had become one of the country's top radio programmes, its prestige was at its height and, if anyone had told me then that within six months I should be producing it, I should have thought they weren't quite right in the head. There is no organization quite like the BBC for giving somebody with limited talent the opportunity for rubbing shoulders with the Great.

I had early in 1951 thrown up my job on the *Western Daily Press*, where I was theatre correspondent, and also military correspondent ('Rather like being racing correspondent of the *Church Times*,' the Master of Hickstead, Douglas Bunn, once remarked to me) in order to produce and introduce a weekly programme about the Festival of Britain from the BBC, Bristol. After six months I went freelance, joining the staff permanently in the autumn of 1952 as a reporter. Nicholas Crocker moved over to television and in February 1953, I was appointed to the vacant job of Outside Broadcasts Producer, which included the production of *Any Questions?*.

April 3, which was Good Friday, was the first occasion my name was printed in *Radio Times* as producer of *Any Questions?*. I put it that way because it was really rather a courtesy title. I spent the broadcast as a member of the audience, although no doubt I assisted in choosing the questions. Frank Gillard sat on the chairman's left on the platform, where the producer always sits.

Frank, and his Assistant Head of Programmes, Bill

Coysh, had been producing the programme between them over the previous year, when Nicky Crocker was away on a television course. Since the programme began, they had exercised a certain amount of supervision over him, and they continued to exercise it over me. It was frustrating, but understandable. The political parties, in particular, scrutinized the programme very closely for any sign of bias. And any idea that the selection of the teams, the choice of locations, the composition of the audience and the selection of questions were all at the whim of a fairly obscure ex-journalist in Bristol was entirely contrary to the BBC's tradition of editorial responsibility resting finally with the Director-General in London down a complicated channel of command through the London hierarchy and the Regional Controller and Head of Programmes in Bristol.

It was quite a relief when, in July 1970, I was appointed Network Radio Editor in Bristol and in effect became my own immediate boss, because I decided to carry on producing *Any Questions?* for the time being. There were still people watching over me but the reins were fairly loose, and in the period between autumn 1970 and autumn 1977, when I handed over the production to one of my staff, Carole Stone, the choice of teams, questions and locations was very largely mine. Whatever was wrong with the programme during that period was my fault, nobody else's. The same cannot be said of my first seventeen years as producer. For example, I was leaned on from above to drop Arthur Street and the farmer and novelist, Robert Henriques, against my own judgement, and I am sorry I didn't put up a stronger fight.

When Carole took over, I continued to exercise the kind of supervision which had been exercised over me, but to a lesser extent. By then the programme had lost much of its power and therefore the pitfalls were shallower. It was, as one distinguished team member is apt to say in another connection, 'entirely a question of numbers'. The number of listeners in November 1977 was about one eighth of the April 1953 total.

Even so, Carole was warned by no less an authority than

the Director-General, Ian Trethowan, that *Any Questions?* was still a hot potato. Unlike the producers of other potentially dangerous programmes which are studio based, the producer of *Any Questions?* is out on a limb, with no advice available from anyone on the spot except the colleague doing the warm-up, with a live broadcast and therefore no escape route through last-minute editing. It is, now I come to think of it, distinctly odd that I, who have always yearned for a quiet life, should have found myself landed with the responsibility for one of the BBC's most controversial programmes. Some time in 1960, I began to get a series of bad headaches, and went to a neurologist. After I had spent days in hospital under observation and undergone numerous tests, he issued his report to my doctor: 'If I had his job, my headaches would be far, far worse.'

1953/54

It was on that Good Friday in 1953 that I first met Freddy Grisewood, by then probably the most popular broadcaster in the country. Freddy was the ideal chairman. He had great charm, a beautiful incisive voice and much experience as an announcer and commentator which he was always ready to pass on to newcomers to the programme. He soothed the nervous ones, and those who had never met him before soon felt they had known him all their lives. He was always calm and courteous and inspired great respect and affection from team, listeners and audiences, who particularly loved the stories he told in Cotswold dialect before each broadcast.

Once, in answer to a question about improvements to the human body, Mary Stocks had suggested grease points for arthritic joints. Freddy must have approved – he suffered dreadfully from arthritis, but bore the continual pain with great fortitude and never complained, though his grey, drawn face often showed he was in a bad way. I can still picture him waving his stick cheerily in greeting as he limped along the station platform where I was meeting him.

There was no problem in establishing friendly relations with Freddy that day in 1953, but it was a strong, somewhat daunting team which confronted me on my first appearance as the producer of *Any Questions?*: Bob Boothby, Lady Violet Bonham Carter, Tom Driberg and Arthur Street. Bob, Lady Violet and Driberg drove down together to Minehead in Somerset and it appeared that Tom, a devout Anglo-Catholic, insisted on stopping at numerous churches on the way and going in to pray. Lady Violet stayed in the car. 'The idea of being *à trois* with God and Tom Driberg did not appeal,' she explained afterwards.

Lady Violet Bonham Carter, whom I tended to call (though never in her presence) 'Lady Vi', was a formidable figure for a young and inexperienced producer to meet on his first outing. The daughter of an earl and former Prime Minister (Asquith) and a leading figure among the Liberals, she was invariably very gracious to me. She tended to speak in italics ('*dear* Mr Bowen') and would thrust her face, with its rather prominent nose, very close to the person she was talking to. Bob told me of someone who, tired of the relentless proximity of her face at the dinner table, took a spoonful of soup and thrust it into her mouth.

I once rather daringly described the delivery of another member of the team to her as 'verbal diarrhoea'. She did not flinch and agreed that it was a very apt phrase. She herself did not relish being interrupted on the programme – few dared make the attempt – and the rules were gladly bent in her favour so that she could talk for as long as she desired. The transcript of her contributions always read like a beautifully constructed essay. When she spoke, you were listening to history. Of all the *Any Questions?* panellists, she was the one who was utterly irreplaceable.

(DJ: *When I first met Lady Violet on the team I thought she might be a bit snooty, but there she was, angular, very warm and friendly, and I got the* dear *Mr Jacobs treatment straight away. I was warned that she was the one person I must never interrupt, but I never found a need, because I was mesmerized by her replies.*)

Tom Driberg, too, was distinguished. The original writer of the William Hickey column in the *Daily Express* and a prominent back-bench left-wing MP, he was a fluent speaker but I found his lugubrious voice distinctly off-putting. He came to resent the fact that I invited him less frequently than Nicky Crocker had. (If it comes to that, hardly anyone appears on *Any Questions?* as often as he feels he should.)

It was a good programme, and one of the questions concerned an issue still controversial twenty-eight years later: 'Does the team consider that the request put forward for an increase of salary for MPs is justified?'

Lady Violet said that, being the trustees of the national income, MPs should be very cautious about voting themselves a fat increase, and if they did do it, they should pledge that when the cost of living went down their salary went down with it.

Tom Driberg said a thousand a year was not enough for an MP to live on and do his job properly because so much of it went on expenses.

Bob Boothby said that when he came into the House of Commons in 1924 it was more of a vocation – now it had become almost completely a profession. It was a hard life and a very dangerous one, because it might end at any General Election. A lot of youngish people who ought to be coming into public life weren't considering it because of the life the MPs had to lead. He thought that the amenities should be improved, and that they should get their secretarial assistance free, as well as postage, note-paper and travel. Then they could think about more cash later on.

Lady Violet agreed they had a hard life 'But whose fault is that? It's partly their own fault. They're the slaves of the Whips. They show no freedom or independence, and they march through the Lobbies like an army of robots. There are none of the old, free minds which used to be in Parliament in the old days.' She advocated devolving some of their work on to other bodies. 'Local governments in Scotland and Wales could take on a lot of it.'

The next programme was from Gosport, Hampshire, where Herbert Morrison, the wartime Home Secretary, was the newcomer. We had a question on the seven-year sentence imposed on Jomo Kenyatta for organizing Mau-Mau. Herbert Morrison at once pointed out that there was an appeal pending against the sentence; it was therefore *sub judice* and in his opinion shouldn't be discussed. It wasn't.

This was the occasion when a questioner turned out to

have a dreadful stammer, but doggedly insisted on persevering to the end. It was, needless to say, the longest question of the evening.

After the last of the series on 17 April, there was a summer break of five months (steadily reduced over the years to six weeks), so my brief association with *Any Questions?* was suspended almost as soon as it had begun. But enough had happened already to show me that there were a lot of submerged rocks for the producer to bark his shins on.

However, at the beginning of the new series, back in Winchester, I was still closely protected from any harm by Frank Gillard, who was usually present, and I stayed in the background. I should no more have considered offering 'production' advice to such seasoned *Any Questions?* performers as Arthur Street, Frank Byers and Lord Hailsham than I should have given hints to Sir Gordon Richards on how to win that year's Derby. Indeed, I was always a little diffident about telling distinguished people how to perform on *Any Questions?* unless they asked for advice. I felt that, if they were sufficiently well known and experienced to be invited, they should instinctively be able to give a performance and pick up the simple rules of the game as they went along. We wanted them to be themselves. It seemed almost an impertinence to 'produce' them.

Nevertheless, as time went on, I did at least advise some newcomers to treat the broadcast like a selection board for a job they didn't particularly want, and on one occasion, while I was pointing out to somebody that the important audience was the one listening at home and he should guard against addressing those in the hall too much like a public meeting (it was unnecessary to project to the back row because the team's voices were carried over the loud-speakers), I noticed that another member of the team, the doyen of all *Any Questions?* politicians, Michael Foot, was absorbing what I was saying. His expression implied that such advice had been denied him in the past and he thought it might be worth considering.

Anyway, his performance that night seemed geared

more to the listener at home than usual.

I also remember sitting on a sofa with Margaret Thatcher in a hotel in Paignton in 1966, suggesting as delicately as possible that her performances on the programme might be even more effective if she spoke with less emphasis and pitched her voice a little lower.

(DJ: *I have newcomers sitting next to me at dinner so that I can give one or two hints. I'm not inhibited by the fact that they may be famous – it's still their first time on the programme and I think they need a run-down of what's going to happen and what's expected of them, and I've never noticed anyone resenting it. I always stress that if they want to speak I will help them – my eyes scour the platform – but once they're in full spate on the air, they then avoid catching my eye! I thought I used to do well to interrupt when they reached a full-stop; then a semi-colon; then a comma. Now when I want to stop them I get in when they draw breath!*)

The newcomer at Winchester at the beginning of the 1953/54 series did not, as far as I remember, get any advice from me, though Frank Gillard may well have spoken to him privately. He was Frank Pakenham, afterwards to reach undying fame as Lord Longford. He caused some consternation by bringing out a copy of a report on capital punishment and reading from it during the broadcast, thus imperilling our reputation for spontaneity and for the team not knowing what the questions were going to be. However, the report had only just been issued and it was an odds-on chance there would be a question on it.

We were in Bristol in November, at a territorial drill hall, and during the afternoon while checking over the arrangements there, I suddenly realized I had never taken any precautions against a power failure. So I asked them to provide a man who knew the location of the fuse-box. Just before we were due to go on the air the lights went out. Rushing to the fuse-box, the man pulled out one fuse after another, sparks flying in all directions, until he found the one that had failed and he replaced it just in time. Ever since then, our engineers have checked.

That evening also showed up my inexperience as a producer. We had the usual dilemma near the end of the programme – whether to keep the existing question going or have a 'quickie'. I always felt it was a good idea to end the programme on a laugh, though the team didn't much care for being expected to be witty against the clock – or indeed at any time.

(DJ: *When I started in the chair I just couldn't believe a whole question could be disposed of so quickly, and thought Michael had gone raving mad when he called for another with only a minute to go.*)

Anyway, on this occasion I decided to have another, but it was a question on myxomatosis – hardly light-hearted and difficult to deal with quickly. As it was, there was only time for Ralph Wightman to reply briefly, no one else spoke, and the programme ended sadly. The Controller of the Light Programme, Kenneth Adam, was rightly critical, but I don't think I made the same mistake again. Lots of others – but not that one!

It was in November that A.J.P. Taylor, the historian, made his début. We were at Camborne in Cornwall, and the team also included Graham Hutton, the economist, and Arthur Street. One of the questioners asked: 'Is it fair to contemplate derationing a commodity, such as butter, while it is still in short supply?'

> HUTTON: I don't know really what 'in short supply' means. Of course, Rolls-Royces are in short supply for everybody who would like to have a Rolls-Royce. It depends upon what one can afford out of one's income as against all the things that one has to buy. I don't think you can judge rationing by relatively short supply. How many people want butter? How many people want margarine? I'll tell you just one factor – in all countries of the world that consume both butter and margarine, when the markets have been freed the demand for margarine has gone up so much that the farmers have had to bring the price of butter down.
>
> TAYLOR: I think it's a mistake for us to suppose that it's the duty of social policy whether under a Conservative government or under a Socialist government to ensure that everybody gets the same amount of

everything. I think that it's the duty of our social policy nowadays to ensure that everybody has enough of the basic necessities of life; that everybody has a warm house, enough clothes to keep himself warm and enough food to give himself an adequate diet. But I've never understood any social reason why people should demand butter when they can get margarine, which I believe is better for you. I've never understood why people should say that whisky should be the same price as beer. But the comparison between whisky and beer is exactly the same as between butter and margarine. Butter is more agreeable, much as whisky is more agreeable; but the fact is that whisky is dearer and butter's dearer, and I cannot understand why butter shouldn't go up to its full market price, so long as there is an adequate supply for everybody of a food which can provide everything which butter provides, except pleasure.

STREET: The question says 'Is it fair to deration butter?' I don't think that it is the purpose of governments to make life absolutely fair. And isn't there going to be anything left to individual effort? Isn't there going to be anything left to chance? If it were fair you'd all win exactly your sixpence back on the pools every week – if you want it fair, life would be very dull. It's very sensible to deration it, because butter has been in short supply for years and it's going to be in short supply for a good many more years. If you want to put it to its right price – as long as you've got plenty of margarine – butter today is made out of British milk, it costs about ten shillings a pound to make, and it has not got the food value of a pound of margarine.

We were in Cornwall again a few weeks later, in Falmouth, and we had a question about the Conservative Government's action over the Buganda problem. The Kabaka of Buganda wanted to secede from Uganda, and the Government had deposed him. The team included Major Lewis Hastings, a fiery, much-travelled warrior, and John Arlott.

HASTINGS: I say, thank goodness we haven't got some weak-kneed sentimentalist at the Colonial Office at this time, since we have to face an extraordinarily difficult position which is none of the making of people in this country – a position which was not anticipated when the war ended – a growth of fanatical nationalism everywhere. If you are to deal with that, in the case of primitive people, by giving them everything they want at once, handing out constitutions as if they were buns to a bear, then I can tell you we will not only lose Africa, but it will be a disaster to the Africans themselves.

And let me say that I'm not speaking only from a party point of view, because there was an expression of opinion given by Mr Attlee, the leader of the Labour Party, some time ago, which I thought was of very great importance. He said, 'It is ridiculous that people who have never had or known anything like responsible government could at once create in Africa a lot of little Westminsters in the bush.'

ARLOTT: We are terribly proud to sing this thing about Britons never never shall be slaves, on the very cheerful assumption that everybody else is very happy to be. The people of Buganda, Uganda or any other race in the world may feel that they are very much happier to govern themselves badly than to be governed by somebody else well. And that, to my mind, is something you must allow to anybody. We could have a much bigger meat ration if we were an American colony, but we don't want it, we prefer to be independent. And for heaven's sake don't let's say that any race mustn't be independent because the English got their claws on them a hundred years ago. Surely this is reasonable. Surely if these people want to be independent, they can. Do face the alternative, that if we do not give these people independence we are producing the perfect breeding ground for Communist propaganda. And realize that the Russian Government, and the Communists in general, are not half witted. Lenin said, 'We do not propose to create revolution, but where the ingredients of revolution exist we will foster them.' And what we're doing when we move out is to say, 'There we leave a nation which does not need to call the Russians in to get rid of us.'

Early in 1954 we were at Glastonbury and I remember giving hoots of derisive laughter when Lord Hailsham described the ghastly railway journey he had endured from London, via various branch lines, each more worthy of being closed by Dr Beeching than the last. But I did rather wonder whether I ought perhaps to have offered some advice as to a less bizarre route. In the early days of the programme, the producer's secretary just told the team where the rendezvous was, and it was left to them to find their way there. After a while we became more helpful and suggested what train they should catch and arranged to have it met. I even went to meet it myself if a team member was particularly illustrious – I cherish the memory of identifying and greeting a mackintoshed, unmade-up and distinctly unglamorous Glenda Jackson at Stevenage station; I imagine she preferred to travel incognito, but she nearly fooled me.

More recently, we've tended to lay on a BBC staff car to bring the team from London and take them back after the broadcast. (The overwhelming urge of any team, like lemmings in reverse, is to return to London at the earliest possible moment.) This is not only convenient but saves money as well, on four or five separate train fares and overnight allowances – my frugal mind at work again! The trouble is that the members of the team are often sick of the sight of each other by the time they arrive. Another snag is that if you arrange for a car, some are likely to complain of car-sickness and insist on going by train, and if you arrange for everybody to go by train some are sure to say, 'Can't you organize a car?'

(DJ: *Some of the most amusing moments have been in the car on these journeys, when the conversation has been scintillating – and the views expressed substantially different from those aired later on the programme! I am thinking particularly of some trade union leaders. I have always enjoyed being privy to the private views of public persons, but my lips are, of course, sealed!*)

But on 29 January 1954 the team travelled again to Cornwall, to St Ives, by train. It included Mary Stocks and Malcolm Muggeridge, then editor of *Punch*, and the first question reflected current unease over the reunification and rearmament of Germany.

STOCKS: Much as I dislike the Russian way of life and the Russian attitude to international affairs, I cannot help having very strong sympathy with the Russians over the question of German rearmament. I am absolutely unable to share the express desire of the British Foreign Office for German reunion. I don't think that a united Germany is likely to make for the peace of Europe – it hasn't done so since 1870, and I don't think there's any guarantee that it's likely to do so in the future.

MUGGERIDGE: One thing is certain – that a divided Germany is not a condition of affairs that can continue indefinitely. If Germany is disunited and if the great majority of Germans, as we all know, wish to unite it, that mere fact is a source of instability in Europe, and it's got to be faced. The scheme of integrating Germany into western Europe through the European Defence Community is a way of doing that. At any rate, it's a way that's worth trying. But it's quite certain that as long as there is a divided Germany there can be no peace and stability in Europe.

STOCKS: Well, as long as you have a divided Germany you have a weak Germany and that is the best guarantee of European peace.

MUGGERIDGE: That's what the French said after the '14–'18 War. They said, 'Let us keep Germany weak; let us keep Germany impoverished and then we shall have peace.' But, my goodness – did we have peace?

STOCKS: We didn't keep Germany impoverished. On the contrary. And the French have been invaded three times by the Germans.

On 5 February we were at an army camp in Wiltshire.

Visiting the services always caused some problems. For one thing, protocol demanded that the front row should be occupied by senior officers lounging in comfortable armchairs, with lesser mortals behind them, in descending order of rank, on chairs of decreasing comfort. I had to point out that the questioners, irrespective of rank, must occupy the front row so that they could get to the microphone to put their question at the right time. I got my way in the end but it often meant an argument.

Then there was the matter of censorship. The Officer Commanding often wanted to vet the questions to see there was nothing likely to be embarrassing to the Army. I would assure him that having been in the Army myself, I was confident I could spot a loaded question a mile off. I would insist that the title of the programme should prevail, and that I should see every question which was submitted, though I was willing to let him have a look at our final list.

When I arrived at the hall that evening I was greeted by a senior officer who produced scraps of paper from every pocket and handed them over, saying: 'I've read them all and these are the only ones that are any good.' However, he finally agreed to hand them all over and we ended up with quite a reasonable selection, including a pointed question about MPs raising ministerial enquiries regarding service discipline for political reasons.

Lewis Hastings was in the team again, and in the closing seconds of the programme, he commented on what he called ridiculous questions asked in the House of Commons about the conduct of the Army in Kenya, 'when some fatuous nonsense was talked by men like Fenner Brockway'. Freddy Grisewood was away that week recovering from a car accident, and Frank Gillard was in the chair, but there was no opportunity for him to make any comment, even if any comment would have been helpful. It doesn't seem to me now that there is anything very remarkable about saying that an MP talks fatuous nonsense, but perhaps MPs were more sensitive in those days, and I was told Fenner Brockway complained to Sir Ian Jacob, the Director-General, and some MPs apparently considered raising the matter as a breach of privilege.

The passage was deleted from the repeat the following Tuesday lunch-time; Sir Ian wrote to apologize to Fenner Brockway; and Freddy Grisewood read out an apology, regretting any pain or annoyance which may have been caused to him, at the beginning of the next live broadcast.

On 5 March, at Watchet in Somerset, Anthony Wedgwood Benn broke some sort of record by anticipating not only several of the topical questions, but also one of the 'funnies' as well. In a recent divorce case one of the grounds had been the wife's habit of squeezing the toothpaste tube in the middle, and the team were asked to comment. Tony's solution: squeeze the wife in the middle.

Later in the same programme (the team also included Jack Longland, by that time Director of Education for Derbyshire, and Collin Brooks, editor of *Truth*.) a rather more serious question was put: 'It is reported that the Government has decided to allot £750,000 a year to commercial television and the Transport Commission have recently launched a public loan for £80,000,000. Why has the Government subsidized private enterprise and left a Government-controlled body to fend for itself?'

> LONGLAND: It seems to me that the raising of the licence-fee to £3 for television is justified. The BBC has always complained that it hasn't had enough money, and sound radio has had to subsidize television, so there is a case for a higher licence revenue. That's why I think it's rather nasty of the Government taking away, if they are going to, this £750,000 in order to bolster up commercial television.
>
> BROOKS: The allotment by the Government is not bolstering up, it's pump priming. If you once agree with the principle, which I strongly support, that there should be competitive television, that television should not be a monopoly, then of course you must get it started. And to get it started you must prime the pump. But don't forget the public is going to get a lot for its money. It's going to get a series of alternative programmes. When competitive tele-

vision is in existence, has begun to make its money, don't forget it will be paying large sums to the revenue; it will be paying its licence fees. And all you are doing is to start a new form of enterprise with a small sum in order to get a large sum back for all generations to come.

LONGLAND: This is dodging something. It's the usual argument that a competitive system is the same as a commercial system. And that again is a kind of confidence trick. It's not true. It's perfectly possible to have a system genuinely competitive with the BBC without its being commercial at all.

BROOKS: The whole point about the monopoly is this – that at the present time, excellent as it is, nobody says a word against it – our television service is a state monopoly. It is in the hands of the State and a bureaucracy. And what is needed is not a competitive system under the same control to break that monopoly: it is a competitive system under another control. Because if you don't do that, the day may come – not this Government, not the next Government – the day may come, as it came in Germany and Italy, when the State monopoly will be used to soften you up for totalitarianism and then you will have the whole ruin of your political and economic system entirely attributable to a monopoly of thought, a monopoly of entertainment and a monopoly of the control of people's minds. That's why a competitive system must be commercial and cannot merely be another department of state.

BENN: The fact is, of course, the only competition commercial television will provide for the BBC is in the field of light entertainment. It'll be Jack Benny and the canned American films coming over from the United States, competing with Terry-Thomas and the home-made variety programmes. So please don't be wooed away by this argument that commercial television is going to put on thought-provoking stuff, breaking the BBC monopoly. The point about the subsidy is an important one. This story of commercial television is a very unhappy one because it was really forced on a Government that didn't much want it and didn't really think it out.

There are three different ways of getting an alternative programme. One is to let the BBC give you an alternative television programme. The other – and this is the one I support – is to break the BBC's monopoly in television, but to have a second television corporation providing your second television programme quite separate from the BBC. And the third way is this hybrid commercial television where great profits are going to be made – let's be frank about it – it wouldn't interest the advertisers if they weren't going to make profits, and these profits are going to be subsidized by the licence fees of people who in many cases won't be able to see the programmes. And I call that unfair and wrong.

What the BBC thought about being inaccurately described as a state monopoly is not recorded!

That spring, for the first time, a future Prime Minister appeared on *Any Questions?*. (At the time of writing, we've never managed to persuade a *former* Prime Minister to appear.) He was introduced by his initials rather than his Christian name – L.J. Callaghan. And, appropriately for one who was to be a future Chancellor of the Exchequer as well, he was asked what his proposals would be if he were presenting the following week's Budget. He replied: 'The thing I'd put top of the list, as a result of what I've seen over the last twelve months, is some relief to the old-age pensioner. We fixed a standard in 1946 below which we said it was not proper that people in this country should fall. They have fallen below that standard, and it's on the conscience of the nation that they should be at least raised up to it again. I don't know how much money the Chancellor's going to have to give away, but what I do hope he won't do is to mess about with the food subsidies once more and so put up the cost of living and provoke wage claims and all the rest of it, because that seems to me to be sheer nonsense.'

Jim Callaghan, whose almost schoolboyish good looks

and manner were being seen frequently on the television programme *In the News* at that time, was apt to complain that he was battling in a minority of one in *Any Questions?* though we always did our best to provide a reasonable balance between Right and Left, because apart from the important consideration of fairness it also makes for a better programme. However, he was generally an affable panellist and, though he was sometimes criticized for introducing party politics more than necessary, I always thought he was one of the most effective politicians on the programme.

On 16 April, in Bristol, we celebrated the 200th edition of the programme. Ralph Wightman and Arthur Street were brought together for the occasion, but the chemistry didn't work. They were so anxious to outdo each other that they neglected their main purpose – to 'play the programme', to provide whatever ingredient was needed at a particular moment, to project earthy common sense in contrast to the flights of fancy from the others, especially the politicians. In brief, to throw a spanner in the works whenever it seemed desirable. Ralph, particularly, was an adept spanner-thrower and made a point of being ostentatiously serious when everybody else was being frivolous and vice versa.

When asked at my appointments board what changes I would make in *Any Questions?*, I replied that I would try to find a third earthy speaker to match Street and Wightman. I never managed to. One problem is that the later breed of farmers don't sound (or indeed look) like farmers. They sound more like businessmen and it is hard to imagine them wearing wellies. Arthur, who frequently described himself as a peasant, was very much the farmer and the countryman, but he had an extra dimension – he was a novelist and he played bridge in London clubs with famous people like the pianist, Moiseiwitsch. Ralph wasn't a farmer at all, but he sounded like one and the listeners liked to picture him ambling among his own cows and pigs. He was an agricultural journalist, with a gift for making edged comments. Arthur's contributions often stood up in their own right as radio essays; Ralph's value was more as a catalyst.

I hadn't been producing the programme long before I realized they had to be treated very differently. Ralph was pliable, Arthur prickly. You could say to Ralph: 'We're a bit shaky on the Right this week, could you help out?' and Ralph, essentially an old-fashioned radical, would obligingly move his convictions several notches towards the Conservatives for the duration of the programme. If you tried the same gambit with Arthur, in either direction, you would get a very dusty answer. Not that it would have been very feasible for him to move consciously to the Right – he was there already.

One result of their different attitudes was that, since the same sort of questions tend to come up periodically, Ralph's answers varied from time to time whereas Arthur's became recognizably similar. But it is impossible to exaggerate their value to the programme.

It was the week before the 200th edition that the war in Vietnam was first mentioned in the programme. A questioner at Honiton in Devon referred to America's warning to China over what was then known as the Indo-China War. In an animated discussion, John Foot, brother of Michael, commented that it might be more serious than Korea, and Bernard Braine, the Conservative MP, forecast that if Indo-China fell, then the whole of South-East Asia would fall, too.

On 21 May at Yeovil in Somerset, the team included Lady Violet Bonham Carter; there had been no woman on the panel since her previous appearance nearly two months earlier. In more recent times, I simply wouldn't have dared select an all-male team, and this is one way the programme reflects the changing social scene over the years. When taxed with the 3–1 ratio which prevailed during much of my tour of duty, I would say I believed in equality between the sexes and that was why I chose three men and one woman. This did not always silence the critics. So I would then become less ingratiating, thus: I believe that women have particular qualities which are valuable in *Any Questions?* but when there are two on the team they somehow manage to cancel out these qualities instead of enhancing them (though Marghanita Laski and Isobel Barnett made an effective pairing). But the overwhelming factor is the question of supply. There just simply are far fewer suitable women to choose from. *Any Questions?* primarily features people at the top of their particular sphere, and when there are as many women cabinet ministers as there are men, as many female bishops as there are male, as many trade union general secretaries who are women, as many editors of national newspapers, as many chairmen (or chairpersons) of nationalized and private industry who are women – one could go on – then there will be 50–50 representation of women on the team.

(DJ: *I can't imagine a team of three women and one man, and that is really the answer. But there was that amusing programme* Petticoat Line *with four women, and that put the woman's point of view. There is such a thing as the woman's point of view whereas I don't believe there's a man's point of view. The men put everybody's point of view!*)

At any rate, those women who still hold that 3–1 ratio against me should recall that I appointed one of their sex as my successor. But, back in 1954, even 3–1 was unusual.

There must have been a lot in the papers that week about proposed changes in the law relating to homosexuality, because I remember asking Lady Violet at Yeovil if she would be embarrassed by discussing the subject – we were less permissive in those days, and it had probably never been mentioned in a question before. She said she wouldn't be. Sure enough, the question came up: should the law be altered? Lady Violet agreed with the others that the answer was 'yes'. But she had one proviso:

> LADY VIOLET: The moral law is one thing; the law of the land is another. There is sometimes a danger that public opinion may think that, because the law of the land has been altered, the moral law is being relaxed to keep step with it. Now I think it would be fatal if that happened in this instance, because in fact I think that we are becoming too tolerant of some offences nowadays. As a Liberal, tolerance is part of my faith, but I do think we are becoming so afraid of being

called intolerant that we do not perhaps sufficiently condemn and outlaw what should be condemned and outlawed. I think that no word has done more harm than the word – I think it's part of the Freudian jargon – 'repression'. We are told that at all costs we must avoid repressions, because they're going to do us such terrible harm. Well, you know, we've all got to repress some things in ourselves constantly. We've got to repress laziness, we've got to repress bad temper, we've got to repress greed – I've got to repress smoking too many cigarettes – and we must repress these things: it's right that we should repress them. We are not doing ourselves harm in repressing, and I think this crusade against repression is really relaxing some fibres in us which we should keep tight.

The next question produced less unanimity:

'The Chairman of the National Coal Board has issued a warning about the fall in coal production. Can the team make any suggestions for raising output?' The team also included Arthur Street and James Cameron, the journalist.

LADY VIOLET: Well, the only suggestion I can make is an appeal to the conscience of the miners. The miners are at present, I think, the best paid workers in the community and they have heavily subsidized houses. They have high wages, they have paid holidays, they have free coal; and we don't grudge them any of it. All we ask is that they should give us the coal in return, but in spite of mechanization and every kind of technical development which has been poured into the mines, the output of coal is steadily falling. I think it's most distressing and disappointing and a most disquieting thing because, after all, our coal is the very basis of our national economy. When coal goes, everything goes. Well, I wouldn't like to be a miner. I think it's a most dangerous and disagreeable occupation, but no one is conscripted into the mines, you needn't be a miner if you don't want to, and if you're going to be a miner, well then, I think you must pull your weight.

STREET: The question is how can you raise the output of coal production today? I think there are two ways. In 1940, a Nottinghamshire miner said to me: 'In the past, whenever we struck, the thing that defeated us was that there was always three months' supply of coal on top of the ground; now you shall never again have more than a fortnight.' So I think we should import six months' supply of coal regardless of price. That is one way. The other way is a rural one. An old age pensioner said to a bunch of people in a Wiltshire pub during the war (they were arguing on the same subject): 'All they wants to do is to bring the miners up top and let they till the land, and take the farm workers and put them down the mines, and then in six months everybody in this country'll be terribly hot and terribly hungry.'

CAMERON: Sooner or later on this sort of a do, us airborne creatures always start talking about the miners and why they aren't doing more. It always seems to crop up and, of course, the problem is that none of us know what we're talking about at all. Unless any of us have in fact tried to dig a ton of coal we do not know quite how hard it is – I believe it's hard – nor how dangerous it is – and I believe it's dangerous. But, above all, none of us have got this curious, historic memory of the last generation when the miner was the chap who was kicked around more than anybody else in the world. And even though not one of the miners who are reflecting on their job today have personal experience of that, their fathers have and mining is a family industry. And I do not think in just half a generation of nationalization we're going to rid the miner of the feeling that one day somebody's going to do him dirt again and for that reason the miner is always going to have a chip on his shoulder. I think there is no answer to that whatever, except sooner or later we've got to do without the coal, and if one day these splendid fellows who are figuring out how to blow up the islands in the Pacific with hydrogen bombs figure

> out a way of making that heat our houses instead of blowing poor Polynesian natives to bits and making Japanese put up umbrellas for radioactive dust, then I think we will have the solution for our fuel problems.

A week later my first full series as producer of *Any Questions?* ended. Very enjoyable, but no innovations. Not many newcomers, and all of them from the traditional stables; the teams male dominated; locations confined to west country towns. It was to be some time before I would be able to make my mark on the programme.

1954/55

There were some innovations at the beginning of the 1954/55 series though I can't claim any credit for them. They were Frank Gillard's ideas. The fortnightly alternation of Wightman and Street was to cease. They were to be joined by two other regulars, Mary Stocks and Jack Longland, and the four of them would each appear, in turn, once a month. There was to be a three-weekly rota of locations. One week a factory, one week a 'closed community' – a community centre, for instance – and only one week in three an audience of the general public. The idea was to counteract the built-in Conservative bias of the average west country town and it was hoped that in two weeks out of the three we should be spared that middle-class audience reaction which so infuriated the Labour Party. There was to be no question of travelling outside the west country.

But the biggest innovation was *Any Answers*.

For six years, *Any Questions?* had inspired lots of letters. Some of them went to the BBC and had to be answered; some went to Freddy who forwarded them to the BBC; some went to the members of the team and it was up to them whether they replied or not. Everyone concerned, BBC staff and team members, welcomed *Any Answers*. It saved them answering the letters.

It also provided a convenient answer to requests for a 'man-in-the-street' to join the panel. If the 'man-in-the-street' could have his considered views broadcast to a comparable audience, why risk complete disaster by putting him alongside experienced panellists in a spontaneous live broadcast? Any political imbalance in the team – sometimes unavoidable when speakers with no party political affiliations were chosen long before you had any idea what they would be talking about – could be corrected by letters putting neglected points of view. Errors of fact could be corrected and relevant points, overlooked by the team, introduced. Above all, it would be a good programme in its own right. This was long before the days of phone-ins, and it was an attractive idea to broadcast to a mass audience the views of some of that audience on the burning issues of the day.

At an appropriate point in *Any Questions?*, Freddy Grisewood explained about *Any Answers* and begged for letters. The response was overwhelming – something like fifteen hundred. All of them had to be read, and a representative selection made to fit into a fifteen-minute script. It was difficult.

The first *Any Answers* was broadcast on Wednesday, 6 October 1954. We managed to include twenty-six letters, which meant that they had to be shortened fairly drastically, but nobody seemed to mind.

It was broadcast live, and it continued to be live for many years. This was a doubtful blessing, I now realize. The increased flow of adrenalin may have caused the readers to give a more vital performance, but if they fluffed they could change the whole meaning of a letter, and if they read more slowly than in the rehearsal I had to make frantic signals towards the end for a letter or part of a letter to be cut so that we could get off the air in time.

One evening, a microphone failed half-way through the broadcast, and we had to tell the readers to move on to the microphone on Freddy Grisewood's table. For the rest of the broadcast they had to stoop in a semi-recumbent posture which was uncomfortable, as well as indecorous.

After struggling through fifteen hundred letters single-handed (I did get some assistance after that), I awaited the second *Any Answers* avalanche with some trepidation. But there were only two hundred letters this time. With such a controversial and outspoken newcomer as George Brown, then Labour MP for Belper, this was surprising. The team also included Lady Violet Bonham Carter. George Brown was less inhibited than I and addressed Lady Violet as 'Lady Vi'. She was not amused.

We were at Lydney, in the Forest of Dean, and it was one of the very few occasions when we didn't have enough questions submitted. (People ask if we carry a supply of spare questions but we can't really do that. The questioner has to be there in person, and questions very quickly become out of date.) We had to solicit questions from the audience during the warm-up period and hand round paper and pencil to encourage them.

That afternoon I had arrived at the hall, had met the chap from the local authority who had distributed the tickets, and had asked him in the usual way, 'D'you think we'll get a good lot of questions?' to which he had replied 'How should I know?' Lydney Council itself had not invited us.

In those days, Frank Gillard looked at the map of the West Region and said, 'It's about time we went to the Forest of Dean'; and we would write off to a suitable council in the area asking if they would like to have *Any Questions?* there. They usually raised no objection, but as it hadn't been their idea they didn't feel any obligation to ensure that the evening was a success.

After this experience I decided never again to solicit an invitation. We would rely on those we received, and, with very few exceptions, that's the way it's been ever since.

One of the questions at Lydney was of considerable local interest then and considerable national interest now: 'There is a possibility that atomic waste will be dumped in the disused mines in the Forest of Dean. How would the members of the team feel about this if they lived here?'

Lady Violet said she knew nothing about atomic energy, but she wondered how much the scientists themselves knew about it. There had been reassurances, and she supposed they had to be accepted. But it raised a problem which seemed to her insoluble – what is going to happen to atomic waste?

George Brown's answer to the question was that he'd feel damned uncomfortable.

After the following week's *Any Questions?* we had two thousand letters, largely because there was a question about the Good Old Days. After that, it settled down to an average of around eight hundred a week. *Any Answers* was immediately given another five minutes, and within three months it was a half-hour programme at the peak listening time of 8 p.m.

The letter-writers had a chance to vote at the beginning of 1955. The last question in *Any Questions?* asked the team to pick a signature tune for the programme. Lord Hailsham suggested *There'll Always be an England* and Graham Hutton *Thanks for the Memory*, but Hugh Gaitskell couldn't think of anything at all and neither could Mary Stocks ('Not the *Dead March* in *Saul*' was all she could manage). With only seconds to think about it, the team were caught on the hop, but, with ample time, the writers to *Any Answers* came up with a wide variety of suggestions. We counted up the votes and this was the result: first – *Question and Answer* (248 votes), second – *Answer me* (77 votes), third – *Jolly Good Company* (33 votes). After them came *Tell Me the Old, Old Story, The Happy Wanderers* and *Bewitched, Bothered and Bewildered.*

But the last word was with Hugh Gaitskell, who sent me a letter several days later – 'I've just thought of the obvious signature tune for *Any Questions?*' he wrote. '*Little White Lies!*'

Around the turn of the year we had two members of the team cry off at the last minute because of illness. This was always liable to happen. When Arthur Street was ill, it was relatively simple. We just rang up Ralph Wightman. This never had to be reciprocated because Ralph, like the utterly professional broadcaster he was, managed to keep at bay any germs which threatened to involve him in a financial loss.

If someone was ill, it often meant a Friday morning spent on the telephone, with anything up to a couple of dozen abortive invitations before we finally struck oil –

and then having to disguise the fact that the chap who had accepted was the twenty-fifth on our list.

There could also be accidents, or delays through the weather or the vagaries of British Rail, and this was one reason why we asked the team to assemble at a hotel anything up to three hours before we were due on the air. The more illustrious the panellists, the more they resented having to be on parade early.

(DJ: *I remember Michael Heseltine nonchalantly strolling on to the platform at Nant-y-moel at the very moment I was beginning my opening remarks to the listeners, and it was five minutes after the broadcast at Axminster had started before David Frost, who was travelling – how else? – by private aircraft, came up the gangway.*)

Newcomers tended to be more punctual. Many of our recruits were invited as a result of word-of-mouth recommendations from those who had themselves appeared on *Any Questions?* and whose judgement we could trust. People may object that this made the programme even more 'clubby' than it was already, but a disinterested hint of this sort was very valuable, and was a regular feature of the conversation over drinks before or after the broadcast. I remember one disgruntled panellist telling a colleague: 'Do stop recommending people – it might mean I shall be asked less often myself!'

Anne Allen was one of the very few people we invited as a result of self-recommendation. She was in any case certainly no 'woman-in-the-street', being a columnist on the *Mirror*. After her début, Frank Gillard's verdict was: 'The best woman newcomer since Mary Stocks.' But she was an exception. The sort of people we most wanted wouldn't dream of asking to be invited.

It was due to Percy Cudlipp, a former editor of the *Daily Herald*, that I invited Lord Mancroft for the first time, and I recall Tony Benn drawing my attention to a lively Conservative backbencher who seemed very much our sort of chap. The name Gerald Nabarro was new to me then.

During this first quarter of 1955, *Any Questions?* was more political than at any other time. There were two

MPs on every single team until the last fortnight in March when we relented to the extent of having only one MP in two weeks. I was still in the minority when it came to choosing teams, the other selectors being Frank Gillard and Bill Coysh. Frank had always had a predilection for including MPs though those who wrote to us tended to be opposed to the appearance of too many on the programme – or even any at all. We asked our Audience Research Department to carry out a survey. It didn't help much. About a third wanted MPs always; a third wanted them never; and a third were prepared to tolerate them sometimes.

There are few questions of the moment which don't involve politics to some extent, and MPs by reason of their background knowledge and experience of debate are especially fitted to discuss them in a stimulating and authoritative manner; thus it would be silly to boycott them altogether. Sometimes we would include one MP instead of two, to avoid predictable party-political bickering which never fails to infuriate the listeners. An MP on his own is less tempted to indulge in the 'Ya, boo' type of comment ('Your lot were worse when they were in power').

I must admit we rather preferred our MPs to be a shade rebellious – much to the annoyance of the headquarters of the two main parties. That was because we liked to feel that members of the team said what they genuinely thought rather than loyally trotting out the party line regardless. We never managed to lure the man regarded by the Labour hierarchy at one time as the arch-rebel – Aneurin Bevan – despite repeated invitations, but most of the Bevanites, the fifty-seven Labour MPs who had voted against their own government's Defence Bill, were good flamboyant performers and they became so effective that their appearances were rationed because the BBC felt obliged to reflect the composition of the Labour Party in Parliament as a whole.

In the same way that rebels are usually more entertaining than loyalists, Labour MPs in general are more entertaining, or at any rate better at the informal cut-and-thrust technique of *Any Questions?* than Conservative MPs, some of whom have a rather strangulated way of speaking and seem unable to establish an intimate relationship with their audience. Perhaps it's something to do with their upbringing.

(DJ: *I think this is a true generalization, but we have weeded out the Tory MPs who speak with a plum in their mouth. It is unfortunate when MPs do their party political thing and turn to the audience and start table-thumping, but we get to know which ones do that and try to avoid them. Recently two opposing MPs bickered so ridiculously that I had to stop them and tell them: 'You are being very silly.'*)

Aneurin Bevan was the subject of a question on 11 March at Devonport dockyard: 'What is the opinion of the team on the proposal of the Parliamentary Labour Party to withdraw the Whip from Mr Aneurin Bevan?' The team included the Labour MP Ian Mikardo and a former editor of the *Daily Herald*, Francis Williams.

> WILLIAMS: Let me begin by saying that I think that Nye Bevan is a damned nuisance. But then, of course, the Labour Party is full of damned nuisances. It never would have been a Labour Party if it hadn't been full of them. But I would also like to say something – a phrase – which I remember Nye Bevan himself used to me on another occasion, when Hugh Dalton resigned from the Chancellorship of the Exchequer following a rather unfortunate mistake he had made. I was travelling in the train with Nye and talking about this, and he said to me, 'But Francis, you know there is no immaculate conception of disaster'; and it is the case that there is no immaculate conception of this disaster. It isn't just due to one particular issue, and to one particular act of apparent disregard, either of the Parliamentary Labour Party or of the leadership of the Parliamentary Labour Party. It's due, or is felt to be due, I believe, by quite a considerable number of the Labour Party, to a consistent course of action which has seemed to be denigrating the elected official leadership of the Labour Party.

Now I would also like to use a phrase which might possibly be misunderstood when I say that it seems to me that Aneurin Bevan has got too big for his boots. Now I don't mean that in the ordinary way in which that phrase is used. I think the natural boots for Nye Bevan to use are those of a rebel and of a prophet in the Labour Party; of one of those who will remind it of its principles, who will rebel against the machinery which a party generates over a period of time. But I don't believe you can both wear those boots of the rebel and the prophet and hope to be a leader of a great organization. You have to make the choice, and I think part of the trouble about Nye Bevan is that until now he never has been able to make the choice. He has wanted to be a prophet without realizing that in any political party practical leadership does depend upon a certain agreement to compromise with the rest of the party, and I believe that much his best course, believing as he does, and having, as I believe he has, great contributions to make to politics in this country, would be to resign and become a leader of a group, or a leader simply of himself, and express what he believes to be the principles which are necessary. I think it's a pity that instead of that he has followed a course of deliberately denigrating the leadership and creating differences within the party.

MIKARDO: It seems to me that what Francis Williams is saying is that if a man is a big man and has got ideas and feels passionately about the issues of the moment, he can't aspire to be a leader of a party; that the only people who can are the little men who are prosaic, correct, never have ideas, never fly off the handle, never drop a brick, always the nice little gentlemen in bowler hats, black jackets and striped trousers. Well, you know, if we get to that stage then the party machines will really have done their damage and have condemned this nation to be ruled by mediocrities. The fact of the matter is that Nye Bevan is a big man, he's got big virtues, and because he's got big virtues he's got big faults, and his friends know it better than those who only get their ideas of him from what they read in the rather unfair Press. He's got big virtues and he's got big faults. Little men have tiny graces and peccadilloes. You just compare Bevan and Winston Churchill on the one hand with Stanley Baldwin and Neville Chamberlain. They're the big men with the big virtues and the big faults and parties always freeze the big men out. They froze Winston Churchill out for years – he would never have been Prime Minister but for the war. Heaven preserve us all, and I say it in desperate seriousness, from the day when the party machines condemn us to be ruled by the correct little men, with only little faults but no ideas.

Winston Churchill retired within a few weeks of this broadcast, and then a General Election was announced for 26 May.

In the last edition before the programme went off the air during the election campaign (it was the last time this happened), the team included Hugh Gaitskell. I rather tactlessly indicated that I did not expect him or his party to be in office after the election, but his normal pleasant manner did not falter. I remember him as being invariably unruffled and approachable, with a rather deprecating way of speaking which seemed odd in a former Chancellor and future Leader of the Opposition.

He became leader later that year when Clement Attlee resigned. He had already accepted an invitation for *Any Questions?* but cried off – unlike Margaret Thatcher who was in the same situation more than twenty years later and kept the engagement.

(DJ: *So did Michael Foot after he became Leader.*)

My prophecy to Hugh Gaitskell proved justified and the Conservatives were returned with an increased majority. On the day after the election we were in Bristol and in answer to the expected first question ('Has the election shown a pro-Conservative or an anti-Labour tendency?'), Mary Stocks said it had shown a pro-Conservative tendency for two reasons: 'One, I think the public has considerable confidence in Sir Anthony Eden – his guidance of foreign affairs at the present rather critical juncture. He has the thing in hand and they don't quite know who they would get as a Foreign Secretary under a Labour government, but I think the other reason is that most people – I won't say everybody – most people are extraordinarily contented. We've got full employment. Purchasing power is fairly evenly spread. National health is good. On the whole, I think most people in the country are more comfortable than they've ever been before.'

Frank Byers thought some of the Labour Party supporters hadn't bothered to vote because they were rather fed up with the troubles there had been with Aneurin Bevan; the disunity and division in the party must have had an effect on Labour chances. He also thought people were getting wary of further nationalization.

Ted Leather, Conservative MP for North Somerset, was grateful for the comments of Mary Stocks (who tartly pointed out that she had said people were contented; she hadn't said they had good reason to be). He thought it was a vote of confidence in Anthony Eden.

Bill Mallalieu, Labour MP for Huddersfield East, who was to provide (indeed had already provided) a future valuable addition to the feminine strength of *Any Questions?* in his daughter Ann, thought they hadn't been decisive enough in saying what future progress they wanted to make.

The following week, at Poole in Dorset, we again had two MPs. I had followed up Tony Benn's suggestion and had invited Gerald Nabarro. The other was Jim Callaghan. The team also included Lady Violet Bonham Carter.

Right at the end of the programme there was a brush between Jim Callaghan and Lady Violet in answer to the question why people in the south of England are generally surrounded by a high wall of shy reserve compared with their counterparts in the north.

> CALLAGHAN: Because people in the south are more snobbish than people in the north. There's still far too much forelock-touching in the south of England, especially in the 'county' areas; still far too many class

distinctions and rigidities that I see on my way around and it's far more pronounced in the rural, agricultural counties of the south than it is anywhere else in Britain.

LADY VIOLET: I entirely disagree. I would say, with all respect to Mr Callaghan, it takes a snob to see a snob.

Jim Callaghan looked somewhat annoyed, and asked: 'Do I get a comeback on that?' but Freddy raised his hands apologetically and said we were right up against our time.

The atmosphere afterwards was somewhat frigid, a comparatively rare occurrence. There is often a great deal of shadow-boxing on *Any Questions?* but the participants shake hands affably the moment the red light goes out. However, I remember William Davis, when editor of *Punch*, saying to his predecessor, Malcolm Muggeridge, that the uproar about permissiveness came from older gentlemen like him who were dreadfully jealous of the young, and there was not a great deal of fraternization after that particular programme. In another, William Davis accused the journalist and broadcaster, Mary Goldring, of making a cheap point, and she was still taking a certain amount of umbrage over the post-programme drinks. A confrontation between Clive Jenkins and the right-winger Robert Moss was also carried on after the programme. But these are exceptions.

Gerald Nabarro made a very promising début. He was a natural for *Any Questions?*, a colourful personality who played to the gallery outrageously. His trademark became his *sotto voce* (which in Gerald Nabarro was like other people's roar) 'Nabárro, Nabárro', correcting the other panellists who persistently failed to pronounce his name the way he wanted it. But not everybody warmed to him. On a later appearance, the team also included Robert Henriques.

'What's this fellow Nabarro like?' asked Robert on arriving at the hotel. 'Shall I like him?'

Then his eyes fell on one particular vehicle in the car park. Its number plate was NAB 1 and some 150 badges adorned its front. With a shaking finger, Robert pointed to it. 'Is that his car?' We said yes, it was. 'Then I *shan't* like him.' And he didn't.

On 24 June at Fawley, a comment from Mary Stocks became part of the *Any Questions?* folklore. A questioner asked: 'What are the team's reactions to the controversy about Colin Cowdrey's feet?'

STOCKS: Who is Colin Cowdrey? And what is his feat?

GRISEWOOD: Colin Cowdrey's one of our Test cricketers. He has been discharged from the RAF because of the state of his feet and he is still able to play cricket.

STOCKS: Oh, F, double-E, T. I thought it was the other sort.

But she remained puzzled. 'I know that you do use your feet in cricket, because you have to run, but do you use your feet in an aeroplane, I mean do you have a clutch or anything like that?' After the rest of the team had explained that a medical board had considered Cowdrey unfit for service in the RAF, she was still unconvinced: 'I should have thought if he'd been let loose to play chess or backgammon or some game that doesn't involve the feet, the explanation would be more convincing!'

1955/56

In the opening programme of the new series, at a factory in Eastleigh, Hampshire, one of the questions dealt with a matter which was of considerable concern to us. The fourteen-day rule, under which subjects due to be discussed in Parliament during the following fourteen days were not supposed to be discussed on radio or television, had been in existence for some time, but only as a sort of gentlemen's agreement. However, the agreement had now given way to a prescription, introduced, appropriately enough, by the former radio doctor, Charles Hill, then Postmaster-General, and this was much more restrictive.

Most of the team, including the Labour MP Christopher Mayhew, thought the ban was outrageous, but Ralph Wightman, perhaps for the sake of being perverse, agreed with it.

> WIGHTMAN: As I see it, this is the Light Programme, we should entertain people up to a point, we should inform them to the best of our ability, but we are not qualified to debate matters of really serious national importance which are before the House, and we should wait at least until the House has debated them, before we put in our – with all respect to all the other three members – our half-witted opinion.
>
> MAYHEW: I don't think it's going to be enforced – because I don't think it can be enforced. I don't think the bulk of people in the country want it. I'm perfectly certain Dr Hill is going to beat a graceful

retreat before many weeks are past.

Chris Mayhew was being unduly optimistic. The ban was enforced, and it was months rather than weeks before Dr Hill beat a graceful retreat.

In the second programme in the new series we had for the first time a television personality. It was Lady Barnett, then at the height of her fame as a panellist in *What's My Line?*. Some of my superiors were a bit snooty about having someone whose main qualification for *Any Questions?* was that she appeared in a successful television panel game; but this was one occasion I got my own way and she proved to have all the attributes for the programme and became one of our mainstays for the next twenty-three years or so.

Having arrived in broadcasting as an amateur, Isobel became the complete professional. For one thing, she was noted for punctuality, and when she was on the team I knew I had to arrive at the hotel in time for tea, because she would be there, having allowed two extra hours in case of a mishap on the journey. I don't believe she ever gave an indifferent performance, and I thought I detected beneath her charming manner quite a hint of toughness – she certainly stood up robustly for her Conservative principles, often against strong opposition, but in the end it became only too clear how vulnerable she was.

(DJ: *It is an unhappy coincidence that three of our best women panellists – Isobel, Jacky Gillott and Anne Allen – should have died in such unexpected, tragic circumstances. All three possessed such wisdom – for other people, but not for themselves. Anne Allen wrote beautifully about the problems of the day which affect other people's lives. Jacky Gillott led one to believe that her religious experience had been so great that she would be able to rationalize anything. And Isobel, whose forthright common sense, which to me was her hallmark, was totally incapable of revealing the one great weakness in her life, that she was lonely. She hid it completely, but I am convinced that that was her downfall.*)

For her début at Tiverton, Devon, Isobel was accompanied by Jack Longland, David Ormsby-Gore (now Lord Harlech) and Hector McNeil, Labour MP for Greenock. Hector approached the programme with some trepidation.

A White Paper had just been issued on the defection of Burgess and Maclean to Russia and a question was inevitable. Guy Burgess had been Hector's personal assistant when he was Minister of State at the Foreign Office and he feared that his political opponent, David Ormsby-Gore, might make political capital out of this.

ORMSBY-GORE: It is a fascinating case, the Maclean and Burgess case. I think one aspect of it which hasn't been put forward so far is what extraordinarily bad spies in a way they must be; we've now heard a good deal about their private lives, and I can't believe that people with private lives such as that could make very good spies. On the other hand it is rather a reflection on our security services that having these rather bad private lives they weren't discovered earlier.

LONGLAND: Ithink in recruiting for any branch of the Civil Service, you're bound to trust people; it's no good beginning by suspecting everybody who comes in, not even into the Foreign Service. The thing which cuts right across this is that patriotism in the twentieth century has crossed frontiers, just as it did in the Middle Ages, when religious wars and religious struggles were going on, in exactly the same way as they're going on today, and in which the frontiers of a country became unimportant; if you were a supporter of the church, or a supporter of Luther, or whoever it happened to be, your patriotism crossed the frontier completely. Now, communism is an international religion, maybe a terribly bad kind of religion, but it is international and I think it's no good supposing that people who took the line Burgess and Maclean did are fundamentally disloyal crooks. They did it because they believed in something which they thought went right across frontiers. There's obviously got to be a post-mortem, but I hope it won't start a great witch-hunt into the members of the Foreign Service, or any other branch of the Civil Service. This is a bit of bad luck, and you've got to have a certain amount of bad luck in trusting individuals.

BARNETT: While I believe in taking people on trust, and while you cannot possibly screen everybody fully, I do think that membership of the Communist Party is something that is fairly easy to trace; and there is no doubt that even as far back as 1937, when Maclean joined the British Foreign Service, that could have been checked. I don't say he shouldn't have been employed, but I do say that a much closer watch should have been kept on him; and anybody you employ who even in his greatest youth has been a Communist should be watched for a period. Against witch-hunting, but pro-watching, that's me!

McNEIL: But if a fellow isn't pretty left wing at eighteen, he's going to be in a miserable position by forty-five. I doubt very much that, in the certainty and enthusiasm of a young man, you should forever judge him by his associations. By all means, Lady Barnett, let's see that our security machine – when they come to offer themselves and be employed in the Service – know about their character, their general associations, which aren't so difficult to find out; but don't say because a man was in this party or that party – not even in the Tory Party, David – I will keep him outside the Foreign Service.

ORMSBY-GORE: We allow the Communist Party to exist in this country; certainly, pre-war, if you belonged to the Communist Party, there was no reason to take any action at all against you. But, of course, if you do that, you do run certain risks; and this is a case where we ran the risk and we've lost out on it; but if you believe in freedom, which we do in this country, you have got occasionally to take these risks. And on the whole it's stood us in pretty good stead.

David Ormsby-Gore was always pleased that he had resisted any temptation to drag up the ancient history which Hector McNeil was dreading, because it was just about Hector's last public appearance – he died soon afterwards.

Almost exactly a year later, Tom Driberg, who had just

returned from a visit to Moscow to see Guy Burgess, was a member of the team at Bovey Tracey in Devon, where this question was put: 'Public opinion denounced Burgess and Maclean as traitors when they fled to Russia. Do members of the team consider it imprudent for a British citizen to associate with them in Russia?'

DRIBERG: I don't myself think that it was imprudent of me to go to Russia and find out what I could about Guy Burgess, his method of life, and what's going on there. The really important thing is not the personal case of Burgess and Maclean so much as the general set-up in Soviet Russia, and the relations between our two countries. And if the study of the particular case can throw some light on that general question, and can help to improve the relations, as I personally believe that it can, then I think that it's worth doing; and I think that purely from the journalistic point of view, if you like, from the point of view of conveying information to the British public, it is the duty of any journalist and any newspaper to make that public.

I do not myself think that Burgess knew any secrets at all at the time when he left Britain for Moscow. He may very well have known many secrets during his period of service as Personal Assistant to Hector McNeil, Minister of State at the Foreign Office; but that was several years before. I don't think he knew any secrets in the technical sense of the word that were of any consequence when he actually went to Moscow; and I'm not sure that the two can be bracketed together and regarded under the law as traitors. I think the law of treason in any case is very obscure indeed. In wartime it's a very different thing, but after all, thank goodness, we are not and have not been at war with Soviet Russia; and I hope we never shall be. And in so far as perhaps misguidedly these two men, and Burgess in particular, because he's the one whom I know and have been talking with, in so far as they were stimulated by a desire to try to do something to better relations between the two countries and to secure peace, I certainly don't think that they were behaving as traitors.

I myself would not have done what they did. I told Burgess quite frankly that I wouldn't have done that; I think it's one's duty if one's a Socialist to stay in this country and work for Socialism through the means that are available here. But I respect his right to do what he did, and I do not believe that he was a traitor.

But back in October 1955 our main concern was the fourteen-day rule. The fact that the business of the House was only announced seven days in advance didn't make life any easier. On 28 October, Freddy had to warn the team that they couldn't discuss that week's Autumn Budget because of the fourteen-day rule. Nor could they discuss housing, for the same reason. The first question I chose was: 'How can the continual rise in the cost of living be stopped?' and Ted Leather seized the opportunity to congratulate the Chancellor for what he had just done in the Budget to stop the rise. Ted also abused the rule. (I understand he was thanked by the Chancellor for what he said about the Budget!)

The teams during this period felt very frustrated at not being allowed to discuss the subjects they wanted to, and they lost no opportunity to have a dig.

A light-hearted question at St Mawes in Cornwall (where the team consisted of Percy Cudlipp, Collin Brooks, Mary Stocks and the writer, Peter Fleming) seemed safe enough: 'Cleanliness is next to godliness; which attribute would the team put third?' Peter Fleming chose honesty and Collin Brooks kindness.

CUDLIPP: I was going to say truthfulness and in that I include speaking out with perfect candour on all occasions which I would love to do on several subjects tonight but am forbidden to do so.

STOCKS: It all depends on what you mean by godliness. Some of my colleagues seem to assume that it doesn't include truth and that it doesn't include kindness, and that it doesn't include honesty, but when we've assumed the existence of a dishonest, untruthful, unkind, godly man who is, nevertheless, clean, then I should say that probably the next attribute that one would wish to see would be courage – to talk about the Budget when he's told not to.

BROOKS: Surely Mary Stocks must have met some clean atheists.

STOCKS: I've met some honest and truthful and kind atheists as well as clean ones. I've also met some very dirty saints.

I got into hot water twice in December. First, as a result of a question on virgin births. There had been a scientific article in the *New Statesman* that week about virgin births, and I decided to open the programme with a question on the subject. Unfortunately, many listeners seemed to think we were discussing *the* Virgin Birth, and as the discussion was a shade facetious, it caused much offence to some committed Christians.

In *Any Answers*, Freddy applied some soothing balm, but London – and Frank Gillard was by that time part of the BBC hierarchy there who frequently caused us in the West Region to use the name of the capital as a derogatory term – felt that I shouldn't have accepted the question, though Desmond Hawkins, Frank's successor as Head of Programmes in Bristol, kindly sheltered me from the blast, and I didn't hear of the adverse London comment until Frank joined us the following Friday at Dulverton, near his home.

It was at Dulverton that Bob Boothby and Francis Williams gave such admirable answers to a question about the purpose of *Any Questions?* :'Do the team feel they have a responsibility for moulding public opinion, or do they regard themselves simply as entertainers?'

BOOTHBY: Let me say at once, ladies and gentlemen, that I do not want to bore you if I can possibly avoid it, and to that extent I am an entertainer. But at the same time, you can't sit at this table, sweating as I am now, looking at this horrible little machine and imagining, if one can, an audience of several million people, without feeling a certain sense of responsibility. And, I think I can truthfully say, I have never said anything that I didn't genuinely believe and sincerely believe. One can have a joke, one can have a crack occasionally, one can try not to be a bore; but I think it would be quite wrong just for the sake of entertaining a very large audience, to say anything on this programme that you didn't believe or that might have the effect of misleading public opinion on an issue of importance.

WILLIAMS: I would say, of course we want to entertain, who doesn't? It is surely one of the essential truths that to be serious it's not necessary to be solemn. Now, on the other question of whether we want to mould public opinion, I wouldn't myself use the word 'mould'. I don't think public opinion is something that one should try and mould. I would much sooner use the word 'inform'; and I would say that according to our abilities, which may vary and which may not be great, we do try to inform the public so far as we are able. I would say, the purpose of the BBC in running a programme of this kind is that it draws together people of varied experience in various walks of life and activities, who may out of that experience be able to contribute something to a discussion of questions which arise; not that anybody in this audience or in the larger listening audience should take anything said by any member of this team as necessarily right or as necessarily the last word on the subject, but simply as an idea thrown into the pool of discussion, to stimulate discussion, because out of discussion a public opinion may emerge.

BOOTHBY: Well, I don't really want to mould opinion, nor do I want to inform my audience. I've always taken the perfectly simple view that people who don't agree with me after they've heard what I've got to say are not quite right in the head! And I thnk really if they're not prepared to agree with me after what I've said, well, that's just their funeral.

The second lot of hot water I got into in December was considerably deeper and hotter than the virgin births affair. It happened at Bream in the Forest of Dean the following Friday. That week the Archbishop of Canterbury had made a pronouncement on the H-bomb, and I accepted a question in these terms: 'What were the reactions of the team when the Archbishop of Canterbury declared that Communism must be subdued, even to the extent of using the H-bomb?'

Anthony Wedgwood Benn spoke first and was critical in general terms about the Archbishop, 'whom I regard as completely reactionary and ignorant in his political pronouncements'.

The other members of the team – Frank Byers, Jack Longland, and Edith Pitt, a Conservative MP – then had their say, each prefacing their remarks with some such phrase as 'if it is a correct report of what he said', and then proceeding to condemn the Archbishop's reported views right heartily. Tony Benn chimed in at the end with: 'I'm thrilled and delighted that this team tonight, which is by no means all one-way politically, should have so thoroughly taken the Archbishop's gaiters down!'

Apparently, the first the Archbishop heard of it was the arrival of sackfuls of mail protesting at his views, and he got on to the BBC to complain that he had been misrepresented. Frank Gillard dealt with the matter at the London end and tried to pour a little oil on very troubled waters. He pointed out to the Archbishop's chaplain that if the Archbishop was going to make pronouncements on political issues he really must make his views clearer, because if the questioner had misunderstood them there was every chance that a lot of other people had misunderstood them as well.

Frank came down to Bristol to discuss the lessons to be learned. As a result, two innovations were made: a copy of the question would be put down in front of the team as it was being read out, in the fond hope that this would encourage them to challenge inaccurate quotations and to keep to the point; and I was to take with me each Friday copies of *The Times* for that week so that I could check the accuracy of any quotation.

We cut the whole question out of the repeat and in *Any*

Answers Freddy admitted that the Archbishop's statement had been misquoted. 'What Dr Fisher in fact said was that every deterrent to Communism, even the hydrogen bomb, was good as long as it deterred. The Archbishop went on to say that when the hydrogen bomb was used it would become absolutely useless. So long as it deterred it would buy time, which was the only thing that was valuable. The BBC apologizes to the Archbishop for the misrepresentation of his statement and expresses its deep regret that the question, in this distorted form, was accepted for discussion.'

Freddy's voice was admirable for this sort of task. It sounded as if the entire BBC was on its knees.

Early in February, 1956, we had a particularly distinguished newcomer, Emanuel Shinwell, who was to become one of our most popular panellists. He was always rather long-winded; Freddy remarked that he was like a car with a cold engine, taking a long time to get into top gear, but once he got there he was a spell-binder with enormous charm, and a twinkle in the eye which somehow communicated itself to the listeners at home. When he was speaking you were conscious of the weight of authority and experience behind him; the many years of political in-fighting; his years as a rebel, a thorn in Churchill's flesh; his post-war years in office when he mellowed and grew in stature; the statesman he became without sacrificing all the aggression of the bonny fighter of his early days.

As he reached his middle eighties I thought he might be beginning to pass his peak, and gradually stopped inviting him. When he approached ninety and was still continuing to give scintillating performances on other programmes, I admitted my mistake and asked him to appear again. This gave him an opportunity he relished and he took the utmost pleasure in refusing the invitation!

He made such a hit on his first appearance that he was back with us three weeks later, at Lympstone, in Devon. In answer to a question about university rags, he said: 'I shouldn't be surprised to find that I'm the only member of the team who hasn't been at a university. I left school at the early age of 11, a fact that filled me with melancholy reflections for many years afterwards, until one day – what do you think happened? I arrived at the House of Commons, and there I saw before me all the products of the universities and the high scholastic institutions and I was immediately consoled!'

The week after his début there was another Labour politician with a strong sense of humour and a strong tendency to be verbose. Michael Foot was at that time out of the House of Commons – he had lost his Plymouth seat in the election – but was as volatile as ever. We were at a factory in Plymouth and with our usual care to avoid advertising had not named it in the introduction, but Michael with great enthusiasm named it three times while urging its workers to demand higher wages. Very quiet beforehand Michael Foot suddenly seems to become switched on when confronted by a live microphone – haranguing the audience, goading the other members of the team, and almost unstoppable in political debate. But whether in private or in public, he has a pleasing, mordant wit.

During the run of television's *In the News*, Bob Boothby arrived one day very much under the weather. 'Look here,' he said to the other members of the team. 'I don't feel at all well today. I think it quite likely that I shall die during the programme. And if I die, I want the programme to continue so that nobody knows what's happened. I want you, Bill, to prop me up on one side, and I want you, Michael, to prop me up on the other and just carry on. That's what you must do, if I should die.'

And Michael Foot asked: 'How shall we know?'

When Bob was leading the campaign to reform the laws on homosexuality, it was Michael who described him as 'the non-playing captain'.

(DJ: *Another characteristic of Michael Foot is affection. He is very affectionate to all those round him before and after the programme. We recently had a broadcast in Wales, and we walked back to the local hostelry together, and it wasn't just a politician's performance – he stopped to talk to the passers-by, because he had a genuine interest in them and affection for them. When we were in the hotel it was difficult to have any privacy at all. We sat in a public room with the local MP and we were besieged by revellers. If it hadn't been for the fact that he had a leg injury, I'm quite sure Michael Foot would have joined them.*)

On 9 March the second of our future Prime Ministers appeared – Harold Wilson. He was friendly and had some entertaining exchanges with Gerald Nabarro on the programme, but I can't pretend that I saw in him the charisma of a potential Prime Minister. (By that time, Attlee had retired and Hugh Gaitskell looked to be in the saddle as Party Leader for many years to come.) Harold Wilson was then Shadow Chancellor of the Exchequer, and was to appear on several more occasions, the last of them in 1963 when he had recently become Shadow Foreign Secretary, but I was unable to persuade him to rejoin the panel after he resigned as Prime Minister.

The Friday after, I was in the chair myself for the first time, Freddy having had a car accident that morning, when he had sustained painful injuries. I had two weeks at it, and I took the chair on several later occasions as deputy for both Freddy and David. I enjoyed it. There is a lot to be said for the producer being in the chair because he can then influence the proceedings directly instead of having to communicate instructions to someone else. On the other hand, it is a little fraught, in a live broadcast, for the producer to be tied to the microphone, unable to deal with any emergency in the hall.

To be frank, I don't think it's very difficult to be an adequate chairman. But what was lacking in me was the personality and charm of a Grisewood or a Jacobs to give the programme colour and authority.

(DJ: *I'm sure it's not difficult to be an adequate chairman. But it's even easier to be an inadequate one and from time to time really quite difficult to be a good one!*)

The newcomer at Brixham in Devon on 27 April was a Liberal who sounded very promising. His name was Jeremy Thorpe. He was not then an MP, having unsuccessfully fought North Devon in the 1955 election. We certainly had no idea that we were inviting the future Liberal Leader – Jo Grimond seemed set in that role indefinitely. (Jeremy would often say that he thought it was wrong for the Leader of the Liberal Party to appear on

Any Questions? – after all, the Leader of the Opposition did not appear – but fortunately he managed to conquer his scruples when he became Leader himself, and David Steel, I'm happy to say, is also willing to come on the programme.

The team that week included Arthur Street who was in tremendous form, especially in answer to the question: 'The price of potatoes has risen beyond what most housewives consider all reason, and we are told it's likely to rise even higher in the next few weeks; what should be done about it?'

> STREET: What should be done about it? Nothing, except that you're going to learn a lesson, and a very much needed lesson; that you are dependent on something nothing to do with politics; you are depending on a higher power than mankind; you are depending upon the yields from the land of your own country; you had a summer last year that gave you a small potato yield. What can you do about it? Nothing at all. You can ration if you like the potatoes that are there; no politician can make any more, you know. You can't ration the ones you'd like to see there. You can only import potatoes; the same crop position took place on the Continent – you can only import them if you are willing to pay an attractive price to make the people over there let them go. But why all this grouse about potatoes? You don't grouse so much, do you, about the price of coal? Sometimes we grow too many potatoes, too much tonnage; you haven't had too much tonnage of coal, have you, in the last few years? If we get a nice wet season this year, we shall have potatoes – you'll have more than you want.
>
> All right, then you say: 'Oh, the Government should compel farmers to grow potatoes' – very good – but we cannot have the children to pick them up because that's interfering with children's education. Therefore, they will have to be picked up by adults and it hurts an adult to bend his back far more than it does a little child, and an adult on a farm now costs

four and fourpence an hour, so that your potatoes, even if you grow a lot, are going to cost a lot of money anyway. And if we are compelled to grow next year a lot more potatoes as an insurance and we get a good crop, then you'll grouse that we're feather-bedded if the Government pays for them having compelled us to grow them. I'm *glad* you're short of potatoes!.

For the last programme in the series, in Bristol, we had two women in the team for the first time since the very first edition in 1948 – Isobel Barnett and Mary Stocks. The men were Bob Boothby and Wilfred Fienburgh, a very bright young Labour MP who was to die tragically in a car accident. The first questioner asked: 'Does the team consider we shall ever have a woman Prime Minister? If so, will the nation be any better or worse off for this change?'

FIENBURGH: I would be terrified if we had a woman Prime Minister, and let me say quite frankly I have not yet seen – with the exception of my mother, who is a very good local councillor – I have not yet seen a successful woman in Parliamentary politics, at all.

STOCKS: Of course, Mr Fienburgh, I gather, hasn't been long in Parliament, because he can't have been there at the time when Eleanor Rathbone and Margaret Bondfield for instance were Members. I don't see why there shouldn't be a woman Prime Minister. Twenty years ago it would have seemed incredible that there should be a woman Cabinet Minister, or a woman vice-chancellor of a university, and I suppose a hundred years ago a woman doctor would have seemed rather queer, but these things happen, and the answer to the question is, it all depends on the woman.

BOOTHBY: I've sat in the House of Commons with both Margaret Bondfield and Eleanor Rathbone, and they were two of the most remarkable women I've ever known, but I'm quite sure of this, that the best work they did was as independent back bench Members of Parliament and not in administration. We owe children's allowances primarily to Eleanor Rathbone, and a lot of other things as well – she was a tremendous girl but I don't think she'd have been an awfully good Cabinet Minister. Her forte was to get things done outside, and go on grinding at the men until you were forced to submit to what she wanted. And I'm not sure that's not the best function that women can perform in politics.

BARNETT: Don't you think they could do that as Prime Minister? Heaven knows, somebody's got to get a few things done, and I should have thought it would have been easier as Prime Minister than as a backbencher.

FIENBURGH: This is a fatal mistake that people make outside politics; you don't get things done as Prime Minister . . .

BOOTHBY: No.

FIENBURGH: . . .you do things as Prime Minister in response to pressure. A Prime Minister's job is essentially one of inertia, trying to prevent things being done . . . but I think the real point about women is this, that to be a woman Prime Minister they shall have had to have succeeded in politics, and to succeed in politics you have to acquire a certain brass neck, rough tactics, a strong arm, arrogance, egotism, which, when women acquire them, they cease to be charming and womanly and cease, therefore, to be effective on that count.

STOCKS: Mr Fienburgh must be even more recent in politics than I supposed, because he doesn't seem to have heard of Winston Churchill as Prime Minister . . .

FIENBURGH: But he wasn't a woman.

BARNETT: He did get things done.

1956/57

When we assembled at Mullion in Cornwall for the start of the new series, our thoughts were very much on the situation in the Middle East. Much had happened in the four months the programme had been off the air, and the first question concerned Britain's policy in relation to the current Suez crisis.

Bob Boothby and Mary Stocks were in the team again, and Manny Shinwell was back. He thought the Government was right to resent the arbitrary action taken by Colonel Nasser, who should have consulted the Suez Canal Company and the Canal users before he nationalized it. He didn't deny the Government had a right to take military precautions, but he was worried about the threat of a possible war and thought the whole matter should have been referred to the Security Council and the Assembly of the United Nations. He ended with this warning: 'We of the western nations have got to find some way of helping the countries in the Middle East to exploit all resources and arrange for effective distribution and at the same time raise the standard of life of the people in that area, and if we fail to do that we'll have problems in that area confronting not only them but the whole world for many years to come.'

The next question was equally topical but less serious: 'Does the team approve of the action by the Watch Committee of certain cities in banning the film *Rock Around the Clock* to the disappointment of many young enthusiasts?'

SHINWELL: Well, I thoroughly disapprove of their action. You see, you get these teddy boys, you get these people who want to – what d'you call it – jive, and dance their heads off, and play all kinds of tricks. Well, you know, there's something happening to the youth of the nation. They're disturbed in mind, they're trying to free themselves of some kind of thraldom, they don't understand what it is, but they're trying to escape from it, they want more liberty, more freedom, and they resent the routine, being in the rut, getting up in the morning, being clocked in, being liberated when the foreman decides and the employer decides they can be liberated, getting their pay on Friday or whenever it is, spending it in the usual way, the same routine morning, noon and night. They're getting a little bit tired of it. And so is the whole world getting tired of routine and being in the rut. That's part of the problem in the Middle East.

And therefore I don't worry about teddy boys and teddy girls, whether they come from the slums of London or elsewhere or whether they come from the universities, and occasionally they indulge in a bit of jiving and a bit of teddy boy action; you can't blame all the teddy boys for what is happening, it seems to be symptomatic – I think that's the right word, but some of the intellectuals on the platform will correct me if I'm wrong. Now, what I object to among these people is when they begin to use coshes and bicycle chains and terrorize people, but if they want to dance their heads off, in the street or elsewhere, well, why not let them have a bit of fun. I know Bob resents that, but he's past having a bit of fun.

BOOTHBY: Well, I must say, that Shinwell should say that I was past having a bit of fun! If that isn't below the belt I don't know what is. But I would only say this, the question says 'enthusiasts', why should we discourage these enthusiasts. Enthusiasts for what? As Manny Shinwell himself has said, for jiving. Jiving!

What a thing to do. Can you see me jiving? I've never had the faintest temptation, I may say. It's not my idea of fun at all. And I think that one of the purposes of us old fogies in life is to stop young people from being silly. And they're being exceedingly silly. There are better things to do in life and much more fun to be had than jiving. And if they cause a lot of trouble and row in cinemas and upset people and if they want to be teddy boys, well, I'd rather they went off to Cairo and started teddy boying around there. But in cinemas in this country, no. And I think the sooner this ridiculous film is banned altogether the better; it's causing a lot of trouble to a lot of people and giving no pleasure except to a few quite harmless, but quite irresponsible, lunatics.

SHINWELL: We were nearly all silly when we were young.

BOOTHBY: Not I.

SHINWELL: No, well, you started rather late in life!

STOCKS: Surely, Mr Shinwell – d'you really think the Middle East is suffering from routine? I mean, have you been there lately? No. Of course that's by the way, we'll get back to the question. Yes, I think the Watch Committees are quite right to ban a film if it causes disturbances of this kind and gives trouble to the police and disturbs audiences and encourages young people to behave in this silly way. But I do agree with Mr Shinwell that there is something more at the back of it, but not, I think, routine. Because I'm quite convinced that the young people of today, on the whole, have more leisure and more money and more variety of leisure pursuits probably than they've ever had before. And I think there are two factors in the situation. One is, I think they have unexpended animal spirits. Now, if those boys had been born rich they would have been at public schools and their brains would have been kept on the stretch most of the day and when they weren't thinking they would be made to take violent exercise. And they would go to bed not exhausted but comfortably tired. Now, I don't think these young people do; I think they work very short hours, at comparatively light jobs, and they've got a lot of animal spirits. The second factor is the popular Press. People are very imitative, and the less educated, the sillier they are, the more they imitate, and they do what's expected of them. They read about this sort of thing happening in one place and they feel that they ought to do it, too. And what can you expect of a generation of young people who are brought up on such literature as *Reveille* and the *Weekend Mail*, let us say?.

BOOTHBY: Steady. Steady.

STOCKS: Well, one advantage of this programme is that one's indiscretions cannot be suppressed.

A fact of which Mary always took the fullest advantage.

The Suez crisis erupted at the end of October, when Britain and France invaded Egypt. And as far as *Any Questions?* was concerned, it brought to a head the controversy over the fourteen-day rule.

On 2 November, the Friday immediately after the invasion, the team assembled at a hotel in Wilton, Wiltshire, in a militant mood. There were two MPs, Stephen McAdden and Francis Noel-Baker, Henry Fairlie, political correspondent of the *Spectator*, and Mary Stocks. There was only one topic they wanted to discuss and that was Suez. It was undoubtedly the most controversial issue since *Any Questions?* had started, and Sir Anthony Eden's decision to invade had divided the country. Everybody was talking about it. Then, on the six o'clock news we heard that there was to be a special sitting of the Commons the following morning, and this meant the fourteen-day rule came into operation and the subject was forbidden to us. We checked with London and were given a ruling that Suez was not to be discussed. When I explained this to the team, they were rebellious, to say the least.

Bill Coysh was with me that evening to do the warm-up and it was decided that he should station himself with the engineers and if the team insisted on talking about Suez he would take the programme off the air by pulling out the appropriate plug. A warning was sent to the Light Programme announcer that this might happen.

At the very beginning of the broadcast it was quite clear that the team were not going to accept the situation tamely. They all protested vigorously when Freddy warned them during his introductory remarks that questions submitted on the Suez crisis could not be dealt with in the programme. However, things were fairly peaceful while the first three questions were discussed. Then we reached the one I had carefully selected. It was calculated to bring to the fore the issue of the fourteen-day rule, and it succeeded. The wording was: 'In our present state of world culture is law possible without the backing of force?'

After another warning from Freddy, Henry Fairlie said: 'We're all under the illusion that Britain has invaded Egypt; I want to talk about the other invasion which has been ignored, which is that Britain has invaded a country called Ruritania. Now, the British Government is being criticized for having invaded this country called Ruritania because it has refused to accept what's called international law and has used force by itself. Now, even if you went to the United Nations, you would soon be invoking force behind the sanction of the United Nations, therefore the simple answer to the question which has been put is that you cannot apply any law without a force which will apply the sanction behind it. The only difficulty about this question of Britain invading Ruritania is whether in fact you could have relied on the United Nations providing the force necessary. I don't think personally that the United Nations would have been willing and ready and able to provide that force and therefore I think that when, three days ago, British forces went into Ruritania, it was perfectly right that they should do so.'

Bill Coysh decided that this was an infringement of the fourteen-day rule, pulled out the plug and the programme went off the air. Despite the warning, the Light Programme announcer sounded rather surprised, but managed to find some suitably angry piano music to play until we sent a message that we were ready to resume.

Taking the programme off the air gave rise to a great

deal of publicity, and we always felt that it was our action which caused the fourteen-day rule to be rescinded early the following year, though I understand the BBC Television Service believe they had a hand in it as well.

Concurrently with the invasion of Egypt by Britain and France, the Russians were invading Hungary and on 9 November the Labour MP Anthony Greenwood, at RAF Chivenor in Devon, commented: 'I'm quite sure there must have been doubts in the Kremlin as to what was the way to handle the situation and as soon as they saw we had defied the rule of law and defied the United Nations, they saw the green light in Hungary to go ahead.'

Suez continued to dominate the programme for several weeks. On 16 November, a questioner at Winterbourne Whitechurch in Dorset asked: 'A Frenchman has said that we set out to explode Nasser and consolidate the Canal, and in the end we have consolidated Nasser and exploded the Canal; does the team agree?' The team didn't agree, which was hardly surprising, as we had three right-wingers in Isobel Barnett, Lewis Hastings and C.A. Joyce. Not one of my better attempts at political balance. When I had first met C.A. Joyce at Ashton Keynes Approved School where he was headmaster we talked about his political leanings. He had described himself as a Liberal. Some *Any Questions?* people are remarkably ill informed about their own political stance. He was certainly one of the most reactionary of all our speakers, but I do not intend this as a term of abuse; it would be a dull team which consisted entirely of anaemic progressives.

Good rich, red blood was invariably donated by Lewis Hastings. In answer to the Nasser question he roared: 'This fourteenth-rate Mussolini, this pinchbeck Napoleon, is now beginning to be recognized for what he is. It's quite obvious that the support for Nasser, the belief in Nasser, has disappeared. Whatever you may think of the action taken by the British and French, the contest is not between ourselves and the Egyptians or the Arabs; it's the perennial, desperate contest between western civilization and these bloodthirsty brutes of Moscow, and it was because Nasser was a Soviet stooge and because he was obviously planning to set the Middle East afire with weapons bought at enormous cost from Moscow that the intervention took place. This action, however you may look upon it, by the British and French forces, put an end to the Soviet plan to dominate the Middle East.'

Gerald Nabarro spoke in the same vein the following week in Bridgwater, but he had stronger opposition, particularly from Jeremy Thorpe. The question was: 'Should British and French troops be withdrawn from Egyptian soil immediately?' and Jeremy replied: 'Yes, of course they should. We're sitting there in twenty miles with our troops exposed; there are forty-nine ships in the Canal; nobody's prepared to start clearing it until we've gone; we're going to have to lose face anyway from this perfectly ridiculous action which was brought on by a weak man trying to be strong and losing his temper; and the sooner we get out and let the United Nations take over and get the Canal cleared, the sooner we shall have genuine peace in the United Nations. We went in to separate the insurgents – Israel is still in possession of the Sinai Desert and the Gaza strip; we went in to keep the Canal open, it's now blocked for the next year. What an abysmal failure it's been. The sooner we get out the better.'

Petrol rationing was introduced after Suez and was discussed in our pre-Christmas edition at Southmead Hospital in Bristol. Mary Stocks was characteristically forthright: 'As far as I can make out, the only people who are really well off under this rationing scheme are MPs and potential MPs who are nursing constituencies and who apparently have as much petrol as they want to drive round about their constituency.'

When the Commons reassembled after the Christmas recess, Mary's remarks were raised as a breach of privilege. Some MPs seemed to think she had accused them of feathering their own nests. I wasn't unduly worried. It seemed to me rather a trivial complaint and indeed nothing came of it. (The only other breach of privilege case the programme has been involved in resulted from Nicky Crocker having ruled that it was perfectly in order to discuss a case which had been referred to the Committee of Privileges, though the two MPs on the team, Anthony Wedgwood Benn and Sir Edward Boyle, opted out. Nothing came of that, either.)

Mary was a bit disappointed. A regular contributor to the *Lift Up Your Hearts* series of religious talks, she had been looking forward to lifting up people's hearts from the Tower of London. When she boasted of her candour in a later programme, the Labour MP Hugh Delargy growled: 'Very lucky to get away with it.' And in fact John Junor, editor of the *Sunday Express*, had to apologize at the Bar of the House of Commons for a leader which included not altogether dissimilar comments.

Trouble had also loomed on 19 October in Southampton, when Ted Leather accused Hugh Gaitskell of knowing that Sir Anthony Eden wanted to go to the United Nations on the Suez issue, but nevertheless deliberately making party capital out of pretending not to know, and making statements that he knew were untrue. Fortunately, Hugh Gaitskell was willing to deny the allegation and set the record straight in a letter to *Any Answers*.

In that same programme, Dr Bronowski found the first question objectionable. It was this: 'With the opening of Calder Hall it was reported that we might be able in five years to produce electricity from atomic power at a cost equal to that of coal firing stations. Considering the rising cost of coal today, will the country's economy stand the strain?'

'Is the remark – will the country's economy stand the strain – intended to be witty?' asked Dr Bronowski icily. 'I'm genuinely at a loss. The cost of electricity is in part that of the fuel and in part that of building the station and in part that of distribution. Calder Hall will produce electricity at a price roughly comparable with that which is produced from coal. That seems to me all that there is to say except that the future cost of atomic electricity will fall and will fall quite fast. I should like to know more about the question.'

On being reassured by Freddy, he continued: 'Calder Hall is one of the great British achievements of this generation. It's in the same class as the poems of Dylan

Thomas and the novels of Graham Greene and the paintings of Graham Sutherland, it's one of the great imaginative achievements of our generation. We are the first nation in the world to have taken atomic power and while everybody else was busy building atomic bombs and hydrogen bombs and all kinds of horrors, to have built a station which is at this moment putting ten thousand kilowatts of electricity into the Grid and which within the next year will be producing ninety-two thousand kilowatts. That's enough electricity to run a town very much larger than Southampton. We lead the world in this, it's an achievement of which I think we should be proud not only as a scientific achievement but because we led the race in the world to turn atomic energy to peaceful use. The cost of making electricity in this way is going to fall, within ten years we shall be making as much electricity from atomic power as would now take six million tons of coal; within less than twenty years we will be making as much electricity from atomic power as is at this moment made by all the power stations in Great Britain. That seems to me to be something to be very proud of.'

On 30 November, in Bath, we had a question asking why normally good-tempered men are bad-tempered drivers. Graham Hutton illustrated the difference between men and women with this story: 'If a man goes out to buy a steak and comes back with the steak and it's cooked and the woman says to the man, "Where did you get this steak?" he'll say, "At Tomkinson's the butchers"; and if the woman goes out to get the steak and comes back and it's cooked, and the man says to the woman, "Where did you get this steak?" she'll say, "Why, what's wrong with it?" '

On 8 February, 1957, we were at Badminton, best known as the home of the Duke of Beaufort. We were beginning to go to smaller places. There is a lot to be said in favour of village audiences. The arrival of a BBC team is a big event, whereas in some of the larger towns of the west country which the programme had visited so often during its first eight years, they were becoming a bit blasé about it. We always enjoy ourselves more with a village audience and this enjoyment is communicated to the listeners. The snag is that it is very difficult to assemble a politically-balanced audience in a small village. Most of them are very Conservative.

(DJ: *What I think is most important is that they come together as a community, and they all know each other, so that when the producer calls out the names of the questioners, they all say, 'I wonder what that silly old so-and-so will ask.' And although they may all vote the same way politically, they may not agree about a lot of other things.*)

Assembling a politically-balanced audience has always been a problem. There seems to be something about *Any Questions?* which appeals to the middle classes. Even on our factory visits, it was largely the white-collar workers who attended; the workers on the shop-floor seemed, perhaps understandably, to prefer to stay at home watching television on Friday evenings rather than return to the factory to watch the *Any Questions?* team. Even when our hosts were the Parent-Teachers Association of a comprehensive school on a council housing estate, it was again the more Conservative-minded parents who turned out on the night. I was told that Sir Geoffrey Howe rather feared he would face a hostile audience on an estate in his native Port Talbot. If so, he needn't have worried.

What to do about it? The local organizer, who distributes the tickets on behalf of the BBC, is always asked to try to ensure a reasonable political balance in the audience and in a Conservative area I used to see that there was a special allocation of tickets to the Labour Party. It is obviously in the programme's interests that there should be a balanced reaction to the varying views on the platform.

In the somewhat feudal atmosphere of Badminton, the team included Percy Cudlipp, John Connell, a leader-writer on the *London Evening News*, and Arthur Street, and the climax to the evening came with this question: 'Does the team think that death duties are too high?'

> CONNELL: There are a number of great estates which, when broken up, a tradition – not of wealth only but of responsibility, of the responsibility the privileged

carry – a great tradition goes; and the connection between a landowner and the farms and the villages that for centuries his family has owned, breaks. Now that I believe to be deeply tragic. We're seeing a dissolution of society and a passing of things as great as the dissolution of the monasteries, and I think that death duties are one of the major factors in this social revolution.

CUDLIPP: You know, I think it's at once picturesque and pathetic to find John Connell here in this splendid feudal state of mind, suggesting that because one is the son of innumerable ancestors, one of whom somehow filched some land or was given it by a king as a reward for heaven knows what, that those people should be regarded by us as the guardians of intelligence and conscience in the twentieth century. It is shameful, John, and I don't really think you mean it, you're acting a part.

CONNELL: It isn't shameful and I'm not acting a part. I'm not feudal. My mind, such as it is, belongs to the eighteenth century and on into the early part of the nineteenth century when I believe our country was great.

STREET: If you destroy by death duties the big house, the landed estate, you chop it up, you make the house into a school or a mental institution or something, what happens? It may be the way that things ought to go, but I'll tell you one thing that will happen. You will get very much less beauty.

The Duke and Duchess of Beaufort were in the audience and did not seem to mind Percy Cudlipp's unflattering reference to the landed gentry, because they kindly invited us all back to Badminton House afterwards.

(DJ: *:Sometimes we finish the programme and nothing happens at all, we just disperse. Other times we have drinks in the Mayor's parlour or in the village hall and enjoy meeting some of the locals. Sometimes we're invited back to a private house – several occasions come to mind, but I remember so well when we were at Silverton, near Exeter, a perfect setting, a lovely evening, we dined at a pub near the river, and after the programme one of the local community* *invited us back to her house. It really was a privilege because when we arrived we found it to be one of the loveliest in the area – a Georgian house nestling on the side of a Devonshire hill. It was the perfect end to a perfect evening – and we were being paid!*)

On 1 March the newcomer was Frank Cousins, General Secretary of the Transport and General Workers Union. Before my time, the only trade unionist to appear on the programme was George Woodcock, General Secretary of the TUC. During those years about fifty MPs had appeared. I gradually changed the emphasis, in order to reflect what I saw as the increasing influence of trade union leaders in comparison with that of back-bench MPs. I wanted the make-up of the teams to correspond to the realities of power, and I invited most of the general secretaries of the largest trade unions, almost all of whom accepted. We normally only see or hear them being po-faced about industrial disputes, so it's interesting to note what views these powerful personalities hold on every conceivable issue, whether they have a sense of humour, what makes them tick. Unfortunately, this interest wanes as soon as they disappear from public life. The producer, emulating Stalin, tends to ask: 'How many block votes has he?'

For Frank Cousins's début, at Okehampton in Devon, I put him up against Arthur Street, judging them to be diagonally opposed in almost everything. My plans for confrontation were foiled by their getting on very well together, as witness their answers to the question: 'Is too much of the taxpayers' money going in subsidies to the farmers?'

> STREET: As a farmer, I say yes. A terrific lot too much. And a terrific lot too much public money going in subsidies to nearly everybody else in the country as well. In January the dairy farmers of this country are to receive 3½d. a gallon less than they received a year ago in January, whereas the public are to pay more money for milk, because the subsidy to the consumer has been taken off. And therefore milk rises in price to the consumer. So the consumer is being subsidized by public money. When the subsidy was taken off

bread because bread went up, again that was a consumer subsidy. I am an unrepentant free-trader, I want no subsidies to farming or to anything else. I want no tariffs to the motor industry or any other industry to protect them. I want everybody to stand on their own feet; as a British farmer I am perfectly willing in a wholly free trade policy to do that and to get away with it very nicely, thank you. And I question very much whether the motor industry in Coventry could face it or any other town industry as well as my own could face absolutely bare free trade all round.

COUSINS: I wonder how genuine Arthur can be in his line that he's a genuine free-trader. Because if he was, he would start by an attack on the Government who make money dear. After all, there isn't much free trading about a Government that says, 'We increase the Bank Rate to a position where costs go up for those of you who have no control over it.'

STREET: I thought they'd just reduced it.

COUSINS: Oh yes, that's a nice political trick. They increase it from 4 per cent up to 5½, knock it down to 5 and say, 'Aren't we clever?' But, you see, the real issue is that subsidies are a way of spreading the burden of costs over those who have high incomes – make no mistake about this, subsidies come out of taxation – and they give the advantages to those who have low incomes. And whilst we all clap about a reduction in tax, surely we don't want a reduction in our taxes at the expense of those who can't afford now the milk that was cheaper before they interfered with the subsidies to the farmers.

STREET: No, the subsidy is to the consumers.

COUSINS: And the farmers.

STREET: No. The farmer gets less money than he got a year ago, and the consumer pays more. The subsidy was to the consumer of milk.

COUSINS: Aye, and in this January, Arthur, he got more milk, too, than he did last January.

STREET: Now that tells you the value of anything Frank Cousins has said on this question. He would even take to himself the power of the Almighty to whether he – oh, Frank, you ought to know better!

COUSINS: Which means we've touched him in the place where it hurts, we've touched him in the tax pocket!

Arthur was at the top of his form that evening. After listening to the others on the subject of fox-hunting, he launched this broadside:

'Is fox-hunting a sport? Yes. It's part of country life. Any man who says they go fox-hunting in order to improve the price of oats or the breed of horses or to exercise the fox, is a liar. When I was able and fit, I went fox-hunting; I was secretary of our local pack at one period. And I went for the only valid reason, that I enjoyed it, call me what you will. It is part of country life, it is part of the seasons. I would never attack fox-hunting and I don't intend to defend it, I would just as soon defend barley harvesting or wheat sowing. Listen. In September, I harvest my barley and I can shoot partridges. In October, I sow my wheat and I can shoot pheasants. And in November, I plough and I hunt the fox. You see? It is part of country life. All right, you say – all my friends on the panel say – we know nothing about it, we think it's dreadful and we would like to abolish it. Let me quote you this:

"The king from the castle, the squire from the hall,
The doctor, the parson, the parish and all,
Oh, see the grand beauty and hear the sweet cry
Of hounds and their music, and then you can die!"

They've never lived!'

Arthur was with us again on 22 March, at Weymouth and one of the questions gave him an opportunity to make capital out of an argument with us some months earlier over fees: 'Would the team strike if the BBC refused to raise their fees?' The team also included Lewis Hastings.

HASTINGS: I think at any rate the people on the platform might show an example to the rest of the country and refuse to take part in this monstrous anachronism of strikes. But, on the other hand, I may say that from my own point of view I'm quite contented with whatever the BBC like to pay on this occasion, to come here and enjoy my stay in Weymouth, especially as I'm already half-way up to North Devon where I intend to do a fortnight's fishing.

STREET: The BBC has a monopoly on sound, not on TV, and the difference is extraordinary. I don't care, you may say I am biting the hand that's fed me for twenty-five years, the rest of my life on this earth I am willing to feed myself, but the difference between sound and television is extraordinary because in television there is competition, in sound there is no competition. When the attitude – I don't say it's said but it's implied by the BBC on sound – if you don't broadcast for us ha, ha, ha, you won't broadcast for anybody. And there is more exploitation by the BBC on sound than the most brassy employer in Britain has ever tried to do.

HASTINGS: Well, I couldn't support that. Here I am, sitting as a client or a servant of the BBC, and I remember a proverb by which I've guided my life for the last twenty years or so which I heard on the Zambesi, and that is 'When crossing the river speak kindly of the crocodile's mother.'

STREET: Which is the best description of the BBC that I've ever heard!

1957/58

Throughout the summer of 1957 I was in London on an attachment to children's television but returned in time to take over *Any Questions?* again at the beginning of its tenth series on 20 September. It was not a particularly distinguished autumn session. For one thing, the international situation hung like a pall of smoke over the discussions. Not only the Suez aftermath which was still smouldering but, even more so, the Russian threat of superior technology in ballistic missiles.

At the end of the year, at Stoke-sub-Hamdon, near Yeovil, there was the customary question about the outstanding event of 1957. One member of the team optimistically voted for the appointment of Sir Hugh Foot as Governor of Cyprus in the hope that this would bring peace to that troubled island, but the other three, Ted Leather, Mary Stocks and Jeremy Thorpe, plumped for the launching of the Sputnik.

LEATHER: It is an event that has upset people's thinking and strategic ideas.

STOCKS: The most significant event is the realization by America that Russia has got an effective intercontinental ballistic missile which has terribly complicated the defence of western Europe. One thing that's followed from it, of course, is the preoccupation of America with the erection of launching bases in western Europe, so that it can get nearer to Russia in the absence of the intercontinental ballistic missile.

THORPE: We have now reached the stage where it isn't a question of one nation being slightly ahead of the other; we've really now reached a position where either side can destroy the other.

It was at that year's Labour Party Conference at Brighton that Aneurin Bevan, who was by then back in the mainstream of Labour politics as Shadow Foreign Secretary, made his famous remark about 'going naked into the conference chamber' if Britain gave up her H-bomb. On that Friday, at Bere Regis in Dorset, the team included the newly elected chairman of the Labour Party, Tom Driberg, and Mary Stocks, and a questioner asked: 'A large group within the Labour Party has always urged that Britain should take a moral stand and renounce the use of the H-bomb; at Brighton, the leaders of this group voted for retention of the bomb; what are the team's views about this sudden change of face?'

STOCKS: I have very great sympathy with Nye Bevan on this. My own feeling is that some nation has got to make a great gesture and refuse not only to use the thing but to make it, or to have it, and it's just possible that that might stimulate a real movement for disarmament because I'm perfectly certain that Russia is terrified of the United States and that the United States is terrified of Russia. So I think – if I'd been going to that conference – I should have gone with a strong feeling in favour of renouncing the manufacture and use of the hydrogen bomb as a lead to the nations of the world. But Nye Bevan may be our future Foreign Secretary and if you tie his hands with a resolution of this sort you rob him of any bargaining power that he may have in the future to deal with the United States on one hand and Russia on the other. And I think that if I'd been at the Labour Party Conference I should have voted with him, with reluctance.

DRIBERG: All of us are against the H-bomb; we all loathe it; the only question is how best to get rid of it. And Bevan made certainly a very strong point when he said after all it's not only the British manufactured or stocks of H-bombs we've got to get rid of, it's also the Russian and the American ones and are we likely to come nearer to doing that by unilaterally saying we will stop making them ourselves? As regards the lead to the world, the example which Mary Stocks mentioned; at any rate he went this far, that we are prepared unilaterally for a period to give up tests. It may be argued, of course, what's the use of having the things unless you test them but at least tests themselves do help to poison the air with this terrible fall-out, and therefore there is some use in giving up tests, partly physical advantage of that kind and partly because that might help to ease the international tension.

To my mind one of the main concrete arguments for the point of view which Bevan expressed yesterday, is this, that the implication of unilateral abandonment of nuclear weapons, their use, manufacture and everything, is that you disengage yourself from all sorts of international commitments, and of course you would have to say to the Americans please remove your bases which are stocked up with nuclear weapons, as one gathers, from England. Well, it has been a popular cry in recent years, 'Yanks go home'; the trouble is now that if the Americans left Britain they would not go home, they would go to West Germany almost certainly, which would be a far, far greater danger potentially to world peace than their presence in Britain even. And therefore this seems to me a very strong argument for the case that Bevan made yesterday and I think the main thing is to try to mitigate the acute suspicion and anxiety and fear that exists between the two great power blocs of East and West.

Tension of a different kind resulted that autumn from criticism of the Queen by Malcolm Muggeridge in an article published in the United States. Only extracts from it appeared over here, and very few people who were so filled with righteous indignation can have read the article in full, but that did not discourage them from condemning the author out of hand.

I found myself unwittingly in the middle of the controversy by having previously invited Malcolm to appear in *Any Questions?* on 1 November. While anxious heart-searching was going on among the BBC hierarchy in London as to whether he should be allowed to take part, Malcolm quietly pleaded a dinner engagement, ironically one hosted by the BBC, and withdrew.

'Well, that problem's solved,' said Desmond Hawkins to me. 'Who have you got in his place?'

'Lord Altrincham,' I replied.

While he was fighting for breath, I realized, rather belatedly, that this was not perhaps the most appropriate replacement. I had previously invited Lord Altrincham for a date later that month and he had been unable to accept. In a moment of mental aberration, I had telephoned him to offer the vacant date, overlooking the fact that he was equally associated in the public mind with criticism of the monarchy. Further horrified deliberations in London followed. Finally, at the same time that BBC television was withdrawing an invitation to Malcolm to appear on *Panorama* to discuss his article, BBC radio decided to withdraw the invitation to Lord Altrincham to appear on *Any Questions?*.

The public sprang into action and, as so often happens when the public is on the rampage, you just can't win. Half of them deplored the fact that we had invited Altrincham in the first place. (Why was it only now that he had been asked to join the panel? It could only be the notoriety he had acquired by his recent attacks on the monarchy.) The other half berated us for having withdrawn the invitation. One correspondent, enclosing a petition signed by forty-six people, pointed out that Lord Altrincham had not spoken against the Queen personally but only against the monarchic system in general. Another complained of the BBC's habit of promulgating regal dispensations as to just what subjects the lower orders might be permitted to hear discussed.

The BBC's official reply to this barrage was that there was no general ban on Lord Altrincham, but it was felt that he might be drawn into a discussion similar to that which was cancelled in *Panorama*.

The Friday after the *Panorama* discussion was to have taken place, I accepted a question about the BBC's action. The team, at Poole, included John Arlott and Christopher Mayhew.

ARLOTT: First of all, I would say that there exists in this country a belief in the freedom of the Press; therefore to my mind any man is free to write anything he likes in the Press which does not come under legal ban as treason, blasphemy or obscenity, and I don't believe that any work should be withheld from him. Secondly, if a particular body, like the BBC, holds a particular view on any subject, then it is entitled not to ask a man to discuss that subject on *its* air, and to violate *its* point of view, but it's not entitled to take his living away from him. Now, may I make a third point: I have all this week been battered by people who are accusing Muggeridge of criticizing the monarchy and I've made the same reply to every one of them. If I live under a monarchy I would sooner live under a monarchy that can take criticism and live it down than a monarchy which can do anything it likes, right, wrong, good, bad or indifferent, and never be criticized.

MAYHEW: I would have liked him to go on *Panorama*. I think that it's not enough for John Arlott to say that just like a newspaper editor the BBC has a right to say that owing to our editorial policy this point of view, or that point of view, may not be put. Now that's all right with a newspaper – one of many – but the BBC, by its charter, has no editorial policy on these questions. It seems to me there is a far greater obligation on the BBC to give a completely free platform even for unpopular ideas if we are really meaning what we say about free speech in this country. Now, I'm not for a moment going to defend anybody – I don't say that Malcolm Muggeridge did – who makes any kind of personal attack on the monarchy, but our right of free speech in this country, our need to keep fresh air blowing through all these things, should have led the BBC to allow this problem to be aired on Monday night.

Malcolm Muggeridge was in the *Any Questions?* team on 6 December, but Lord Altrincham did not make his début until December 1963, by which time he had renounced his peerage and appeared as John Grigg.

Early in 1958, the Rochdale by-election gave the Conservative Government a shock. The Liberal candidate, Ludovic Kennedy, later to become a valued *Any Questions?* contributor, did unexpectedly well, and this gave rise to a pointed discussion on 14 February, the result of a crafty bit of casting on my part.

Some time previously, Dingle Foot had written to Frank Gillard to warn us that he was about to leave the Liberal Party and he thought it only fair that we should be aware of this in assessing the political balance of our teams; he would understand if we felt we had to drop him. Frank replied reassuringly: 'We love you for yourself alone.'

By the time we met in Plymouth in February, Dingle Foot had become Labour MP for Ipswich, and I thought it might be rather a good idea to pair him with that doyen of the Liberal Party, Lady Violet Bonham Carter. I thought this might give the programme a certain edge. It did. (The others were Gerald Nabarro and Arthur Street.) A questioner asked: 'Does the result of the Rochdale by-election indicate a revival of the Liberal Party or merely a lack of confidence in the present Government?'

NABARRO: Of course this was a very great success for the Liberal Party. It was a failure for the Socialist Party, because their total vote went down, and the Labour member was elected on a minority vote. Looking at it as a Tory I think that this result shows one important thing: that the Liberal candidate was the residuary legatee of a large number of Tory malcontents – possibly ten thousand of them. Something of that order. They were fed up with the Government, thought it wasn't Tory enough. They were to the right of the Tory Party in the House of

Commons; But, as a private member of the House of Commons and a strong Tory supporter, it always seems to me that it's a very good thing that governments are given a hard kick in the pants from time to time. That's what democracy, after all, is all about. And, you needn't think the Tory Party is going to lose the next election, because it's not.

STREET: I think the result of the Rochdale by-election shows, yes, a Liberal revival to some extent, but a definite lack of confidence in politicians generally. I think that today very few people care who gets in, so they put in a TV personality, that's what Rochdale shows. Politicians today stand lower, I think, in public opinion than ever before in my lifetime. They yap about restraint in profits, restraint in wages and then they put their own salaries up. That is something which is not done – it comes into that category of the things that are not done by decent people. And a gesture is wanted from politicians of all parties to put their wages down and show that they believe what they say, because nobody else believes it. And there's an economic argument, too, ladies and gentlemen. You see advertisements now, don't you, for farm-workers, typists, electricians, washer-uppers, everybody – no one has ever yet seen an advertisement for a politician. Politicians today in this country are surplus to requirements. There were three put up for the one seat at Rochdale. There are at least ten times more would-be MPs than there are seats in the House of Commons. There is an enormous surplus of would-be politicians, and when there is a surplus the price should go down. And the deposit should go up. There's a surplus of milk at the present time, and during the last few months the price of milk to the farmer has gone down – but while you can make useful things like butter and cheese from surplus milk, if anybody can tell me anything useful that you can make out of surplus politicians, I'd like to know.

LADY VIOLET: This Rochdale result is only the climax of what's been a steady trend in all the recent by-elections – a soaring Liberal vote, a slumping Tory vote, and Labour being unable to pick up on the swings what the Tories have lost on the roundabouts. Well now, Mr Nabarro here has said that the Liberal success is due to the fact that these ten thousand-odd Tory malcontents think the Tories ought to be more Tory than they are. Well, in that case it's very odd they've voted Liberal, because they can hardly expect the Liberals to be more Tory than the Tories.

Now what is the cause? There's no doubt that the cause is partly what is suggested by the questioner – a lack of confidence, not merely, I should say, in the present Government – that is obvious – but a weariness and a disillusion with both the great parties, these great powerful machines grinding against each other. And both harnessed to the service of particular interests, of particular classes. I think what the Liberal stood for, and what he got support for was as a man who would stand for the needs and the rights of the ordinary man and woman, as citizen and as consumer. A man not belonging to any particular class. They don't want to divide the nation, they want to unite the nation. They want to stop this sterile cold war which is going on in industry, and which is one of the greatest menaces, I think, to our national solvency. And the way they do that is by building peace in industry through partnership.

Now, I think I can't do better than to end with a short quotation from Mr Dingle Foot. I couldn't possibly put it better or as well myself, which is that there are millions of people in this country who dislike the Tory past and who dislike the Socialist present, and that's why there must be a Liberal future. I agree with every word and so did Rochdale.

FOOT: Lady Violet quoted from some speech of mine. I don't remember the exact date but I think it must have been several years ago. And things change in the course of years. Lady Violet said, just now, that people who wanted the Government to be more Tory wouldn't vote Liberal. I'm not at all sure about that. When you look at the record of Liberal members over the recent years – when you look, for instance, at the recent by-election at Carmarthen, where the Liberal candidate supported the Tory Suez policy, I think it may very well be that disgruntled Tories now can safely support Liberal candidates.

Lady Violet was on the team again on 2 May at Westward Ho! in Devon, where a questioner asked how they would overcome the London parking problems. 'Are they in favour of meters or do they approve of the police driving away owners' cars without authority?' The question was greeted with loud laughter. Lady Violet's trial of strength with Sabrina and her car had been much publicized. (In case you have forgotten, or are too young to know, Sabrina appeared on television in the late Fifties doing not very much else besides brandishing her bosom.)

LADY VIOLET: I have been the victim of this problem almost for the last year. I have had a car of immense dimensions parked practically permanently, with short intervals, in front of my own front door; and when I say my own front door I'm not being accurate, because it's the front door of a block of flats inhabited by twenty-two other unfortunate tenants as well as myself, who have been denied access and egress from this house. I cannot tell you how thankful I was when I discovered – all too late – that I could appeal to the police. Every kind of courteous representation had been made through the right authorities and had been met with a blank refusal, and then I was suddenly and mercifully informed by the managers of the flat of a lady known as Miss Spinks, but better known as Sabrina, that I ought to telephone for the police, and that I did. They appeared within a very few minutes, and the car vanished – I've not set eyes on it since.

So I am very much in favour of the police. Of course, the meter system might do the trick as well. I might add that I've never seen or had any personal truck with the owner of the car, but I was very interested when I was told it was her car; I knew she was very famous, in the entertaining business, and I asked what she did, how she entertained people. And I was rather surprised at being told that she was famous for her measurements – I don't know what measurements. And one of her measurements – S.41 – was the number of the car. Well, I've never seen her measurements, but I have seen the measurements of her car, and if her own measurements correspond to that of the car they must present a very formidable obstruction.

During the first few months of 1958, I was also working in television. After getting some experience during my attachment to children's television the previous year, I now set to work on an *Any Questions?* -type television programme. In Nicky Crocker's time, two or three editions had been televised simultaneously with the radio broadcast. But, as Freddy himself pointed out, it was rather a let-down to see some of the speakers. It was, alas, by 1958, rather a let-down to see Freddy. He looked older and more frail than his voice, unchanged over the years, led people to expect. It was also doubtful whether he could cope with the mechanics of the medium. So when we devised the new programme, specially for television, we had other people in the chair. In a later series we had the youthful David Dimbleby, but the chairman early in 1958 was Jeremy Thorpe. Mercifully, the programme was only on in the west of England, because on his first appearance there was a failure of communication between us which resulted in him starting off the live broadcast with a rehearsal of his closing remarks. My frenzied shout, 'You're on the air!' haunted him for years afterwards.

The new programme was called *It's My Opinion*, and members of the audience expressed an opinion instead of putting a question, and were encouraged to join in the discussion with the team.

(DJ: *I encouraged them to do the same in* Any Questions? *when I took over the chair.*)

Unfortunately, the programme never quite caught on.

The London television hierarchy preferred to try and devise their own formula. Finally, after many years, they ended up with *Question Time*, with Robin Day in the chair, and a formula not all that dissimilar to *It's My Opinion*.

(DJ: *For years I've been trying to persuade my masters at Television Centre to let me do* Any Questions? *on television, and they've always said it wasn't suitable for the schedules. I still think they are wrong and I don't consider* Question Time *is* Any Questions? *on TV – indeed, it probably isn't intended to be. It has an invited audience in a BBC theatre and that's the difference. With us, the audience feel at home and we are the strangers. I shall continue to press for* Any Questions? *to be on television, although I am likely to be disappointed because if they ever did it they would probably use another chairman and I should be disappointed, as Julie Andrews must have been when Audrey Hepburn got her part in the film version of* My Fair Lady*!*)

1958/59

In October, the programme reached its tenth anniversary. I was by then working full time on a television series, *Command in Battle*, in which Field-Marshal Montgomery revealed how he had won the war, but I temporarily deserted Monty to produce the birthday edition.

We went back to Winchester and had a strong team: Lady Violet Bonham Carter, Bob Boothby, newly ennobled, Anthony Wedgwood Benn and Arthur Street. The first question, not unexpectedly, asked them to recall their outstanding memories of the programme.

> BENN: My actual happy memory is the day Ralph Wightman told me how to do *Any Questions?*. He said, 'It's very simple, old boy. If there's only one obvious thing to say, say it before the others can and if there's nothing you can think of, wait till the others have started and disagree with them, and once you know that, you can't go wrong!'

> LADY VIOLET: My memories are a happy blur, it's awfully difficult to pick out one from another. But I remember one which was only a year or two ago. It was rather a heated programme; it was soon after the Suez incident and I'd been engaged in rather hot controversy with a member of the team, Mr John Connell, who is a great personal friend – there was no bad blood, but we shouted at each other a good deal. Well, the programme was just over when he was summoned to the telephone and I was filled with

anxiety and compunction, I was afraid it was a message to say 'SOS, your wife has been taken seriously ill.'

Another colleague, Mr Victor Mishcon, comforted me. 'Don't worry,' he said, 'it's only some old colonel ringing up to say, "It needed saying, sir, and by gad, you've said it." ' When Mr Connell returned and I rushed solicitously to ask him if he'd had any bad news, he said: 'No, it was just a message from a strong supporter – a major – and this is what he said to me: "It needed saying, sir, and by gad, you've said it."

BOOTHBY: I was travelling down in the train to Bournemouth with Hugh Gaitskell and he said: 'This is my first appearance on *Any Questions?*. I know you don't care a damn what you say, but I've just been Chancellor of the Exchequer and I've got a certain sense of responsibility and I must really be a little careful – you don't think they'll ask any embarrassing questions, do you?' And I said: 'Not at Bournemouth, you needn't worry about that.' Well, down we sat and the first question was: 'What would the team do if they woke up tomorrow morning and found they'd changed their sex?' And Freddy Grisewood looked at me and most unfairly said, 'What would you do?' and I said: 'Go for a walk and see what happened.'

I had chosen that team but had no say in the rest of the teams that autumn. In some of them, I thought, the basic principles of *Any Questions?* team-building had been overlooked. In my opinion there should always be someone, experienced in *Any Questions?*, who will 'play the programme' in the way Street and Wightman did, saying the sort of thing that is needed at any particular point instead of being wholly concerned with his or her own performance. Practising politicians can't fill this role; they have to look over their shoulders at their constituents and their agents. First there was one regular, then there were two, then there were four. Eventually I built up a 'hard core' of about a couple of dozen people with the qualities of regulars and so closely associated with the programme that their obituaries would mention it. I thought that one of them should be included in every team.

There should also be a newcomer, preferably someone who will inspire the comment: 'I *must* listen to *Any Questions?* tonight; so-and-so is on.' But not more than one.

Then the producer must ask himself several questions. For instance, who is going to speak up for the Government? (One needn't worry so much over who is going to speak up for the Opposition. It is the Government who is actually *doing* something and the politically uncommitted, as well as the Opposition, are likely to be critical.) Who's going to speak up for the workers? (Necessary in order to overcome the tendency for team members to be middle-class and fairly comfortably off.) Do they all speak slowly – or all speak quickly? Do two people's voices sound similar? Do two people, alike in style and background, have similar views? (The stronger will inevitably swamp the weaker.) If there is a real star, is there someone else on the team who will bring out the best in him (or her)?

Finally, each team should of course include at least one woman, and if there are two, they should be opposed politically.

During my absence from the programme, an all-male team were asked by a questioner at Marshfield in Gloucestershire whether they thought they could answer questions properly without a lady on the team.

> BRONOWSKI: This problem of women on teams, *Brains Trust*, *Any Questions?* teams and so on, is constantly with us and I am very much depressed by it. I enjoy the company of women enormously more than the company of men; I enjoy the conversation of women much more than the conversation of men. And when women have something interesting and individual to say I find it far more penetrating than what men have to say, because in general I know what men are going to say. And yet it's so sad that our education of women in public debate has lagged so far behind that in general it's extremely difficult to take a woman out of the private context of the home and get her to

say in public, on an occasion like this, what she says intelligently and charmingly with great penetration at home. And if there are any remarks to be made to girls' schools it's simply this: 'For goodness sake, let's teach the girls to speak to men as if they were persons, and let's stop getting them to talk to men as if they were ladies.'

The next question resulted in our losing Bronowski from *Any Questions?* for many months: 'We read that there are tremendous stocks of coal in the country, and that there is redundancy in the industry. Does the team consider it would be a good thing if the Coal Board sold some of these stocks at a cheaper rate to the general public, who in many cases are barely able to afford enough fuel for their present needs at today's prices?'

BRONOWSKI: I should warn you that I am an interested party in what I'm going to say, but it happens that on the subject of prices I have very deep feelings, which I can back up with facts. The average price paid per year in each household in the south of England for coal is nine pounds for their total consumption for a year. The average amount paid per household in the north of England for coal is fourteen pounds per year. To talk in the face of that of the cheaper rate, and the public barely able to afford enough fuel for their present needs seems to me, if the questioner won't mind my saying so, an impertinence.

The fact is that each of you in this hall and each of you listening to me all over the country is spending on coal somewhere between four shillings and six shillings a week. That is the price of somewhere between twenty and thirty cigarettes. If any one of you wishes to double your standard of comfort in the home, and to buy twice as much coal as you use at this moment, so that the stuff would be running out of your ears – at any rate out of the bedroom window – it would still only be the equivalent of buying yourself another twenty or thirty cigarettes a week. Considering that the average consumption of cigarettes in this country per week, for each woman, is

> now nearly fifty and for each man is now nearly a hundred, how can you talk to me about the price of coal? Every household in this country spends more on cigarettes than on coal, nearly twice as much, and spends nearly three times as much on drink as on coal. Now in the face of that you can't persuade me that what's keeping coal on the ground is its price.

Dr Bronowski worked for the National Coal Board and he was not a man to make an error of fact, but his remarks caused listeners to seize their pens and send off white-hot letters to *Any Answers* and at the end of thirteen minutes of correspondence filled with umbrage came the pay-off line: 'Doctor? He's a flaming quack!'

I don't know whether Bronowski complained at once – certainly the closing announcement included a reference to an independent report by the Department of Scientific and Industrial Research having very largely borne out his figures – but he was exceedingly annoyed by the final comment and refused subsequent invitations for *Any Questions?*. It was not until the following summer, when I was temporarily producing the television *Brains Trust* in which Bronowski regularly appeared, that I was able to win him over by apologizing – which was fairly easy for me, as I had not been involved in the controversy.

Newcomers in the first half of 1959 included Peter Walker, then National Chairman of the Young Conservatives; Lady Lewisham, now the Princess of Wales's stepmother, who arrived at Southampton station, where I met her, wearing a huge, wide-brimmed hat more suited to Ascot than my open Morris Minor and who hurried to the exit at the end of the broadcast and shook hands with the audience as they left; and Vic Feather, then Assistant General Secretary of the TUC. Vic, amiable, full of humour, his face normally creased with a smile, had a voice which sounded as though he were speaking through a blanket. His début at Carisbrooke Castle, Isle of Wight, coincided with a demarcation dispute at Cammell Laird. Vic did his best, but John Arlott wiped the floor with him.

'This is not protecting workers against the employers, this is the boilermakers, because their numbers are bigger, trying to stop the shipwrights from drawing a chalk line on an iron plate. I never heard of such bunkum in my life. If the employers had done this years ago when it was the trade unions who were in the underdog position they'd have screamed their heads off – and I'd have been on their side – at the crying injustice of throwing yesterday another one thousand, two hundred men out of work, different men, because they couldn't agree who was going to draw a chalk line. These chaps aren't out of work; there it is, good, rich work, right at their fingertips, but it isn't going to stay there long if they put the people who provide the money for them to do the work out of business by folding up on a job that's due for delivery in June. This is sheer murder; this is a new sort of tyranny and it's a fantastically ignorant sort of tyranny, and whether you fight it through what Victor Feather calls the appropriate machinery or whether you fight it through what he says has the appearance of a strike, but which *is* a strike and which is throwing other men out of work, whatever you do it's sheer, utter, absolute and tyrannical nonsense and it makes me throw up.'

On Good Friday 1959 we had a bishop on the team for the first time. It was the much loved Wilfrid Westall, the Bishop of Crediton, who was to become almost our resident Bishop, appearing in the programme altogether about forty times. A warm, human man, unhappily accident prone, hardly a visit passed without some mishap, often, I suspected, the result of his performance at the wheel of a motor-car which those who had witnessed it assured me was an experience worth missing.

(DJ: *The Bishop drove me eastwards to Exeter station on a Good Friday so I could catch the sleeper home. On a Good Friday driving eastwards you meet one car pulling a caravan after another. This Good Friday was no exception. The Bishop seemed concerned with driving straight at the oncoming traffic on the wrong side of the road! I have never been so frightened in my life. We got to Exeter station safe and sound, however, and as soon as we got into the station yard, the Bishop drove straight into a wall. I think his employer had been looking after him for the journey, but had given up when we arrived.*)

Wilfrid always seemed to me apolitical (though Jeremy Thorpe claimed him as a supporter), but the same could not be said for the bishop we recruited for the last programme in the series, Mervyn Stockwood, newly consecrated Bishop of Southwark and a fervent Socialist.

We were at Littlehampton with Bob Boothby, Isobel Barnett and Percy Cudlipp, and a few seconds before we went on the air the power supply in the town failed without any warning, and the entire broadcast took place in complete darkness. The engineers promptly went over to their emergency battery supply, and listeners had no idea that anything had gone wrong until Freddy mentioned it right at the end of the programme. Some people moved cars so that their headlights shone directly through the windows of the Pavilion, and one or two torches were produced so that the questioners could see to read the copies of their questions.

In the darkness the Bishop took advantage of a question about clergymen becoming too involved in politics to make a public apology for having criticized a magistrate in a way which, he said, may have been unjust and unkind (this made front-page news the next morning). And when Bob Boothby was the mystery guest in *What's My Line?* Isobel Barnett guessed his identity with the words: 'I think we spent the evening together in the dark at Littlehampton!'

1959/60

There was a General Election on 8 October 1959. The Conservatives won, with an increased majority. It was the era of Harold Macmillan's 'You've never had it so good'. For the first time, *Any Questions?* remained on the air during the election campaign, but with a difference: a team of three – candidates from the main political parties – no regular. But I wasn't there to produce these programmes. I was in London on an attachment to television talks department to help in the election coverage. I also produced some other programmes, including the television version of the *Brains Trust*, and I adopted the *Brains Trust* set-up when I returned to *Any Questions?*, with the chairman in the centre and two of the team on each side of him, at an angle. Previously, the team had all sat at one long table and I hoped the new formation would encourage them to work as a team rather than address the audience as individuals. Ideally, the team should make short contributions, sparking each other off, so that the discussion develops naturally as a conversation, but it is not easy to ensure this.

In the 1959/60 series, the subject of apartheid recurred several times. Harold Macmillan made his trip to Cape Town and delivered his 'wind of change' speech there, and in April 1960, at Bishop's Sutton, Hampshire, John Arlott was a member of the team which faced this question: 'It would seem that the non-whites in South Africa are having a very rough passage at the present time; what methods would the team adopt if they were whites in South Africa to solve the problem of apartheid?'

John Began his answer by recalling that he had got into very hot water, ten years earlier, for saying on the programme exactly what everybody in England was saying now. (He was then a BBC Talks Producer, and as a result of the fuss caused by his remarks, no permanent member of the BBC staff has appeared on *Any Questions?* since that time.)

He continued: 'I have been in South Africa and I've been very, very harrowed by what I've seen. Since then I've been very harrowed by what I've heard. Mr Macmillan said, believing, I fancy, that he was very strong, that the wind of change was blowing through South Africa. This is no wind, this is the great big strong certain river of history, and Dr Verwoerd isn't going to hold that back with a race card, nor a British representative at the United Nations with a blank order paper. So what will I do if I'm a white man in South Africa? And I've got to think a bit hard about this. I looked at the funny old telly last night and they were wondering if assassination could ever be right. I'd shoot this chap, if I didn't think another one would come up in his place, and think I'd done well if I did any good for the ten million black men, but I don't think it would help. It would assuage my conscience by going to the police and saying, "I reckon the people who are in the majority in this country, their own country, have got to be given a break, now lock me up" – and they would, and they'd knock me senseless with their gun barrels, and that wouldn't do any good. And if I went over to the Africans they wouldn't have me because my colour is wrong.

'I reckon what I would try to do would be to come to England and reach the Prime Minister and say, "This is not a wind, it's a torrent. Recognize it, recognize the right of human beings and have the courage to come out in the United Nations and say: 'This thing is evil even if it does contribute to my country's Stock Exchange income through the gold and diamond shares; it's wrong, and because I'm English, I've got the courage to condemn it and hope that when the Africans eventually rule, on an ordinary democratic basis of a majority, they may remember that there was one white race that thought they were entitled to do it.' " '

There was great heart-searching in London as to whether the bit about assassinating Dr Verwoerd should be deleted from the repeat, but the hierarchy wisely came to the conclusion that it was not inflammatory to say that one would *not* assassinate somebody.

In that series there was a notable newcomer – our third future Prime Minister, Margaret Thatcher. She made her début on 8 January at Portishead, near Bristol, just three months after entering the House of Commons. The rest of the team were Woodrow Wyatt, Jack Longland and Graham Hutton. She displayed a touch of iron very early on, in answer to a question which Freddy described as the most original we have ever had: 'You have, we hope, been enjoying a good dinner. We have been sitting like good children waiting for titbits from your table. What did you discuss at dinner?'

> WYATT: We talked for quite a long time about a gentleman called Mr Gerald Nabarro. And I was saying what a pity it was, for him, that he was in the Tory Party, because of course the poor chap can't get a job. Because he's really rather too non-U, if you know what I mean, and Miss Mitford means, by that, to count as a kind of Old Etonian or a peer in order to get a job from Mr Macmillan on those grounds. And he's not sufficiently working class to be paraded as a working-class member of the Government, on the other hand. So the poor fellow's stranded like a fish on the bank, much more able than half the Government, who'll never get a job. And I rather like Mr Nabarro who makes very funny jokes.
>
> GRISEWOOD: If he was here he'd say Nabárro.
>
> WYATT: And it's one of the great sadnesses of British politics that the Conservative Party at the moment, which proclaims itself as a classless party, when it comes to choosing members for Government, in fact chooses them either from the very upper upper crust, or from the very obviously non-upper crust

and working class. Well, it's chaps like poor Mr Nabarro or Nabárro that get left out. And that's what we were talking about for quite a long time.

THATCHER: May I make one thing quite clear, Mr Chairman – we weren't discussing very much at dinner, we were mostly listening to Mr Woodrow Wyatt.

LONGLAND: I would remind Woodrow Wyatt there is such a thing as nature's Etonian, and perhaps the label might apply very well to our mutual friend.

WYATT: Well, you must pass that on to Mr Macmillan.

LONGLAND: We did – let's be quite fair and we're not flattering you – we did discuss you, we discussed the audience. We wondered what sort of audience we'd get, we wondered what sort of questions you'd ask. We wondered whether you'd have a whole heap of terribly passionate questions about Africa and about Mr Macmillan there, or whether you'd only be interested in Portishead, for instance. We wondered whether you read evening papers of London, or mainly the local papers and therefore whether the things we'd seen in the London papers would come into your questions here. We discussed Woodrow Wyatt's dog for quite a bit, that was a jolly good subject. As usual every time we get together before *Any Questions?*, we discussed famous occasions on *Any Questions?* programmes, involving people as diverse as Lady Violet Bonham Carter and Mr George Brown MP and Colonel Robert Henriques' driving habits across the landscape in deep snow when he disregards the hedges and doesn't stick to the roads at all. And the famous MP who at that time I think was father of the House of Commons, who fell asleep actually during an *Any Questions?* programme, and I had to keep on butting him from behind to make him wake up for the next question.

HUTTON: All I can say is, in the words of the gentleman who was asked how he enjoyed the conversation with Lord Macaulay, 'We had a wonderful conversation – it was lit by some glorious flashes of silence.'

THATCHER: Not from Mr Woodrow Wyatt.

Around St Valentine's Day, the team, as often happened, were required to suggest to whom they would send a Valentine. Jeremy Thorpe had an inspiration: 'My old friend Queen Salote of the Tongas. You know, they are a great lot of people over there. They always used to indulge in cannibalism – that's why they all look so healthy. And the story that I like about her most is when she went up to a very belted Earl, with a walrus-type moustache, and all the rest of it, and she said: "I'm very pleased to meet you, Lord So-and-So, because we have some family connection." And he said, "Oh really, Ma'am, what is it?" "Well," she said, "my great-grandfather ate yours." '

On 11 March at Bath we had another notable newcomer, who has for the following twenty years and more displayed all the attributes of an *Any Questions?* regular – the provocative, humorous, Australian writer, Russell Braddon. He was recommended to me by Freddy, who took the chair for some non-broadcast *Any Questions?* organized by groups like Aims of Industry, on which Russell often appeared, and he was an instant success on the programme, not least with the correspondent who wrote to him every day for most of the next twenty years, or with another admirer, who came to every *Any Questions?* he was on, even pursuing him to Germany when he was on the team there.

At Bath, where his companions included C. A. Joyce and the writer, Macdonald Hastings, a questioner asked: 'Would the team favour the rewriting of the National Anthem, having regard to Lord Hailsham's remarks that with the coming of the nuclear bomb, parts of it were meaningless?'

> HASTINGS: I quite agree with Lord Hailsham that the National Anthem – which happens to have an abominably bad tune – ought to be abolished; and having said that, I think I ought to suggest what the alternative should be, I would like to see our National Anthem, which is a magnificent tune and a magnificent verse, I would choose Blake's *Jerusalem*.

BRADDON: I will not have Mr Macdonald Hastings or the rest of this team mucking up my National Anthem. You see, it isn't just yours – it's ours, too. And as for the bomb, I do have the feeling that so long as we go on pointing them at one another none of us are going to use them so that the bomb doesn't really affect the National Anthem at all, whereas the National Anthem might affect the bomb.

JOYCE: I don't want to mess about with the National Anthem; I think we want to think about the words and sing them rather more sincerely. Of course, if I may just interpolate one small story – did you ever hear that nice story of our present Queen when she was a little girl, and she said to her father: 'Daddy, when they sing the National Anthem, do you sing *God Save my Gracious Me?*'

BRADDON: The National Anthem, played after every film in cinemas in Australia also, is not in my country the signal to bolt for the bus. It is in this country, and indeed I've been to the films with my grandfather who was then aged ninety-four, and there was a misguided new Australian who had just arrived from Yugoslavia, who didn't realize the significance of this piece of music, who started to move as soon as the music was played and was hooked round the throat by me grandpappy's walking stick and there he stayed at attention like the rest.

The following week a large audience at Hove, Sussex, stimulated a strong team, which included Bob Boothby, Ted Leather and Frank Cousins. Bob revelled in a question which allowed him to talk about his health and his legendary supply of pills. The question was: 'Does the panel consider that private patients should be able to obtain their drugs under the National Health Service?'

BOOTHBY: Yes, it would save me about five hundred pounds a year, I reckon. I'm a tremendous believer in pills. I take pills on principle. I don't much care what they're for, and I don't care what their colour is. If ever I feel ill, I take pills. The other night I didn't feel very well so I took eight pills of different colours, entirely by the colour, and the next morning I was completely recovered.

LEATHER: I've sat through the debates on the National Health Act over the years, as Bob has done. The terms of the thing originally were perfectly clear; this argument put forward by some people that it would produce two classes of patients I find quite impossible to understand. It seems to me you've got two classes of patients at the moment, and they both pay their National Insurance contributions for exactly the same thing, and I cannot see why they should not both be treated equally.

COUSINS: What I like is the naivety with which representatives of the Tory group always approach these questions. He says, well of course they'll have equal rights and they both pay their contributions. He's not suggesting, surely, that all the doctors in the country don't give privileged treatment to the people who pay their private bills? And I would like to suggest to Bob Boothby there's a certain way in which you can get these drugs on the National Health, give over paying a private doctor. Go on the panel like I do. Go to the doctor and get his treatment in the same way that you and I do. Why should the service of the doctors be bartered for by people who can afford to pay for it? Why should they be put under this temptation? I don't think you can allow private patients to contract in for part of the scheme and out for part of the scheme.

BOOTHBY: I'll give Frank Cousins the answer. Sometimes I suffer from recurring fits of nerves, and when I get a fit of nerves in the morning I ring up my private doctor – who's a great friend of mine – and I say I'm feeling nervous, and he comes round to my flat and he says you're quite all right. Now I think that's well worthwhile paying the extra money. Otherwise I would have to go to a surgery and sit for an hour and by the time that hour had ended I really would be suffering.

COUSINS: Now, Lord Boothby, don't you try and get

the sympathy of the audience on your nerves. You shouldn't go to your own doctor, you should go to a psychiatrist! I suffer from recurring bouts of all sorts of things, but I don't ring up my doctor and say, well because I'm going to pay you for this call will you come and pat me on the head and comfort me? And, if I did and he recommended that I ought to have a double Scotch or a couple of aspirins, I would expect to pay for them.

There was a bit of an argument after that programme about whether I was wrong in not choosing a question submitted on the lines of 'Should one always keep one's temper or lose it occasionally?' On reflection, I think I should have chosen it. Questions of human and social behaviour are an important ingredient in *Any Questions?*. The programme suffers if *all* the questions are either topical or funny.

The boundary between 'funny' and 'human interest' may, however, be a trifle blurred. For example, a question at Kingsbridge in Devon, where a pretty lady asked: 'My husband likes to see other ladies wearing bikinis, but does not like the thought of other gentlemen seeing me in one. Does the team think that the majority of husbands hold this view?'

The team included Dr Frank George, then Lecturer in Psychology at the University of Bristol, John Connell and Mary Stocks.

STOCKS: I'm in rather an awkward position. I was wondering whether one couldn't put this question from the wife's point of view. I don't like seeing anybody's husband in a bikini. You know, these hairy chests . . . I think possibly that the majority of husbands do hold this view because husbands tend to be possessive, they like to keep a good thing to themselves. But, it's very difficult for me to deal with it from the husband's point of view – I mean, I've never been one.

CONNELL: There is a certain aesthetic aspect to this, that in both sexes there are bodies that one is only too thankful to see as clothed as possible. And I think, therefore, Mary Stocks was so right in bringing up this other side to it. I wouldn't know whether women are possessive or not, but I would suspect that they would be deeply shocked and horrified to see my sort of tubby figure disarrayed in this fascinating costume.

STOCKS: I would hate to see you in a bikini.

GEORGE: I can't help thinking the whole team would look horrible in bikinis.

STOCKS: To tell the truth, I don't believe I should look so bad!

1960/61

With the Conservatives firmly in power for the next four years or so, *Any Questions?* could look forward to a steady run, undisturbed by any likelihood of a General Election. It was a time of consolidation rather than innovation. The quartet of regulars – Street, Wightman, Longland and Stocks – remained, though on a less rigid pattern. Several others, like John Arlott, Isobel Barnett, Sir John Wolfenden (Vice-Chancellor of Reading University) and C.A. Joyce, were able to fill this role. The proportion of women in the teams increased slightly; the proportion of MPs decreased. There were more newcomers, some of them destined for great prominence: Shirley Williams (not then an MP), Judith Hart, Richard Marsh, John Freeman and Gilbert Harding.

I had delayed inviting Gilbert Harding, one of the best known men in the country because of his appearances in *What's My Line?*, as his reputation for irascibility had put me off. I needn't have worried. He couldn't have been milder or more charming. He had sought advice from his fellow television panellist, Isobel Barnett, and she had impressed on him the need to arrive punctually at the hotel and to listen intently to the six o'clock news. The only time he showed any irritation was when another member of the team talked during the news. Gilbert Harding glared at him with the expression which struck terror into many a *What's My Line?* challenger.

On the programme itself he was equable, civilized, not especially outspoken. I've no doubt I should have been glad to have him on again. But it was not to be. He died three weeks later.

(DJ: *I only met Gilbert Harding once. It was at a reception at Broadcasting House. I introduced myself, and he said, 'What are you doing here?' I said I was invited. He replied, 'I know you; you are the cloakroom attendant at Grosvenor House Hotel.' I never did know what he meant.*)

It must have been about that time that the word 'unilateralist' came into common usage and questions on nuclear disarmament cropped up frequently during that series. On 30 September at Fremington, Devon, the team included John Foot and Ted Leather.

FOOT: The only way in which the deadlock which now exists can be broken is by one nation having the courage to say: 'We, having this weapon, will of our own accord discard it.'

LEATHER: Do you really believe that if Britain did discard it, and obviously that's what we'd all like to do if we could, that it would have the slightest effect on Russian policy?

FOOT: I'm in favour of discarding it even if it had *no* effect upon Russian policy, for different reasons; but if one nation were to discard it voluntarily of their own accord, I am quite certain that that would meet with an enormous response – not in Russia, I don't suppose that for a moment.

LEATHER: What else matters?

FOOT: I believe we should give ourselves the moral leadership of the world. Now you may say, well, the moral leadership, what does it count for? It counts for a good deal because we are engaged at the moment in two struggles; one is a military struggle or competition with the USSR and the other one is the cold war which is the struggle for men's minds. I believe that in that sphere the unilateral renunciation of the weapon by us would have enormous consequences.

LEATHER: I hope entirely you're right, but I can't help thinking of that terribly cynical but true remark attributed to Stalin when somebody asked him about the influence of the Roman Catholic Church during the war and he simply said: 'How many divisions has the Pope got?'

FOOT: Well, I'm not going to defend the Catholic Church, but nevertheless the Catholic Church has survived for nearly two thousand years. Soviet Communism has only survived for about forty and it may not last very long. And it may very well be that the victory will be with the Pope and not with the Soviet Union.

On 21 October at Buckfastleigh, Devon, John's brother, Michael, put the unilateralist's argument still more forcefully: 'When we went to war with Hitler we could survive the war, as we have done. If we go to war with nuclear weapons, none of us will survive. Nobody can deny it. This country is more defenceless than we've ever been in our history owing to the invention of these weapons, and that changes the situation entirely. It is a new situation in the history of the world. These weapons – they're not weapons of defence at all – they're boomerangs; if they're ever used we're utterly destroyed, so we have to discover some new method and it's no use anyone saying that this is an idea of a few little cranks.'

And on 4 November in Dorchester, Margaret Thatcher and Manny Shinwell crossed swords over the proposed American Polaris nuclear submarine base in Scotland.

SHINWELL: I'm definitely opposed to the establishment of this base, in Scotland or any other part of the United Kingdom. We're becoming an aircraft carrier in Britain for the United States. And there is no real and effective measure of control over the use of the Polaris missile, or indeed over any of the missiles that have been furnished by the United States to the United Kingdom. Now, it is argued that this is a very valuable and effective means of preventing war, preventing an attack on this country. I'm very doubtful about this deterrent value. If the Russians wanted to attack us they could have attacked us before there was any deterrent at all, any nuclear deterrent. Why didn't they do it? They were strong enough to do it, for we only had conventional forces at our disposal. Why didn't they do it? Because they don't require to go to war in order to get what they want. And what they want is economic development and possibly economic domination. And they can get that without going to war. If there are to be bases of that kind let them be established in the United States of America. Because in my judgement these bases are primarily intended to protect the United States. And I'm doubtful if they're likely ever to protect this country. And if they're going to be used – and God forbid that they should ever be used – in my judgement it means suicide for the people of this country.

THATCHER: I believe fundamentally in the system of collective defence, as operated through NATO. As part of the NATO system we have the nuclear deterrent, which is one of the most striking and most powerful parts of that particular system. We already have in this country the deterrent in the form of a strategic bomber force. I believe that the establishment of the Polaris submarine base here will make the deterrent much more effective and more operative than it has been to date. Now may I say one word on the positioning of this particular base? It's next door to the loch which has the British submarine base there. So that in any case would make that area a suitable target for any attack. Also in that area are NATO installations worth fifteen million pounds, another reason why that particular place is vulnerable to attack. Now I do not believe that Russia could ever get what she wanted in this island, that is domination, through underground communism only. I think there would be a point when, if she had to go further, she would have to attack. And I believe therefore that the existence of a powerful deterrent would stop her from attacking. And if you believe in the deterrent at all, then you must believe that the more powerful it is, the more effective it is likely to be.

SHINWELL: I'm not against defence. I think a country

like ours must adopt defence measures, must have defence organization. And I'm not against some collective means of defence, in association with NATO. But what we're engaged in now, and what the United States is engaged in, is a nuclear arms race. And does anyone suppose that the Polaris missile, and the submarine, and all the rest of it, is not going to be matched by something the Russians produce? And only this morning, in the newspapers, I read that the Americans now are developing something even more drastic, more dangerous, more effective, than the Polaris missile. That's how it goes. We're going crazy over this business, and in the end I think there's going to be disaster for us all.

The issue of unilateral nuclear disarmament tore the Labour Party down the middle. It was in such disarray that hardly anyone could have believed that Labour would be in power again within four years.

The Labour Party's problems occupied a strong team at Pensford, near Bristol, on 16 December. Frank Byers, Anthony Wedgwood Benn, Christopher Chataway and Bob Boothby were asked whether they considered there was any prospect of the Labour Party being able to supply an effective Opposition in the foreseeable future; if not, did they think the Liberal Party would be able to do so?

BYERS: I don't believe that the Labour Party is going to be able to produce an effective Opposition for many years to come, if ever, and the split in the Labour Party is not just on the question of defence, they're split on the question of the leadership, they're split on the question as to whether Members of Parliament should take their orders from the Labour Party Conference or not, and they're split on a number of other issues too. And in these circumstances you are not, within any foreseeable future, going to get a really healthy, effective Opposition which you've got to have if you're going to shake the Government out of its complacency. Now the Liberal Party can produce this effective Opposition if only people will vote in sufficient numbers to put more

Liberals back.

BENN: If you look at the country at the moment, and the various areas of policy, of course the only effective political Opposition is coming from the Labour Party. What is really happening is a fundamental change in the character of British politics, which I for one welcome; and, as you would expect, it's emerging through the Left – changes in politics don't emerge through the Right, they work themselves out through the Left, and what is happening in Britain today is that a demand for an entirely new foreign policy, quite different from the cold war policy, is emerging from the Left, also a new attitude to African questions is emerging from the Left, and also a growing realization which the Sputnik began to put in our minds that in the world of today Socialism as a means of economic planning is more efficient than Capitalism, and this is proved by the comparison between the eastern European advance and western European advance.

CHATAWAY: I don't believe that this country is swinging to unilateralism, if that's what Anthony Wedgwood Benn means by a great change and a demand for a new policy in foreign affairs. I'm sure that it's a very, very small minority who want to discard our defences. And my personal opinion is that the Labour Party is bound to split before long, and that this will be a good thing for British politics because it will lead to an effective Opposition. My guess would be that before long we shall see the Gaitskellite wing of the Labour Party, the Right, coming to some sort of a deal with the Liberal Party and a new Opposition emerging. Because it is clear that the small left wing faction does speak for a minority view on defence and on Socialism too, because of course, far from there being a trend towards Socialism in the world, every single Democratic nation in the world has given up the ideas of Socialism that are held by the left wing of the Labour Party.

BOOTHBY: What has happened is that certain divisions

of opinion have arisen, as they often do in the party of the Left, the Labour Party. But what has now arisen as the result of them is bitter internecine strife ending in searing personal hatreds. Now I lunched the day before yesterday with one of the leaders of the Labour Party whose name must obviously be kept quiet, but he said to me, 'The hatreds in our party have now become so great, so vicious, that they transcend any divisions about policies whatsoever.' The people who are determined to get rid of Gaitskell and his crowd, that is their overwhelming motive – I mean, nuclear disarmament and all that kind of thing really fades into the background, and as for being an Opposition, or talking about the Tory Party, it bores them stiff. All they're determined to do is to cut each other's throats. Now I think this is a very bad thing for British Democracy. I'm old enough to have watched the Liberal Party destroy itself by the Asquith–Lloyd George feud. It seems to me that on a far greater scale exactly the same thing is happening in the Labour Party today.

BENN: The personal row is there, nobody denies this, but what is important and interesting is the political movement of our times, and there's absolutely no question at all that Socialism in the world as a method of economic planning is overtaking Capitalism hand over fist. The economic planning is nothing whatsoever to do with the political tyranny that has lain behind it in the past and still lies behind it to some extent in the present. The Soviet Union is spending three times as much on education as this country, although its standard of living is half as high, and within about ten or fifteen years people are going to be asking why on earth it was that Britain was allowed to get behind; and it was because of the 'never had it so good' philosophy. I'm not a unilateralist, but I think what is interesting and important about unilateralism is that the younger generation are rejecting the order of priorities that puts the cold war top on the list of the dangers that face the world –

nuclear weapons, rise of population, the revolution in Africa, these are much more important than the cold war – and these forces are working themselves out in the Labour Party, and they're leaving us in the short run weak but in the long run these are the forces that will ultimately win the support of the majority of the people in this country, and that's why I'm more of a Socialist now and not less of one.

In the introduction to that team which I wrote for Freddy (I got very bored with writing these introductions for some fifteen years, and was delighted when David took over the task himself), he said: '. . . and finally, Lord Boothby, who went quietly to the House of Lords.' This was an arch reference to Tony Benn's fight not to suffer a similar fate, after the death of his father, Viscount Stansgate. Tony was determined to stay in the Commons and fought a long parliamentary campaign which he eventually won. Writing the introductions during that period when he was insisting he was still an MP and Parliament said he wasn't, called for a certain amount of tact.

Tony stayed the night with us after the Pensford broadcast. He stayed with us several times. We cherish memories of him setting off in the mornings, wearing a beret and carrying his old RAF haversack, to hitch a lift into Bristol.

The last programme of 1960, in Plympton, Devon, caused some controversy, but it was internal rather than external. The team included C.A. Joyce, Mary Stocks and the Cornish poet and schoolmaster, Charles Causley. Against the advice of Bill Coysh, who feared the discussion might take an unpleasant turn, I selected the question: 'Does today's punishment fit today's crime?'

JOYCE: I don't think so. I think we've got to the stage when it's time we made it clear to certain people that the reaction that will follow an action is inevitable. I hate violence in every single form. But that doesn't mean that I think that thugs ought to have the monopoly of it. I think the time has come when we ought to say to these young men who commit deliberate violence, 'That is going to happen to you.' I don't want it. I don't want people to put their hands in the fire and be burnt. But if they stick their fingers in the fire they're going to be burnt, and that's not my fault. And I think we'd be much wiser to protect the public, instead of trying to go the whole hog so often in saying, 'Oh well, the poor little child was raped and killed. But of course you mustn't do anything to the young boy because he's got a chip on his shoulder.' So what? Let him carry his chip.

STOCKS: No. I think today's punishment doesn't sufficiently fit today's crimes. I think that people who are convicted of being drunk in charge of cars should have their licences taken away, not for a year but for five, ten years, perhaps for ever, if it's a second offence. They're a danger to other people. I don't think they should be put in prison. That doesn't do them any good. I think that boys, or for that matter girls, who commit vandalism and destroy property should be made to pay for what they destroyed, if necessary week after week, month after month, until they know what it is to do damage to property. And I think that men who commit repeated sex offences and cannot control that particular impulse, but otherwise might make quite reasonable citizens, should be castrated . . . on the principle, 'If thine eye offend thee, pluck it out'.

CAUSLEY: I am appalled, in the year 1960, to hear such shockingly reactionary, emotional, sentimental words spoken about crime and criminals. We're talking about a minority when we talk about sexual offenders.

STOCKS: We're talking about punishing a minority.

CAUSLEY: Quite so. Let's get on with it then and see what we mean by that. Let's abandon then, if you wish to do so, Christian charity. Let's not turn the other cheek. Let's be vindictive. And let's seek vengeance. We have a man who says he hates violence. D'you condone hanging, Joyce? How violent is that?

JOYCE: I don't want to hang anybody.
CAUSLEY: Good.
JOYCE: But I'm telling you quite fairly that you can prevent me hanging you if you won't kill anybody, and the people who can abolish capital punishment are murderers for a start. If they don't murder people we shan't hang them. But I don't want to get on to capital punishment. I want to raise this question over Christian charity. I want a bit of Christian charity for the child as well as the fellow that committed the rape.
CAUSLEY: Of course we deplore the murder and the rape of young children. Of course we do. And to use this as a pivot, as a hinge, as the central theme of an argument seems to me to be quite wrong. And I must say that I am appalled, Mary Stocks. I hope you won't take exception to this, but to hear a woman advocate castration seems to me to be primitive, mediaeval, and quite disgusting.
STOCKS: Mr Causley, what I suggested was not retribution, but prevention. I don't suggest putting these people in prison or flogging them. I suggest doing something to them which will prevent their particular weakness from harming the public, as in fact now it does. Reckless driving.
CAUSLEY: Yes.
STOCKS: Destruction of property.
CAUSLEY: Yes. Agreed.
STOCKS: And the awful crimes that are committed on girls and women, repeatedly, by men who can't control a particular impulse. I don't want to put those men in prison. I don't want to hurt them. I think they might live as quite good citizens, and be happier.
CAUSLEY: Well, I'm glad to hear you amplify your words a bit anyway. But I still, personally, deplore violence. I deplore murder, whether it is the action of a madman or whether it is planned, or whether it is ritual and performed by the State.

The controversy within the BBC that followed this

discussion concerned *Any Answers*. There were, as you can imagine, very many letters reacting to Mary Stocks's recommendation that sexual offenders should be castrated, and I wrote into Freddy's script an indication that the large majority took Mary's side. This was disallowed on the grounds that the letters were not a true reflection of public opinion.

I objected. I pointed out that many newspapers indicated the number of letters they received for and against a particular issue. I said that we were bound to give *some* impression in the broadcast of the correspondence received, whatever we said or did not say, and it was better to give an accurate impression than a deliberately false one. On this occasion, in the revised script, we gave a false impression that the letters received were roughly 50–50 for and against Mrs Stocks, whereas they were in fact roughly 90–10 in her favour. For one thing, this seemed unfair to Mrs Stocks (who subsequently wrote to ask for the information). I thought it was arrogant of the BBC to judge the character and motives of its correspondents. Admittedly, all correspondence columns attracted some cranks, but a large number of these letters seemed to be from rational, perfectly normal people who were deeply disturbed about the prevalence of this particular crime and thought Mary's idea might be a possible solution. But I don't think we reached any conclusion for the future.

In February 1961, Freddy Grisewood was voted Radio Personality of the Year and at the beginning of that week's programme, in Bristol, Bob Boothby congratulated him 'on behalf of the team and on behalf of the millions of people in this country who admire you and love you'.

(DJ: *I was voted TV Personality of the Year and Freddy and I were sitting at the same table. When I made my speech of acceptance I said that if I had modelled myself as a broadcaster on anybody it was on him, little thinking that one day I would take his place.*)

Towards the end of the 1960/61 series, a team including Russell Braddon, Lady Barnett and Jeremy Thorpe were asked: 'Why is it that so many of the public, when being interviewed by members of the BBC, address them by their Christian names?'

THORPE: I think we are, possibly, a little too prone to call people by their Christian names whom we've never seen before and are never likely to see again. I think perhaps the use of the Christian name should signify that you know somebody fairly well; that it represents the next step in your acquaintanceship. I think if you say: 'May I introduce Mr William So and So', and an American says: 'Glad to meet you, Bill', that's a little premature.

BARNETT: Both radio and television are very, very intimate media: they come to you in your homes. You're not at the theatre or the cinema – you're sitting at home, and there are those people literally in the sitting-room with you, and you do think of them as friends and as people you know well. You get rather a shock when you meet them and find they don't know you. But I must admit, it does irritate me slightly, because I feel, as Jeremy Thorpe does, that for the thing to look natural, you address people on television or radio in the same way as you address them in private. If you know them well enough in private to call them by their Christian names, you do, on the radio or on television: if you don't, you call them Mr or Mrs, or whatever they are. I think it sounds much more natural, and I do hate people who've obviously met somebody for the very first time, to say: 'Yes, Eamonn', 'No, Eamonn'.

BRADDON: I agree with Lady Barnett. But I not only agree with her that there is this familiarity. These people, as she says, are in your sitting-room with you. Sometimes one wishes that they weren't. But they are there, and you can't get rid of them, because you're too lazy to get out of the chair and turn them off. So there is this tremendous familiarity. But there is also another thing in interviews which causes this, I'm quite certain, in this class-ridden country of yours – and that is an intense and snobbish desire to appear to be on familiar first-name terms with celebrities whom one doesn't know from a bar of soap, and who don't know you either.

(DJ: *Very often team members who have met for the first time get on so well at dinner that by the time they are half-way through the meal they start calling each other by their first names or ask each other how they would like to be called on the air. I hate being referred to as 'Mr Chairman'; the only person I know who does it frequently is a good friend of mine, Tom Jackson, the General Secretary of the Post Office Workers Union, but I suppose that is the trade union upbringing. On the air, I couldn't say 'Lord Willis', for example, all the time, but in the course of the programme I would give his title occasionally so that people switching on late will know who it is.*)

That programme was at St Merryn, in Cornwall. It was a lovely June evening, and after the broadcast Jeremy drove Freddy down to the beach to show him the sunset over the sea. We, more prosaic, went back to the hotel for a drink. After about ten minutes, the bar door burst open and an ashen-faced Jeremy strode in. He looked at us grimly and enumerated several articles he required, marking them on his fingers one by one: 'Tow-rope... torches... shovels...'

In his enthusiasm for the beauties of Nature he had omitted to notice that the sand was very soft and his car was well and truly stuck on the beach. Eventually he got a tow from a local garage. The proprietor was a prominent local Conservative, so presumably the bill did not err on the side of under-charging.

1961/62

We had our first libel action during the 1961/62 series. Considering the nature of the programme – live, spontaneous, controversial, often critical of the actions of well-known people – it wasn't perhaps a bad record that we had managed to keep out of this sort of trouble for more than thirteen years. Once the programme was on the air, we had virtually no control over what was said. What had saved us so far was the team members' experience, integrity and sense of responsibility. But there were occasions when things went wrong and this was one of them.

Ironically, it was a very special occasion. I've always been one for statistics and anniversaries and in those years I allowed no excuse for a beano to pass by unnoticed. The five-hundredth edition, on 23 March 1962, was to be the biggest celebration so far. We decided to go to Freddy Grisewood's own village, Liphook in Hampshire, with a team consisting of three of the regulars (Stocks, Wightman, Longland) plus Bob Boothby. Most of the top brass from the BBC in London were invited. And it ended in near-disaster.

As there were libel actions arising out of one of the questions, the discussion cannot be reproduced here. But the preamble before it got under way can be quoted, and it turned out to be of some significance. That week, the Duke of Edinburgh had been widely reported as describing the *Daily Express* as a 'bloody awful newspaper', and the team were asked for their reactions.

STOCKS: Can I ask a question? It's really a point of order. Supposing a member of this team were to make a remark which was, say, indictable for slander, would the member of the team be responsible for saying it, or the BBC for putting it on the air – I'd like to know first. (*Laughter*)

GRISEWOOD: Well, we've got a lot of very important heads of the BBC here. I think they'll have to answer that. (*Laughter, in which the very important heads of the BBC, sitting in the second row, lustily joined. However, they showed no sign of leaping to their feet and issuing an instant ruling.*)

STOCKS: Yes, but I want to know now! (*Renewed laughter*)

GRISEWOOD: No idea. Anybody – Jack, would you think anything about that? I think probably the BBC. (*More laughter*)

STOCKS: Oh, that's all right.

BOOTHBY: Yes, that's right, and they've got plenty of money!

I was sitting on Freddy's left and should have chipped in myself. But I suppose I didn't know the answer either.

Subsequently, as a bit of stable-door locking after this rather expensive horse had bolted, I had with me, ready to be quoted, a copy of the contract in which the team agree not to say anything defamatory. So in theory they are as liable for what they say as the BBC is for publishing it – I understand it is no defence in law that the programme is unscripted and live. If the BBC chooses to broadcast the programme live, then that is their headache.

Therefore, the answer to Mary Stocks's question was 'both'.

What happened was that certain remarks were made about the *Express* newspapers, and the *Sunday Express* in particular, to which those working on the paper took exception. Mary Stocks and Ralph Wightman were in the clear, but Bob Boothby and Jack Longland received several writs.

At the end of the discussion, Freddy said, none too

helpfully, 'All I can say is, I think we shall be jolly lucky if we get out of this without some trouble.' When he got home, a friend in the legal profession rang him and said: 'I advise you to get Gerald Gardiner immediately!' Gerald Gardiner was, of course, well known to Freddy as one of the most eminent advocates in this country.

There was a brief paragraph in the *Sunday Express* indicating that legal action was being taken, and in Broadcasting House on Monday all hell was let loose, with particular reference to what exactly Freddy had said about the BBC paying. The entire question was deleted from the repeat on Tuesday and in *Any Answers* no letters were read on the subject. After that, I ceased to be involved and it became entirely a matter for our legal department. I only knew that the thing was dragging on because Jack Longland told me when he next appeared on the programme. In the end, the matter was settled out of court. I was never officially informed what the settlement was. I believe it cost the BBC's insurers about £20,000.

Several years later I welcomed the editor of the *Sunday Express*, John Junor, as an *Any Questions?* panellist. He was flattering about the programme and we established a friendly relationship. I wish he could have taken part more often, but Friday evenings are a busy time for the editors of Sunday newspapers and he can only be with us when the programme makes one of its rare visits to London.

Boothby, Stocks and Wightman were included in the opening programme of the 1961/62 series, in Southwick, Sussex, but nothing untoward occurred. The fourth member was Donald Soper and this was one of the questions: 'When is the age of discretion, and what is the discretion for?'

> WIGHTMAN: Merely, I imagine, frustration, and you just give up because you're no longer capable of most of the pleasant sins of the flesh. That's when I reached the age of discretion, I should think about fifty-nine.
>
> SOPER: My age is fifty-eight, and I have to speak professionally; there is no word like discretion in the

catalogue of the Christian virtues, in fact, I think discretion is a very poor quality anyhow; I think courage, enterprise, pertinacity, goodwill, they ought to be Christian virtues – but discretion I think is that age at which you think you must keep up with the Joneses and you musn't do anything that would put you out of your status form. And that I believe to be a very bad thing, and as a revolutionary – and this probably will draw Lord Boothby – as a revolutionary I think that discretion is a thoroughly disagreeable thing to attain and it's mainly a Capitalist experience.

BOOTHBY: My worst enemy, I think, would not claim that I had yet reached the age of discretion. All I can say on that matter is that I hope whether I finish up a Capitalist or a Socialist, that I never will reach the age of discretion. It won't be my fault if I do, I'll have to go really senile before I reach the age of discretion. I agree it's a disastrous quality, I'm absolutely with Dr Soper on this.

STOCKS: Judging from my own experience on this programme it's obvious that I reached the age of discretion a long time ago. I never advertise, I never slander; I've obviously reached it. But what worries me is what Ralph said. Ralph, you say you no longer enjoy the pleasures of the flesh.

WIGHTMAN: Sins of the flesh I said.

BOOTHBY: What's the difference? Tell us the difference between sins and pleasures.

WIGHTMAN: Pleasure is something that you feel that you should really enjoy, which is really virtuous but you don't; and sin's something that you're quite sure you shouldn't enjoy, but do.

SOPER: Theologically, the only difference is that the sins are those pleasures which are found out.

GRISEWOOD: Lord Boothby does run true to form; a good many years ago there was some question that came up about whether the team should see the questions before they came on to the platform. I said to him, 'Bob, what do you feel about it, would you like to see the questions before you had to talk about them?' He said, 'My dear Freddy, I should never be so indiscreet if I knew what the questions were.'

BOOTHBY: But if I got a chance of looking at them I would. And that would be a sin.

STOCKS: Oddly enough, you know, it wouldn't be a pleasure, it would merely spoil your enjoyment of the programme, you'd always be thinking ahead what you're going to say, and the result wouldn't be good.

BOOTHBY: I think you're right.

Mary Stocks was with us again a few weeks later at Saltford near Bristol. The others were Anthony Greenwood, then Labour MP for Rossendale, Peter Rawlinson, a lawyer, then Conservative MP for Epsom, and Kenneth Kendall, who had abandoned television newsreading – only temporarily as it turned out – in order to seek a political career. They were asked to suggest ways of overcoming absent-mindedness.

KENDALL: I'm thoroughly absent-minded. I wish to goodness that somebody would teach me a way of overcoming it. Two days ago I was interviewing somebody for a programme and just before we went on the air I could not remember his name at all. He was a very important man. I knew him very well – I'd seen him before. Fortunately, there was a newspaper in front of me and it had a quotation from the speech he'd just made, so without embarrassing him or myself I was able to pick up the newspaper – but you can't always have a newspaper handy.

GREENWOOD: Once in the course of one week I stood on the platform of the Underground station with my umbrella up, and in the same week I went to the ticket office and repeated my telephone number. And once on a television programme I said to Lord Hailsham: There are three things that are absolutely essential – (1) . . . (2) . . . And then said 'I'm terribly sorry, I can't remember the third.' I think the only real solution is only to have one idea in one's mind at a time, and therefore it's much easier for Conservatives.

RAWLINSON: It's usually the right thing in your mind.

My worst occasion was in the House of Commons, and I was going strong in a speech, and I turned to Mr Speaker – whom we should address as 'Mr Speaker', but I called him My Lord. I think the way of overcoming it is to have a terribly good wife, who tells you exactly where you ought to be and what you ought to do, *and* what you ought to say.

GRISEWOOD: We've had three very interesting solutions to this – a newspaper for Kenneth Kendall; I've forgotten what you said –

GREENWOOD: One idea only.

STOCKS: I don't think I'm absent-minded, but the only example I can give is my memory of getting on to a Manchester tram and saying to the ticket collector: 'Third return to York.' And he said, 'We don't go there.' And that was true, of course. But I don't think that absent-mindedness is the right word for what we're talking about, because I really think that that sort of action – not mine, but those of my colleagues and other people that I know – is the result of concentration on a particular subject of some importance, and the details, therefore, escape you. And I think you don't necessarily want to overcome it, because I think concentration of thought is a wonderful thing. Now, in some ways the most absent-minded person I've ever come across was the late Eleanor Rathbone, who on one occasion bowed in a cold manner to a gentleman sitting opposite her in the tram, who turned out to be her own brother, who wondered why he was treated in that way, but the thing was that she was thinking with great concentration about something and with the kind of really constructive results that her concentrated thought had.

RAWLINSON: There was the well-known peer in the nineteenth century, who was a very absent-minded man. He went to dinner with somebody, and half-way through dinner, forgetting where he was, he apologized to the lady on his right for the execrable dinner. He said the cook was on holiday.

GRISEWOOD: You know the classic example? Dear old G.K. Chesterton was sent a telegram from his wife: 'Am at Crewe – where should I be?'

STOCKS: I was once Principal of Westfield College, and I had a very distinguished predecessor in Miss Lodge, formerly of Lady Margaret Hall, and it's alleged that on one occasion she remained for quite a long time in her bath, because she couldn't remember whether she was having a bath at night and going to bed, or having a bath in the morning and going to get up.

There was another amusing edition in February 1962 at Portchester in Hampshire. (The early Sixties were really vintage *Any Questions?* years!) Bob was on again, this time with Russell Braddon, Jack Longland, and, making his début, the broadcaster, Wynford Vaughan Thomas.

This was one of the questions: 'Dame Edith Sitwell has stated that the sin of pride was one of her favourite virtues. Would members of the team say what particular deadly sin they favour?'

BRADDON: Covetousness. I think covetousness should be made part of Lord Boothby's constitution. I want his title. I'm very tired of being Mr Braddon. I'd like to be Lord Braddon of Pimlico and Portchester. See when he came in here – Lord Boothby – you clapped like mad –

BOOTHBY: Yes, quite right, too!

BRADDON: – while I came in, just a crummy Mr Australian backwoods – feeble little spatter of applause. But for Lord Braddon of Portchester and Pimlico you would have clapped even more than for Boothby.

BOOTHBY: Well, I don't like pride very much, but I'm all in favour of general, genuine all-round self-indulgence. That's what I'd go in for, and I love it – and I am a Lord! And I am Lord Boothby of Buchan and Rattray Head, and it's simply splendid!

VAUGHAN THOMAS: D'you know, I was brought up so firmly on the paths of righteousness that I can't remember what the deadly sins are!

GRISEWOOD: Sloth is one of them.
VAUGHAN THOMAS: Sloth – that's the one I covet – sloth, indeed! I am basically and fundamentally a lazy man. I've always been ashamed of it. I wish I could become suddenly proud of being lazy. It's when people are busy about things that they really do wrong. It would be so much better if half the busybodies in this world got corrupted by the sin of sloth. No, a deep snore is one of the great social virtues, I think, and I shall cultivate sloth.
LONGLAND: It's all very well to talk about sloth: it says nothing about snoring – I mean snoring is by way of being a quite extra deadly sin. You ask your wife! Now, I think we've got to make gluttony respectable, and I think there have been far too many high-minded people wearing homespun and drinking orange juice who've said that it's wrong for us to like what we eat and drink. I don't mean by 'gluttony' to go stuffing yourself disgustingly or getting disgustingly tight, but I do think that one of the gifts of Nature is first of all the raw materials, and then what human beings – chefs, and what not – have been clever enough to do with it.
VAUGHAN THOMAS: It all depends on where you practise this sin of gluttony. In some of the hotels that I know in this country, you start to try and practise the sin of gluttony, you're in for a very great shock. I never forget taking a Frenchman once to a certain Welsh hotel, where we were served with Yorkshire pudding, and when he saw this little disconsolate yellow raft floating in a sea of congealed gravy, he turned and he said: 'Mon Dieu – c'est du plastique!'
BOOTHBY: If we all had Jack Longland's svelte figure it would be easy enough to agree with what he says, because I'm a very, very greedy man. But I am a fat man, and I'm told that if I get any fatter I'll die quite soon. And my doctor has ordered me to breakfast – God save me! – off orange juice and tea every morning – and the first makes me sick, and the second makes me sicker, and I've now reached the

stage when I dread waking up in the morning.

BRADDON: You eat a big breakfast, Lord Boothby, die, and leave me your title!

The next questioner asked whether British Railways should be run as a public service, and this gave Bob an opportunity he was never shy of taking: being rude about British Railways. Towards the end of the discussion, Russell Braddon joined in:

BRADDON: I have one other very sore point, and that is the lavatories on British Railways.

BOOTHBY: Hear Hear! I'm with you there.

BRADDON: They're always filthy; and there's a most disconcerting sign which says: 'Gentlemen lift the seat.' Now, does this imply that if I don't lift the seat I'm not a gentleman? Or, does this mean because I'm not a gentleman, I may not lift the seat?

BOOTHBY: They never do, on British Railways. I can tell you this: No seat has been lifted in a British Railways train for twenty years.

An interested listener to that exchange was Jeremy Thorpe, who was a member of the team the following week. And when the question came up, 'Does the team think that entertainment has deteriorated over the last five to ten years?' he said: 'I don't think so at all. You take, for example, *Any Questions?*. Last week you could hear Bob Boothby say: "I don't think, Freddy, for the last twenty years a lavatory seat has been lifted in British Railways!" This said in a lifelike imitation of Bob's voice. Jeremy then proceeded to imitate Ralph Wightman equally realistically: 'You know, Freddy, I don't think there is anything more beautiful in life than a cow's udders at dawn.' Ralph was on the team, and many listeners thought it was him talking.

This was the first time Jeremy had done some of his impersonations on *Any Questions?*, but he had been entertaining us with them before and after the broadcasts for several years. His great speciality was the Foot family, differentiating between them all, Hugh, Michael, Dingle, John, as well as their wives, and also their illustrious, lovable father, Isaac, with his sonorous west country tones. Unfortunately for listeners, Jeremy decided when he became Liberal Leader that it would be undignified for him to indulge in any of his impersonations on the air, but he relented on the occasion of Freddy's eightieth birthday, and 'did' Bob and Ralph for Freddy and the listeners.

During the second half of that series, Britain was negotiating to join the Common Market and there were questions submitted on the subject virtually every week. One of the most memorable discussions came on 8 June in Weymouth. The team included Lady Violet Bonham Carter, Russell Braddon and Edward du Cann, and the question was: 'Should Britain enter the Common Market, and if we do, how does the panel think this will affect the average household budget?'

> DU CANN: I think we should enter the Common Market provided that we can get terms which are satisfactory to this very important industry of agriculture of ours which employs more than a million people; providing we can get terms which are satisfactory for maintaining and strengthening the Commonwealth relationship, and provided we can get terms which are fair to our partners in the European Free Trade Association and that is what we're negotiating at the present moment. And the reasons why we should go in are: first, that the Common Market presents us with a tremendous trading opportunity, fastest growing market in the world, two hundred and fifty million people; and second, because it will enable us to influence developments in Europe maybe over the next hundred years or so. As to the question of a household budget if we do go into the Common Market, food is likely to cost us a little bit more because we shall have to go over to the Continental system of price support. On the other hand, other commodities may well be cheaper and I think probably the housewife will gain in the long run through the benefits of increased competition.
>
> BRADDON: I would like to speak first of all from a more emotional angle. In the first place, I don't want my temperatures in future read in centigrade. I don't

want to read that a beautiful day like today the temperature is 23 degrees, because when I read that the temperature is 23 degrees I go to bed for a month and I stay there. I don't want to see decimal coinage. I don't care if it does confuse Europeans, our coinage of guineas and half crowns – their language confuses us and they make no attempt to oblige us by changing that. I don't see that there is any reason when we go in why we should say categorically and with some arrogance that we shall influence them. I'm much more alarmed by the fact that they might influence us – the French at this moment with the Algerians have not a particularly savoury record; the Germans with their attitude have an equally unsavoury record. Italy and France have huge Communist parties. None of these countries, as idealistic countries, appeals to me as peoples with whom we wish to associate our future so closely. And if you ask me, if you do go in, whether your fellow-countrymen, your fellow-Britons in Australia and the other Dominions who are English-speaking and white will feel somehow, although you're entitled to do this, that they have been betrayed, the answer is 'yes'. And if you ask me whether you go in with the best will and the greatest ideals in the world, whether those Dominions will feel that somehow you as Anglo-Saxons have lost status, the answer is 'yes'. And if you ask me whether we're afraid that if you go in the Commonwealth will be lost, the answer is again 'yes'. I don't want to see you becoming less British by joining the European Common Market, I want to see you becoming more British. This to me is a tremendous ideal and it seems to be the one ideal which is lacking in all your leaders today. Furthermore, it has been said in the House of Commons, that the figure of an increased expense for each of you per week will be a minimum three shillings a week up to one pound a week.

LADY VIOLET: I am absolutely convinced that it will be for the long-term good of the Commonwealth that we should go in rather than that we should stay out. We in this small island can never provide these dynamic growing countries like Australia and Canada, either the markets or the capital investment which they need. Let me tell you one fact. Do you know that the Common Market countries are at present giving India just double the aid for her five-year plan that we are giving her? And that is not because we are ungenerous. It's not because we do not feel for India as we should, it is because we haven't got the capital resources to do it. Do let us realize that the day of small units – and I love small units, I hate these monstrous monopolies – the day of small units, even among nations, is over.

We have two great masses – one is an ally, America, the other – I won't say it is an enemy, I would hate to say that, but we have Russia to face and to deal with. And we must do that, the West must do that together; and to some extent we must pool our sovereignty if we are going to do it successfully.

Now in Europe I am sure we can make an enormous contribution. Mr Russell Braddon says that we can't influence Europe. I think we can. I think we can link Europe with the Commonwealth. I think we are already a link between Europe and America. One of the reasons I feel most deeply about this European unity is that I am old enough to have lived through two world wars and both started in Europe, and tore Europe to bits. This union of France and Germany, which is almost a miracle, they were bitter enemies – this coming together of the whole core of Europe, and we want to bring in the EFTA countries too, and the neutrals, as well as Norway and Denmark – I believe it is a tremendous safeguard against another European war and that is why I want it most of all.

1962/63

Hardly had we embarked on the new series in September 1962, when the Cuban crisis, which had been rumbling during the past year, erupted with devastating suddenness. On 21 September, a questioner at Braunton in Devon asked: 'If the build-up of Soviet arms continues in Cuba, does the panel think that war hysteria amongst the American population could bring about an invasion of Cuban soil by American troops?'

Bernard Levin said: 'What do people imagine that the Soviet advisers and technicians, and shortly no doubt the troops, are actually doing in Cuba? Sending back post-cards to Kiev saying, "Having a wonderful time, wish you were here"? They're setting up a Communist base, military base, ninety miles from the American mainland. Of course America is right to be deeply concerned about this problem and to take steps to deal with it. I can't see any remote possibility of an invasion of Cuba by American troops in these circumstances, but for goodness sake, let's look at the reality of the situation. This is not something that simply concerns the Americans; it's closest to the Americans geographically, but Soviet penetration and Soviet expansion concerns all of us, whether it's happening ninety miles from our doorstep, or ninety miles from the American doorstep.'

A fortnight later in Petworth, Sussex, there was a question asking whether Britain should co-operate with a request from the USA for an economic boycott of Cuba.

The team were dubious about this, especially Richard Crossman: 'One's got to be careful about repercussions. The Americans are really claiming that they are allowed to throttle a Communist state which is very near to them. If they claim that right, then the next thing is that the Russians claim the right to throttle Persia – I mean, somebody says, "I'll do it to the similar problem I have"; and Persia under American control, so to speak, is just as objectionable to Russia as Cuba is under Russian control; and I think we've got to say to both of them: "Now, for heaven's sake, don't lay down this law that you have the right to throttle rival systems you don't like, merely because they're close to your shores." '

Towards the end of October, the situation deteriorated alarmingly. Missile sites had been spotted in Cuba and Russian missile ships were on their way there. The American navy was poised to turn them back and imposed a naval blockade of Cuba. A head-on clash seemed imminent. The Third World War was nearer than ever before.

We met for *Any Questions?* at Trowbridge in Wiltshire on 26 October in the utmost despondency. The team included Colin Welch, of the *Daily Telegraph*, inaugurator of the Peter Simple column, and the first question asked: 'What does the team consider should be the policy of the British people towards the naval blockade of Cuba by the United States?'

> WELCH: President Kennedy's action in blockading Cuba I would regard as necessary, entirely justified and it will have most salutary effects. Therefore, I think if we have any policy it should be to back up President Kennedy in his resolution. I think it's perhaps the best thing that has happened since the War. Many people have discussed the various risks involved in this operation. Now does anybody seriously think that Mr Khrushchev would have risked a nuclear war over a thing as really unimportant to him as Cuba? It isn't important to him; it is important to Mr Kennedy. This, I think, was designed as a test of President Kennedy, who may conceivably have given

Mr Khrushchev the impression that he was a weak and timid man. Now in these circumstances the risks of doing nothing are very much greater. If President Kennedy had tolerated what went on in Cuba without protest or without resistance of any kind, I think we would certainly have to face a very much more grave and appalling crisis in Berlin, or perhaps somewhere else within the next six months. The impression would have got around to Mr Khrushchev and others that America would stand for anything; if she stands for rockets in Cuba she might well stand for rockets in Florida! You can make various points that this is analagous in a way to the Americans placing bases in Turkey. Though the point about this Cuba thing which makes it quite different to anything that has happened in Turkey is this: that this is a fresh threat, a new threat, it is a disturbance of an existing status quo which has been implicitly accepted by both parties.

Colin Welch's optimism was clearly regarded by some other members of the team as misguided, but he was proved right. The Russian ships did turn back and the crisis subsided even more suddenly than it had begun.

The Cuban crisis was perhaps at the back of my mind later in this series, when I chose a question about the end of the world. We were at Mitcheldean in the Forest of Dean, with William Rodgers, who had been recently elected Labour MP for Stockton-on-Tees in a by-election, Gerald Nabarro, recently made a Knight in the Honours List, the musician, Antony Hopkins, and Mary Stocks. The question was: 'If the world were doomed to end on Sunday, what would the team do tomorrow?'

RODGERS: I simply wouldn't accept it. I wouldn't care if anybody told me the world was ending on Sunday, I would say, I don't believe you, I intend to do tomorrow what I intended originally to do, go back to London, take my constituents round the House of Commons, and then go back to my family and spend the remainder of tomorrow and Sunday until the end of the world with my wife and my three children, pottering about the house, doing something in the garden, and generally carrying on living my life as if it wasn't going to end at all.

HOPKINS: I would certainly practise the piano strenuously. This sounds an absolutely ridiculous thing to say, but it's something which I don't on the whole have enough time to do in a crowded and busy life, and I enjoy practising the piano enormously, and I think I'll really have a crack at the first movement of the Hammerclavier which I've been putting off for a very long time. And having done that for about four hours, I would get into my very fast motor car, and I would drive down to a racing circuit on which I'm not allowed to race, normally speaking, and I would break in, and I would do about a hundred laps because I would enjoy doing that enormously. Then I would come home, and I would have an extremely good meal, starting with smoked salmon, and going on to a few other things, and whatever the price was, I'd finish up with strawberries and cream. And – well, I think the rest of the day you'd better draw a veil over.

GRISEWOOD: Antony, when you began your story I thought you were going to say you were going to practise the harp.

HOPKINS: Where I'm going it wouldn't be needed.

STOCKS: My first thought was that I should have to do the washing because it might not be possible to do it on Monday. I think I should read some novels – I shouldn't do much, I should really enjoy doing nothing.

NABARRO: Well, one thing I wouldn't do is have anything to do with my constituents on my last days! They might grumble at me about teachers' pay, or the local rates, or some other current controversy. No, what I'd do would be to have a whale of a party at home, so that I had such a hell of a hang-over on Sunday morning I wouldn't mind the world ending.

The previous question had been distinctly more serious and concerned the dissolution of the Central African

Federation.

NABARRO: I'm a realist, and the reason I supported the Central African Federation in 1953 was that it seemed to me to be the only civilized formula for building a multi-racial society in the Rhodesias and Nyasaland. That's why I supported it, and people who've got hindsight and look back on it all now and say, 'Well, of course it was an impossible proposition or formula in the first place, and should never have been embarked upon by the Government,' are being unrealistic in their approach. The problem in Little Rock, Arkansas, or in Notting Hill Gate, or in Rhodesia, is one and the same. And it is a problem which has afflicted the white races and the civilizing influences in the world – and the white races *are* civilizing influences in the world – for hundreds of years. It is white versus black. That's all. And if anybody disagrees with that, I say to them straight away, if they are a parent here in England: Would you be happy if your blonde, blue-eyed daughter, aged 21, the apple of her father's eye, came home with a great big buck nigger and said: 'I'm going to marry this man' and you had a prospect of some coffee-coloured grandchildren?

Gerald's use of the words 'big buck nigger' came in for much criticism, and Frank Gillard, by then back in Bristol as the Controller of the West Region, decided that the offending passage should be deleted from the repeat. When I telephoned Gerald to let him know of this decision, he tried to justify the phrase by making out that it was widely used.

'What about the BBC putting on the Nigger Minstrel Show?' he asked.

'It's called the Black and White Minstrel Show,' I replied, somewhat coldly.

Anyway, we cut it from the repeat. Then the words came up again in an item on the satirical TV show *That Was The Week That Was* the following Saturday, and Gerald wrote me a letter complaining that there did not seem to be any continuity of policy.

'The precise evaluation of my correspondence which has been carried out in my office shows the following results: to date there are 117 letters, 72 for me and 45 against me, the latter including doubtfuls,' he wrote. 'I am not for myself in any doubt at all that I represent a majority opinion in what I said and it is now confirmed to me from innumerable sources that there is nothing contemptuous or offensive in the term "big buck nigger"; a number of journalists are trying to read into what I said things which are not there, but I shall put them into good order as we go along.'

Frank replied that the cut was made because he had the impression that Nabarro was being misunderstood and to some extent pilloried because of a phrase used off the cuff. He thought, on reflection, that it might have been a mistake to order the cut, and that *Any Answers* could be expected to take adequate care of the whole incident. (In the event, *Any Answers* maintained a stony silence.) There was, of course, no Race Relations Act at that time.

On 16 November 1962, we marked the BBC's fortieth anniversary by taking the programme to London, to the BBC's old Savoy Hill premises where Freddy had gone as an announcer in 1929. Part of the building was leased to the BBC by the Institution of Electrical Engineers before Broadcasting House was built, and the audience was provided that evening by some of the members of the Institution.

We thought we ought to have a special team, and that really boiled down to including people we couldn't normally have, i.e. a minister of the Conservative Government, and the Leader of the Opposition. We couldn't normally have Government ministers because Downing Street, whichever party was in power, wouldn't allow them to appear. Shirley Williams once explained to me that it would be awkward for a minister to have to discuss off-the-cuff matters which were the proper concern of other ministers, though Tony Benn often told me he could see no reason why ministers shouldn't take part in the programme. In 1977 we thought at last we had made a break-through when a junior minister, Leslie Huckfield, joined the team in his birthplace, Pershore in Worcestershire. But although the evening passed without either the heavens or the Government falling, we were not able to repeat the experiment.

However, on that special occasion in November 1962, Hugh Gaitskell was willing to appear and the most appropriate minister, who was also willing, was Lord Hailsham, whose first appearance in the programme dated back to 1950, when he was Quintin Hogg, MP for Oxford. The other two were Lady Violet Bonham Carter, a former BBC Governor, and Ralph Wightman.

Hailsham, concerned about discussing Government policy, did in fact try to insist that no political questions were accepted. Hugh Gaitskell, on the other hand, was very much in favour of a political discussion and so was Lady Violet. We couldn't, of course, accept Hailsham's restriction, but in the event there were no party politics. A politician in the audience, Hugh Delargy, put a light-hearted question: 'Last night a play by Graham Greene was barracked off the stage in Paris by French dentists because it described dentistry as an unromantic profession. Does the team agree, and what is their version of a romantic profession?' In his reply, Hugh Gaitskell showed a pleasant sense of humour.

'I think this is a very good illustration of the difference between the French and the British. Only in France could the dentists have organized themselves to barrack a playwright because he described the profession of dentistry as unromantic. Now that is because of course "unromantic" is an offensive word in France; but in England it's entirely the other way round. If in fact in England Graham Greene had put on a play which described dentists as engaged in a romantic profession, this would be regarded as libellous. Indeed it would imply that all sorts of things happened in the dentist's chair that in fact people are supposed to be thrown out of their job for over here. Totally different in France. You see, there are all these problems that are going to arise when we go into the Common Market!'

After the programme I had a friendly talk with Hugh Gaitskell about the relationship between the Labour

Party and *Any Questions?*, complaints about political bias in the audiences and so on. He thought it might be a good idea to arrange for me to meet a senior member of his staff to discuss the problems, but within two months he was dead.

On 14 December a questioner asked: 'Most of us have a great number of friends in every walk of life. Occasionally one meets with somebody who's bloody awkward. What is it that produces awkwardness in mankind?' Freddy's inclination to repeat every question word for word was severely tested, though any swear word, however crude, would have been neutered by Freddy's golden tones. However, he cautiously repeated 'b— awkward' and the team all followed his example.

Funny thing about this word 'bloody'. You would think as time went on that its occasional inadvertent use in the programme would gradually pass almost unnoticed, that the listeners would become more tolerant, but you would be wrong. Some listeners persisted in objecting very strongly indeed. Team members could express the most unpopular opinions and escape relatively unscathed in *Any Answers*, but just one 'bloody' and there would be shoals of angry letters.

Bob Boothby was one of the most regular offenders, and when I mildly reproached him he would argue that it wasn't really a swear word. However, he did concede that the word irritated some listeners and he made strenuous efforts to avoid using it, and indeed made some capital out of not doing so. ('Hell. I think I can safely say that.')

(DJ: *I think some listeners have this reaction because we are the last outpost of good behaviour. There has to be a line of good taste and our line has always been thickly drawn, perhaps pompously so; but it doesn't alter the fact that somebody has to keep the flag flying and it very often seems to be left to us. But I did notice a 'bloody' get in recently without any reaction, so perhaps the standards are beginning to be eroded at home anyway.*)

From the beginning of 1963, there was a change in the timing of the programme. We were on the air at 8.40 – more chance for me to grab my pudding before rushing for the hall – and we had an extra five minutes, giving us fifty instead of forty-five. I welcomed this very much. It meant we could have at least one more question and could allow a little more elbow room when there was a discussion which looked as if it might really take off. I was sorry when the extra minutes were clawed back five years later.

On Good Friday at Clevedon, Somerset, Arthur Street made what was to be his final appearance in *Any Questions?* though I didn't know it at the time. He was in a rather truculent mood and one of the questioners asked: 'If Christ walked this earth this Easter time, what things do the panel think would delight or sadden Him?'

Arthur nearly hit the roof: 'Surely to goodness, it is a private thing, if you have any religion. And I'm sorry, I think it is unfair to ask us – you might ask me whether I'm a Christian or a Jew or a Buddhist or what you will – that is my business, and I will see the BBC and all you in a hotter place than this before I'll answer.'

That's all there was to it, but the rest of the team seemed to have no difficulty in attempting the question, and the result of it was that I failed to put up a fight when some of my masters decided that Arthur had outlived his usefulness to the programme. I still regret that I submitted so tamely. Arthur was unique. He lacked Ralph's sly humour and flexibility, but there is a magnificent string of his superbly constructed solo pieces on a variety of subjects in the BBC archives which are still trotted out from time to time; and for pithy, down-to-earth, pungent comment he had no peer.

1963/64

In the autumn of 1963 four mop-haired young men from Liverpool were busy revolutionizing pop music, and on 18 October, at Wootton Bassett in Wiltshire, a team including Russell Braddon, the writer, Gwyn Thomas, making his début, and Isobel Barnett, were asked if they could explain why a bunch of unattractive, unkempt youths bawling down a microphone could drive young girls to a frenzy.

BRADDON: No. But equally I can't understand why girls dressed in what look like slung-on ex-railwaymen's clothes and wearing the kind of jackboots that would be very popular with the Irma Grises of this world who had human skin on their lampshades – I can't understand why these girls should drive all the scruffy males to distraction either. In other words you, ma'am, who asked the question, and I, we're getting on a bit, you know, we're past it, we're not driven to distraction often enough, and I suppose if this mob that's kicking around, driving one another to distraction at the moment, saw what we picked up with in our youth they'd be pretty horrified, too.

THOMAS: I think there's a terrible revenge involved here. It is, of course, part of the whole tempo of education; we drive our reluctant species into the light at the best speed we can, and we have actually driven this particular generation into a kind of affluence that possibly we didn't know in the past, and of course its done on the basis of a great mass of romantic pop fiction which doesn't instil a single decent, human value. And, after all, let's not forget the terrible, pathetic validity of this experience – the need for some kind of expression and projection of oneself. There are very few Carusos; there can be very many young crooners. There can be very few Ladies of the Camellias, but there can be a great horde of girls who can scream at the behest of the gramophone companies. I mean, this has created a kind of hysteria, but I don't think we should ignore what lies behind it. It is a great hunger for articulacy, for beauty, for being in the light; because so many of these people, after all, are the first generation who have actually got their voices before the public. Let's not forget that for a million years before this they were silent people. So don't let's criticize the quality of the sound they make at the moment. It is squalid, it is bestial, but in an appalled sort of way I'm for it.

BARNETT: I'm not screaming in the aisles – I hope to heavens I never shall be screaming in the aisles – but you know, I can see it, this terrible adolescent desire to release an enthusiasm of some kind; and if you can't catch their imagination with something more worthwhile, they've got to let it loose somehow. And I'd rather they let it loose screaming in the aisles, with pudding-basin haircuts and four guitars plugged into something on the stage than that they tore up railway trains or landed up in the Juvenile Courts. And you know, getting back to something Russell Braddon said, we've had it, we're past it, and I do remember skipping round in my youth to something that was called 'A tisket, a tasket, I've lost my yellow basket'. I know my mother thought that was the ultimate low. And so presumably what I think the ultimate low now, my son thinks is absolutely deli cious. This is just a generation on, and I'm sure that those who are swooning in the aisles now will presumably go on to (ha! ha!) 'enjoy better things'.

THOMAS: Well, I would like to point out a certain

difference in idiom between themselves and ourselves, because when I was a boy, my madness was to imitate the posture and walk of film stars – silent film stars, because we couldn't hear their voices. And I was passionately involved with the gait of an actor called George Bancroft, who kind of walked about like that, you know, and William S. Hart, the cowboy; and I imitated the walk and posture of these two men so well that on sixteen occasions I was whipped into the local clinic for rickets and pigeon-chest. They cured me, too.

BRADDON: In a way, you know, the success of these screaming kids is our fault, the older ones' fault. We're a lousy audience, now; we're no longer capable of being a good theatrical audience, we're so obsessed with television, which you sit watching alone, your eyes channelled on to the screen; if anyone comes in, you don't take your eyes off the screen, you just send out little hate rays at them, saying, 'Shut up or drop dead, shut up or drop dead' – and you look at the screen all the time. We don't know what to do with a performance on the stage, but the kids know – they're sick to death of television, they go to see live shows and they're doing what we're not doing, they're creating stars. And if we don't like the stars, it's our own ruddy fault, we're a lousy audience, we don't know how to make 'em any longer.

On 22 November 1963, we assembled at a hotel in Wellington, Somerset. It seemed much like any other Friday. I rather think it was here that Bob Boothby claimed some credit for Harold Wilson's effective television appearances. ('I told him, "Look straight at the camera; if your eyes wander round, it makes you look shifty!" ') Mr Wilson looked like being the next Prime Minister after the General Election, due some time the following year. 'He won't be *too bad*, you know,' Bob said encouragingly.

I remember going with Wynford Vaughan Thomas to explore the resources of the hotel's wine cellar. Marghanita Laski probably disappeared to have a bath on arrival – she usually does. The newcomer, the writer Michael Frayn, joined us and was unostentatiously given the producer's pep talk. Like most newcomers, he doubtless found it enervating. We had some drinks, we listened to the six o'clock news – nothing of any great significance – we wondered what questions might come up, we drifted in to dinner. It was just like any other Friday evening.

As usual, I left the dinner table early with Bill Coysh and my secretary Janet Robertson, leaving Freddy Grisewood and the team to linger over their coffee. We arrived at the school where the broadcast was taking place, went into the office and began reading through the questions. One of them asked: 'What punishment would the team recommend for the man who assassinated President Kennedy?'

It was our first intimation of surely the most shattering news item since *Any Questions?* had begun fifteen years earlier. The news must have come through on the radio just as the questioner was leaving for the hall.

The team heard the news at much the same moment. They were still sitting at the dinner table when Edward du Cann, in whose constituency we were, happened to walk in and asked them 'Have you heard . . .?' They were so horrified they decided then and there that it would be quite impossible for them to do the programme. They all felt they couldn't discuss other issues that evening, and the tragic news was too recent, too shocking, for them to discuss it dispassionately. 'We can't go on,' Bob told me categorically over the telephone. He had known President Kennedy as a personal friend.

A compromise was reached. The team agreed to come to the hall, and each of them would pay a short tribute to the President, and that would be all. By this time, the audience had been told the news and what had been decided. One of them suggested that they should stand for one minute's silence as a mark of respect. They all seemed to accept that a normal *Any Questions?* broadcast that evening was impossible. The team arrived, the audience stood and the short broadcast began.

In his tribute, Bob said: 'President Kennedy seemed to stand for all that is good and hopeful for the future of the

Freddy Grisewood, travelling question master October 1948 to November 1967. (BBC)

Sir Jack Longland, a member of the first Any Questions? *team and a regular for many years.*

The team for the second edition of Any Questions? *at Taunton on 26 October 1948. L to R: Major Lewis Hastings, Lady Violet Bonham Carter, Ralph Wightman and the writer and critic St John Ervine.* (BBC)

L to R: Walter Elliot MP, James Griffiths MP, Lady Violet Bonham Carter and Ralph Wightman with Freddy Grisewood and Michael Bowen at Stroud, Gloucestershire, on 28 January 1955. (Stroud News)

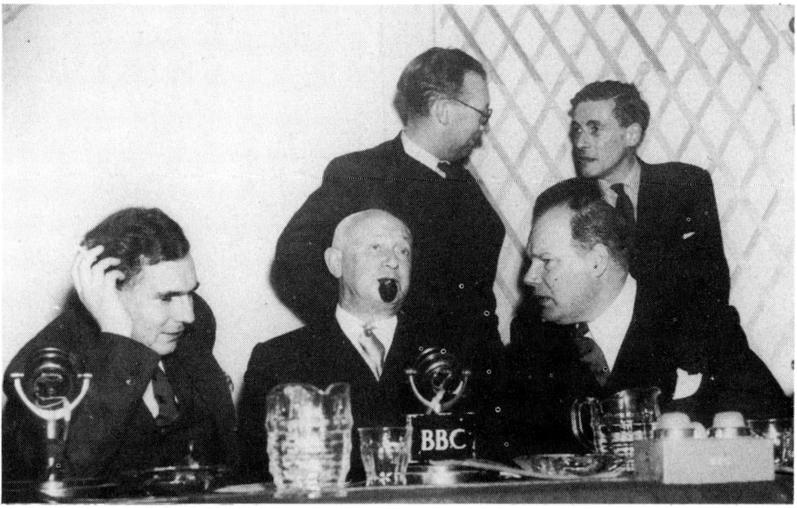

A post-programme discussion in Bristol, 21 February 1958. L to R: Peter Kirk MP, Emanuel Shinwell MP and Alan Villiers the sailor; (standing) Michael Bowen and Desmond Hawkins, Head of West Regional Programme. (Bristol Evening Post)

The tenth birthday edition, 10 October 1958. L to R: Lord Boothby, Anthony Wedgwood Benn MP, Lady Violet Bonham Carter and Arthur Street, with Freddy Grisewood and Michael Bowen. (Hampshire Chronicle)

L to R: Gerald Nabarro MP, Patrick Gordon Walker MP, the farmer Jack Houghton-Brown, and Mary Stocks with Freddy Grisewood and Michael Bowen at Combe Martin, Devon, 17 April 1959. (Powell's)

'I adopted the Brains Trust *set-up when I returned to* Any Questions?, *with the chairman in the centre and two of the team on each side of him, at an angle.' L to R: Edward du Cann MP, Bernard Levin, Freddy Grisewood, Michael Bowen, Mary Stocks and Anthony Wedgwood Benn MP in Exeter on 4 December 1959.* (British Rail)

The pre-dinner drinks in a Bournemouth hotel on 26 February 1960. L to R: Freddy Grisewood, Lady Barnett, Arthur Street, Francis Williams, Professor Asa Briggs and Michael Bowen. (Rowland Adams)

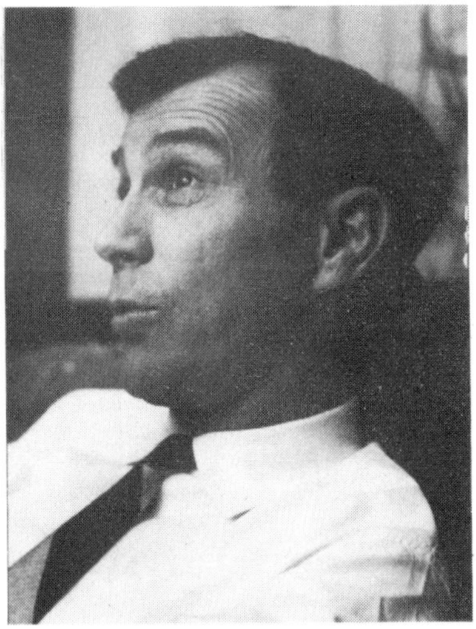

'On 11 March 1960 at Bath we had another newcomer—the provocative, humorous Australian writer, Russell Braddon.'

Michael Bowen and Freddy Grisewood face the audience at the Ralph Allen School, Claverton Down, Somerset, on 11 November 1960. (Radio Times)

The team at Savoy Hill, London, during the BBC's fortieth birthday celebrations. L to R: Viscount Hailsham, Ralph Wightman, Freddy Grisewood, Michael Bowen, Lady Violet Bonham Carter and Hugh Gaitskell MP. (BBC)

L to R: Dorian Williams, Ralph Wightman, Freddy Grisewood, Michael Bowen, Mary Trevelyan and the Bishop of Crediton. In the foreground is Janet Robertson with one of the questioners at West Hill, near Ottery St Mary, Devon, on 12 March 1965. (BBC)

'During the summer break I had what seemed to be a bright idea that we should tie up with The Archers *and take* Any Questions? *to Ambridge.' L to R: Lady Barnett, Chris Gittins (Walter Gabriel), Steve Race, Monte Crick (Dan Archer), Ralph Wightman, Anne Cullen (Carol Grenville), Godfrey Basley (editor of* The Archers*), Michael Bowen and C. A. Joyce at Inkberrow, Worcestershire, 9 September 1966.* (Redditch Indicator and Alcester Chronicle)

Freddy Grisewood's eightieth birthday at Liphook in Hampshire, 11 April 1968. L to R: John Arlott, C. A. Joyce, Freddy and Michael Bowen. (BBC)

The three 'surprise' guests talk to Freddy after his eightieth birthday programme. L to R: Anthony Greenwood MP, Jeremy Thorpe MP with his future wife Caroline, and Quintin Hogg MP. (Donald Eades)

The team at Plymouth where Paul Foot made his début and 'started us off on the bumpy road to trouble with London'. L to R: Margaret Thatcher MP, Tom Salmon (BBC Plymouth), Malcolm Muggeridge, David Jacobs, Michael Bowen, Paul Foot and Dr John Dunwoody MP on 4 October 1968.

L to R: Anthony Hopkins, the thriller writer and former champion jockey Dick Francis, David Jacobs, Michael Bowen, Mary Stocks and Ned Sherrin at Saltford, near Bristol, on 4 April 1969. In the foreground is Alison Brady (secretary of Any Questions?*).* (BBC)

Alison Brady, Michael Bowen and David Jacobs discuss the questions.

(Berrow's Newspapers Ltd., Worcester)

Lord Mancroft, Vic Feather (centre) and Irene Handl meet some of the officials of Wills's Sports and Social Club in Swindon, Wiltshire, after the broadcast on 21 January 1972.

Some of the distinguished members of the audience for the twenty-fifth birthday edition in Bristol on 12 October 1973. L to R: Lady Plowden (Vice-Chairman of the BBC Board of Governors), Ian Trethowan (Managing Director, Radio), Frank Gillard, Alderman and Mrs J. W. M. Willcox and Stuart Wyton (Head of the Bristol Network Production Centre).

The team for the twenty-fifth birthday edition waiting in the wings. L to R: Lady Barnett, David Jacobs, Mary Stocks, Sir Richard Marsh and Kenneth Williams.

(BBC)

David Jacobs talks to Mary Stocks after what proved to be her final appearance in Any Questions?, *the twenty-fifth birthday edition in Bristol.* (BBC)

The team share a pre-programme joke at Nantyglo Community College and Sports Complex in Gwent, where Enoch Powell revealed his ambition to lead the Tory Party. L to R: Powell, John Cole, David Jacobs, Michael Bowen, Norman St John-Stevas MP and Baroness Wootton on 8 March 1974.

Michael Bowen, no longer producer of Any Questions?, *talks to Patrick Moore after the programme from Filton High School, Bristol, on 25 November 1977. His successor as producer, Carole Stone, is on the left.*

world. And I think that in the hour of his death we realize now what stature he really had, what hope he held for the future of us all.'

Marghanita Laski spoke of the great loss – the feeling that here was a man who could perhaps lead us on the way to peace.

Wynford Vaughan Thomas hoped that the feeling of continuity built up in the comradeship between the two countries during the war would go on with Kennedy's successor and, if that was so, then his death would not have been in vain.

And that was the end of the broadcast. The audience quietly dispersed and we packed up our things and went home. Before leaving, I promised the headmaster that we would return within a few months. We did so, on 3 April, with a different team, including Russell Braddon and Frank Cousins. But there seemed to be a jinx about Wellington. When we went on the air, Freddy prefaced his introduction thus:

'*Any Questions?* normally has a team of four speakers. At the moment we only have three, because Mr Russell Braddon unfortunately went to the wrong Wellington, the one in Shropshire, but a fast car has been driving him to the right one for the past three and a half hours. Whether he will get here in time we don't know, but we're hoping he'll arrive at any minute, and thank heaven he didn't set out for Wellington, New Zealand.'

Russell had caught the train his manager had told him to catch (our letter of instructions unfortunately didn't specify the county) and gradually became concerned at the behaviour of the sun in setting on his left. At that time *Any Questions?* was invariably broadcast from the west country and therefore his train should be travelling straight into the setting sun. He wrote out a message on a bit of paper, wrapped it round a British Rail bun and threw it out of the window. The message asked the finder to ring the BBC or look in *Radio Times*. When the train pulled in to Birmingham he asked a porter to ring the BBC and find out where he should be going, but the train pulled out again before he got the answer.

At Wolverhampton, a reception committee awaited him, bearing grim tidings. He had caught the wrong train and was well on his way to the wrong Wellington. They got him a taxi and he started on his epic journey to the right Wellington, some 150 miles away

There was, unfortunately, a snag. When Freddy spoke of 'a fast car', he was overstating the case. Russell's taxi was governed not to travel above a certain speed and that certain speed seemed desperately slow. If they weren't actually overtaken by bicycles, it must very often have seemed like it. And so we went on the air with a team of three for the first forty minutes of the programme. Then, just as we had given him up for lost, Russell appeared at the back of the hall and made his way up on to the stage. 'I'm awfully sorry to be late,' he said. 'There are apparently about seven other Wellingtons in Great Britain. And I've come via the lot.'

There was one question I had been saving in case he arrived, because I suspected he had strong views on it, and there was just time to get it in: 'Given a free hand, how would the team deal with the Mods and Rockers who smashed up Clacton last week-end?'

BRADDON: The first thing to do is to smash up all their motor bikes so that they're irretrievably done in, then fine them so much that those that can be mended can't be paid for so that the finance companies reclaim the bikes. Finally, send someone from Clacton round to the homes of the parents of all the kids and smash their windows in too, so that they know what it's like.

COUSINS: The real problem that worries me is the kind of comments that were made by one or two of the youngsters who were asked why they got involved in it at all, that they were bored, they wanted a giggle, they wanted to do something because there was nothing to do in Clacton. Now, what sort of a system of society are we developing where youngsters feel that the only way to relieve boredom is to break things or to fight, or to have what they describe as a 'punch-up', or a night out with 'birds', as they described it? And I think that we are quite as much responsible as the children, that we lead them to a set of circumstances where, unless they're willing to go to one of these fun palaces, one of these places where they can look at the machines, or play for coins on machines, or go to a bingo hall, there is nothing of any substance worthwhile in many of the places that the kids go to.

BRADDON: Well, why do they go there?

COUSINS: Wouldn't you go if you were living in certain parts of the East End of London, wouldn't you go somewhere else?

BRADDON: I could look after myself, entertain myself or I got a hiding from my parents for not looking after and entertaining myself, and I don't see why this lot don't, too. I'm sick to death of 'we've got to entertain the kids'.

COUSINS: I'm not saying 'entertain the kids'. We have closed down many of the places where the kids found their own entertainment. We have made it impossible . . .

BRADDON: But Frank, they could have gone somewhere else where they could have found entertainment. They just jolly well didn't want to. They didn't have to go to Clacton and lie in the fog. Don't forget there's nothing new in this. The first juvenile delinquent was a fellow called Cain; this is no reflection on modern society.

In one of the programmes in this series, the Bishop of Crediton mentioned his admiration for the producer in often contriving, well in advance, to include a panel member on a week when he or she turned out to be in the news. I must admit I had a fair bit of good fortune over this; never more than in the case of Lord Mancroft and the Norwich Union.

It had been suggested that we might sometimes keep a place vacant and then call in at the last minute a fourth member of the team who happened to be in the news, but people in the news are often there for some disagreeable or embarrassing reason and are unlikely to welcome an invitation to appear – quite apart from the difficulty of maintaining political balance in such a team. The very last thing Lord Mancroft wanted to do was to take part in *Any Questions?* that particular week, but as he had accepted the invitation several weeks earlier, long before the story broke, he was good enough to keep the appointment, unlike some who were apt to send telegrams pleading a judicious illness or a subsequent engagement.

What had caused Lord Mancroft, who is Jewish, to be in the news was that he had been asked to resign from the Board of the Norwich Union insurance company, apparently because of pressure brought by Arab states who objected to the fact that he was also a director of a body which dealt with Israel. All that week there had been great pressure on Mancroft to make a statement to the media. He had resolutely refused to do so. When it was realized that he was due to appear on *Any Questions?* there was intense interest. BBC television even considered sending a crew to the broadcast to film his reply to the inevitable question.

Over drinks that evening I discussed with him at what stage it would be best to bring in the question. He thought about number four. So I went off to the hall to choose the questions, intending to place this one at number four. There was just one small difficulty. Nobody submitted a question on it.

We were at the Royal Naval Engineering College in Plymouth, and I said casually to the young naval officer who was ferrying the questions to us, 'I rather thought we might get a question about Lord Mancroft as he's on the team.'

'Oh?' he replied. 'I imagine everybody thought that would be rather bad form.'

'Oh, I don't think it would be considered bad form; I don't think Lord Mancroft would consider it was bad form at all,' I said, as meaningfully as possible.

A minute or two later a question duly arrived. I had no compunction about dropping this tiny hint. It is one thing to 'plant' a question; it is quite another to reassure potential questioners that their inhibitions are misguided.

If we hadn't had the question it would have been a let-down. Everybody would be waiting for it, not least Lord Mancroft himself.

In the event, he cleverly managed to say very little about his former colleagues with whom he had, much to his grief, to part company: 'Perhaps I can say one thing and one thing only firmly in their defence: I'm absolutely certain that they were in no way motivated by the slightest degree of anti-semitism. They knew my religion when they asked me to join the Board; they knew that the travel firm of which I am Chairman trades actively with Israel – they've known that all along; they've asked relations of mine over many years to join them on the Board knowing their religion too, so any accusation that the Norwich Union was motivated by anti-semitism is wholly unjustified. I'm very sorry that they should find themselves in this difficulty. I wish that the time would soon come when a bit more can be said in their defence, and there is something to be said in their defence, but not, I think, either in their defence or to attack them by me here this evening.'

In April 1964, Freddy suffered a serious illness, more serious than we at first realized, and what was expected to be a week or two's absence extended into two months. During that time we had several different chairmen – Steve Race, Wynford Vaughan Thomas, William Hardcastle, Lionel Hale, Alan Melville and Robert Robinson. They all took their turn in introducing *Any Answers* as well. I was writing the presenter's linking material at that time and had to try to capture their very different styles. I told them they could alter anything they wanted to. None of them altered a single word, except Robert Robinson, who altered every single word.

In the *Any Questions?* chair he was the one who least resembled Freddy Grisewood. His astringent style was very distinctive. He made clear his impatience with the traditional word-for-word repetition of the question. ('Well, I'll just say that again, you know, in the sort of ritual way.') He didn't call in each speaker by name, but allowed the discussion to develop of its own volition, unless no one volunteered to speak next. He could be caustic with the team – he said to Gwyn Thomas: 'What are you labouring to say there?' – and he prodded them with penetrating supplementary questions and entered into the discussion himself in a way which anticipated *Stop the Week.*

It ended up as quite a jokey sort of programme. Philip Haskell, a lecturer in mathematics at the Portsmouth College of Technology, a witty, fluent talker, had some very good moments. In discussing the question 'Does the panel think that a decline in students' morals would necessarily result from living in a mixed hall of residence?' (the programme was coming from the University of Southampton), he said: 'Whenever we say morals, we mean sexual morals. I remember quite distinctly a film being advertised in a town where I lived not so very long ago in which it said "the most primitive instincts are appealed to in this film" and I visualized the whole audience sitting there getting hungrier and hungrier. I'm quite sure that wasn't what the people who were selling the film were trying to say, I'm quite certain they weren't serving chocolates there, they were supposed to be appealing to something more primitive. I think this is absolutely false emphasis and I don't think there's any reason at all to suppose that if you're close to women, your sexual morals would necessarily decline. I think there are quite a lot of women, with whom chastity is not merely a duty but a downright pleasure.'

In discussing a question about individual hospitality to students from overseas, Gwyn Thomas had this cautionary tale: 'I remember some years ago in South Wales I wanted to make welcome an African student, and I took him to a local Eisteddfod in Treorchy which was held in a disused waggon shed, and even at the best an Eisteddfod can wear a sullen face, but in a waggon shed it really comes to its ripest. And my African friend and I were trapped between a very large audience and the platform, and he had to listen to eighteen male voice choirs singing a very lowering piece called *The Martyrs of the Arena*. He was under drugs for months and within a fortnight he was the leader of the Nationalist Party back in his own country.'

1964/65

The long-awaited General Election came on 15 October. It was a real cliff-hanger, and I remember listening to the results on the car radio during the long drive to Brighton on the Friday afternoon. At the beginning of the journey, I didn't know which of the MPs on the team would be a member of the governing party. At the end of the journey, it was clear that Labour was in with a small majority and that Harold Wilson was now Prime Minister. I remembered Bob Boothby's prophecy.

At Brighton, one of the team, Ray Gunter, told us: 'I've got the bed of nails', which was his way of saying he'd been appointed Minister of Labour. A delightful man, Ray Gunter.

The other members of the team were William Deedes, Conservative MP, later to become editor of the *Daily Telegraph*, Frank Byers, who had been in the thick of things running the Liberal campaign and was shortly to be made a life peer; and Bob Boothby, who had by then left the Conservative Party and had been much in demand as a pundit on television. Bob was an exception to the general rule that *Any Questions?* panellists tend to become more right wing as they grow older.

We started with the inevitable question: 'Why did the Conservative Party lose the General Election?'

Ray Gunter thought they had chosen the wrong leader in Sir Alec Douglas Home. William Deedes thought the leadership made a big difference in the Conservatives' favour and considered the main factor was a desire for change. Frank Byers thought the nation had been faced with the prospect of a further term of a tired and complacent Government. Bob Boothby said the answer to the question could be summed up in one word – boredom. 'We've been looking at these same old dreary faces and there is no great enthusiasm, as has been proved by the polls, for the Labour Party, but everybody hopes it might be a bit better, and at least it will be different.

As always after a General Election, party politics became a more dominant feature of *Any Questions?*. I increased the number of MPs during the period before and after an election and gave the teams a distinctly less political character mid-way between elections.

On 23 October, a questioner at Cam in Gloucestershire asked, 'In my opinion, a Lib-Lab alliance would weaken rather than strengthen the Government – what are the team's views?' The team included Bamber Gascoigne, the writer and TV chairman, making his début, Isobel Barnett, and Michael Foot, by that time MP for Aneurin Bevan's old constituency of Ebbw Vale.

BARNETT: When the Conservative Party said at this election that the Socialist Party were without prices on their menu, my feelings about is was that they were without a menu at all because those who voted for them weren't certain whether they were voting for the Right, the Left or the Centre, and that what was going to come out at the end nobody quite knew, and we're waiting with bated breath now to find out. And I think there may well be a coalition of the Liberals and the right-wing Socialists, and a left-wing group making, what I think is a good thing in this country, three parties and not only two.

GASCOIGNE: If the Liberal Party and the right wing of the Labour Party made a new radical party they would certainly be joined by a great many people on the left wing of the Conservative Party. You say, Lady Barnett, that this leads to a three-party system – it does. I think personally it leads to a very dangerous three-party system in that you get, I suspect, a gigantic central party which is a lot of people with moderate views, from all the Liberals and the two halves of each of the other parties so far, and you get outside them, to the Right and to the Left, parties whose main tenet of belief is something much more extreme than, at the moment, sways either the Conservative or the Labour Party. And so the electorate's choice is between a moderate party, or extremists on either side. I personally would be in a moderate party, but I feel that sooner or later people will want a change and they will be forced to vote for a party which is more extreme than really England tends to operate with or wants, whether it's extreme to the Right or extreme to the Left.

FOOT: I was rather surprised at Lady Barnett's remark that she didn't know what was on the menu. I thought the complaint is that they know that the first item in the dish is the public ownership of the steel industry. And so we're going to go ahead with that, of course, as soon as we've cleared up the economic crisis which the Tories said didn't exist anyhow and which everybody agrees now does exist, but we'll do the two things together, we'll go along on the menu, and it will be the menu that was presented to the public at the election. I think it's extremely important that political parties should stick to their principles and not try and get them muddled up with the principles of other parties, because one of the things that causes so much cynicism in politics is the abandonment of the principles on which politicians have stood, and if the Labour Party were to abandon its programme now in order to adopt Mr Grimond's, then I think that the cynics would be justified, which would be extremely injurious, not merely to the Labour Party but to the whole health of British politics.

It was in 1964 that the number of listeners to the repeat for the first time exceeded the number listening to the live broadcast on Friday evenings, and at the beginning of the 1964/65 series the repeat was moved from its time-honoured Tuesday lunch-time to Sunday lunch-time. There were far more listeners available on Sunday and I was all for the change, but it gave me less time to seek top level advice over cutting anything. From then on, the onus fell very much more on me; it was worse still when the repeat was moved to Saturday and I had to dictate over. the telephone details of a cut to a tape editor in London, with the minutes ticking away to one o'clock.

In December we went for the first time to a prison. It was an open prison, Leyhill in Gloucestershire, and we included in the team a former prison governor, C.A. Joyce. Apart from the fact that the questioners identified themselves by their Christian names only, it sounded very much like a normal *Any Questions?*. A moving moment came when 'Gilbert' asked the team: 'Which old adage is the truer, that absence makes the heart grow fonder, or out of sight, out of mind? I know what *I* think.' At the end of the discussion, Gilbert himself summed up: 'I'm happy to say that in my own case the former is the answer, that absence *does* make the heart grow fonder.'

In the New Year we went to another sort of closed community, a girls' boarding school in Wiltshire, where one of the questions was put by a future *Any Questions?* secretary, Fiona Watson, daughter of the actor Jack Watson. Most of our secretaries have had charm and have been 'a bit of a character'. One of their most important jobs is to look after the questioners, to brief them, to soothe them if they are nervous, as they usually are, and to hold the microphone while the question is put.

(DJ: *They did this anonymously in Freddy's time, but when I took over I thought it might be good publicity to build them up a bit. I mentioned Alison Brady, Fiona's predecessor, on the air at regular intervals, until she became quite a household name. She was even interviewed in the* Daily Mirror.)

On 2 April there was a major change of policy. For nearly seventeen years, *Any Questions?* had been restricted to west country locations, despite pressure from London and the other regions. The Bristol hierarchy had declared that it was quite impossible for their staff to spend the time travelling all over the country. I had never found this particularly convincing – after all, you could get from Bristol to Birmingham or South Wales more quickly than to Cornwall.

The most valid arguments against taking *Any Questions?* all over the country were that most of the other BBC regions had their own similar programmes; that most of the raw material, the questions and the teams, would be much the same; and that the west country flavour of the programme, personified in Ralph Wightman and Arthur Street, was an essential part of its charm. The main argument in favour of moving it around was that the west country audiences were not typical of the country as a whole and that audiences in the industrial North, for example, would give the programme a shot in the arm – or a kick up the backside.

Anyway, on 2 April 1965, we finally dipped a cautious toe in the stormy waters outside the sheltered West by taking the programme to Manchester, and we followed this up with a trip to Wales on 30 April. The number of visits outside the region steadily increased until eventually it became comparatively rare for the programme to be broadcast from the west country. (There had been some trips to London before April 1965, but they were special occasions, not part of a declared policy.)

The programme was undeniably revitalized. To have the questions put in a north country or Welsh accent instead of the usual west country burr and the different reactions from the different audiences seemed to give the programme a new dimension.

We were, however, in familiar surroundings on 14 May, in the village hall at Pulborough in Sussex, with a team that included Bob Boothby and Lord Robens.

Asked what aspects of political life irritated him most, Bob replied, 'Listening to speeches other than my own – which has really become almost unendurable.'

Lord Robens said, 'The thing that irritated me perhaps the most was sometimes when I heard a very good speech from somebody on the opposite benches with which I entirely agreed; then I had to get up and say I disagreed with every single word.' A remark which anticipated by several years his resignation from the Labour Party.

Robens, one of the most popular of all *Any Questions?* panellists, created difficulties of political balance while he was still accepting the Labour Whip in the House of Lords but uttering distinctly non-Labour opinions on *Any Questions?*. I should have stuck more firmly to my rule of ignoring what politics people said they held and going by the politics they displayed on the programme. But then, having belatedly placed him mentally on the *Any Questions?* Right, I noticed with some alarm in one particular programme after Jim Callaghan had became Prime Minister (and when the Right was otherwise thinly represented) he appeared to swing back towards the Left. It became clear that his admiration for Callaghan was somewhat greater than it had been for Harold Wilson. Truly, contriving a political balance in the *Any Questions?* teams can never be an exact science.

Our final programme of this 1964/65 series was a cracker. We were at Lovedean near Portsmouth, with a team that included Mary Stocks, Russell Braddon and Bob Boothby again, and this was one of the questions: 'Why is it that some ailments or afflictions of the human body may be sympathetically mentioned, while others are regarded as indelicate or even comic?'

> STOCKS: I remember a relative of mine who went for a rowing honeymoon, and he wasn't accustomed to rowing and at the end of his honeymoon he had an unfortunate affliction which prevented him from sitting very comfortably. And he was mocked at. It was very sad. But it isn't only afflictions which affect certain parts of the body that are regarded as comic. Nobody will take mumps seriously, and it's a very painful disease. But people do mock at it. Why should they? They don't behave like that over measles or over whooping cough. Why mumps? The word is a bit odd, certainly.
>
> GRISEWOOD: And there is that queer swelling all round your ears.
>
> STOCKS: You can swell in other places!
>
> BOOTHBY: I regard all ailments with fascinated interest.

I think they're tremendously interesting. I don't think any of them are comic, with the possible exception of hay fever. And I don't think any of them are in the least indelicate – not even piles. I think you can have many jolly jokes and much interesting and useful conversation on the subject of piles. I don't see why you shouldn't talk about them absolutely freely.

STOCKS: Bob, there's a wonderful chapter about piles in the Bible. Do you remember?

BOOTHBY: It's one of the few bits of the Bible I do know.

BRADDON: I don't think the question really is right, because you don't get sympathetic attention, you only give it to yourself. There are some complaints of your own that you feel deserve sympathetic attention, but other peoples' never deserve sympathy. They're just a bore. I mean, I've had the mumps and I've had the swellings in that other place – not just in the neck – a truly intimidating experience, but I don't find that anyone is sympathetic when I tell them about it. Equally, I asked a girl once how her grandfather was and she burst into tears at once, because her grandfather had died. So I said I was terribly sorry; how had it happened? And she said, well, he hadn't been terribly well, he was terribly old, he'd gone to the lavatory, sat down, when he'd finished he pulled the chain, the cistern had come down, hit him on the head and killed him. Well, I did what you're all doing – I fell about, and she expected me to burst into tears like she had.

1965/66

The main news story of the autumn of 1965 was the situation in Rhodesia. A few weeks after UDI, a team in Bristol that included Russell Braddon and David Ennals, then Labour MP for Dover, was asked: 'Would it be better to negotiate with Rhodesia now, even with Mr Ian Smith, rather than wait until sanctions have ruined his country, his authority and this country's reputation in Rhodesia?'

ENNALS: My case against Mr Ian Smith is not simply that he is a rebel, that he has taken independence against the law and outside the Constitution. It is that he is a man who, I believe, is committed, and I believe that most of his supporters are committed, to the maintenance of white supremacy, who do not in fact want to see even the gradual advance of the African people.

BRADDON: The answer to the question, as far as I'm concerned, is yes. You can't from this country throw Mr Smith into jail like you threw Nkrumah into jail, or Gandhi into jail or Nehru or Makarios or De Valera. Since you can't throw him into jail you can in no way control him except by sanctions. And before you imagine that sanctions are going to defeat Smith and his Government and the Rhodesians, try and understand the Rhodesian temperament. The Rhodesians with whom you're dealing are people like yourselves who have left this country – usually because they're disconsolate with it – and gone to conditions infinitely superior, and I'm not arguing the morality of their position, I'm arguing the stubbornness of their position. They've gone to conditions that are better and they intend to keep them better, and if to keep them better they have to go without petrol and ride bicycles for five years, they'll do it. They will be as stubborn as the Boers were and Great Britain did not defeat the Boers for a long long time and then only with a Commonwealth army, which this time she will not have. Therefore in the field you are not going to beat the Rhodesians, and by sanctions I don't think you are going to beat the Rhodesians. But by sanctions you are going to ruin Central Africa, the whole of it. As for world opinion, I think apart from the black Commonwealth, the coloured Commonwealth and the Afro-Asian bloc, no one in the world of any nationality really gives a hoot whether the Rhodesians win or lose, whether we beat them or not. This is a question of morality we've raised in our own minds that doesn't exist outside. Where there are opinions outside they are not opinions of a morality, they are opinions of Afro-Asian coloured hostility, as venomous and as virulent as the racism Mr Ennals finds in Rhodesia of the whites towards the blacks.

ENNALS: I think it's greatly over-simplifying the situation to compare Mr Smith with Gandhi and Nehru. Those two men were the leaders of all their people, not just a part of their people. This is why you've got to remember the composition of Rhodesian society. We have to think of the Africans as much as we have to think of the Europeans. Now, of course, we must get this thing over as quickly as we can. But there is really no point in starting a policy of sanctions and then just as it is having effect cutting it off. I do believe in fact that this is going to end; I do believe that there are Rhodesians who will be able to take over and who will be able to guide the country towards a really multi-racial state. But if at this stage we just give in and follow a policy of appeasement, then I believe the tragedy for Rhodesia would be far greater than the short-term economic tragedy that we're facing now.

An almost equally emotive subject was raised in Gloucester on 3 December – abortion. It was in the days before David Steel's Abortion Act, though a Bill had just been introduced into the House of Lords by Lord Silkin, and there were very strong feelings on both sides. When the question came up we unfortunately had an all-male team, though during this series there were only six all-male teams, a considerable improvement.

However, Gerald Nabarro made some thoughtful points: 'My views, very shortly, are these. That abortion should be legalized if the health or physical or mental welfare of the mother is prejudiced by the bearing of that child. Second, that if the social environment of the child is likely to be so bad as to cause the child to grow up in miserable conditions and surroundings; subject to very stern safeguards, and I mean by that five magistrates sitting in camera to decide the case and hear the evidence, then I would allow abortion to take place. And thirdly and lastly, if the child is likely to be born deformed beyond repair or mentally deficient then I would again, subject to the most strict medical safeguards, allow an abortion to occur.'

The other three men simply agreed and left it at that. When the subject came up again, in Bristol on 4 February, Anne Allen was a member of the team. The question was: 'Do the members of the team think that the conditions of Lord Silkin's Bill, which seeks to reform the laws concerning abortion, adequately protect the potential life of the unborn child?'

ALLEN: If potential life means more than just breathing and means a proper existence, yes I do think so. I think that a child has the right to expect loving parents and a welcoming home. I also think that a woman has the right to decide if she will bear a child. Now, I don't mean that every time a baby comes and it's not quite planned to fit in with the down payment for the car or fridge, that she should rush off and say,

'I don't want this baby, I want one in six months' time,' because I don't think that this is any good either to woman, child, family or anything else, only perhaps to the people receiving the money for the car or the fridge. But I think the time has come when we have got to face up squarely to the fact that the world is over-populated, and that many of this population are unloved, unwanted, uncared for and, in fact, starving, and I would have liked the Bill to include those children who are conceived as a result of rape or of intercourse with a child under the age of sixteen. Some time ago I wrote about abortion in my paper, and to my amazement there was an overwhelming response in favour of liberalization of the law, and it came from married people. It didn't come from people who found themselves in a jam because they were expecting an illegitimate baby, and with one or two tragic exceptions it didn't come from people who were the subject of criminal assaults, because fortunately these aren't that common. But it came from ordinary people, like you and me, women who had come completely to the end of their tether, financially, physically, emotionally; their marriage was cracking, their relationship with their present children was fading, some of them were even suicidal. Who are we to say, 'You must go on and bear a child.' What arrogance!

Sensibilities were shocked that autumn when Kenneth Tynan used a four-letter word on television, and a questioner at North Wootton, Somerset, asked: 'We hear of terms like "Clean up TV" and "Sex and Violence on TV"; are the team in favour of TV censorship?' The team included Marghanita Laski, C.A. Joyce and Donald Baverstock, former Controller of BBC 1 Television.

BAVERSTOCK: The answer, very quickly and very adamantly is No. Because I think the health of television in this country depends on self-censorship of those professional people engaged in making the programmes, and that self-censorship depends, of course, on measuring, judging and accepting the reactions which their programmes produce in the public. I don't think they should operate in a kind of professional vacuum, inattentive to the general reaction of the public. The trouble with censorship is that it tends to make the producers, the programmers, the writers, irresponsible rather than responsible. They can then say, 'Well, we've just tried it on, old boy. The censors agreed it, and that's their responsibility.' Secondly, I think it's very difficult for the censorship body, whoever it is – with, no doubt, seven people nominated by the Civil Service, and the statutory woman – as they call her – on the panel, to judge this voluminous output of material, and to see it all, to formulate opinions on all the different questions and judgements and thoughts that go into the making of a programme. It is far better, by argument, by public discussion, to allow the producers, the programmers, the officials, the writers, to worry about their work, to do their work and in the course of this to develop a kind of tradition of good standards and honest reporting, and good creative writing – to develop their own tradition. And it is in the tradition of conduct that the security lies.

LASKI: I think it is the duty of any moral educational body, as I believe the BBC – though not the ITV – to be, to carry the public forward and not to stay within its limits. To shock the public is very often necessary. And there is another side to this question. Those of us who are not, with a small C, conservative – those of us who do desire to see more progressive ideas put forward constantly – are as much repressed and as much shocked as those of you who are shocked when Ken Tynan says a word that all of you know and had in your minds when he said it.

JOYCE: Well, I'm sorry, but I don't believe that because a thing is a fact and that you and I know about it, you want to bring it into the public eye. I know what a bucket of cow-manure looks like, but I don't want it in the drawing-room. Are we having a censorship? That's the question. If all the producers and the people who did these things were indeed the folks they should be, we wouldn't need the censor that is asked for by the questioner. But I doubt very much whether some of the people who are in charge have got the standards that are necessary. I'm not going to stand for this business of four-letter words. It's not true that everybody knows them, I may say. I know four people who don't, and I shan't tell 'em, either.

LASKI: Oh, come.

JOYCE: No, Marghanita. When you say, 'Oh, come,' I'm not coming, because I'm one of the people who does know.

LASKI: Please, forgive me, we don't know each other, and my name is Miss Laski.

JOYCE: I beg your pardon. The real essence of it surely is this. If the people who are going to produce these things are going to say, 'We don't need a censorship and we don't need static, standard rules' – then I want to mention the Bible. We weren't told to go and live just how we like, and how we feel at the moment, and all the rest of it. We were given specific standards and rules, and if we live by those we shan't go far wrong, and if we don't we shall go very badly wrong.

LASKI: If we're going to live by the Bible, by all means let us live by the Bible. Let us, then, stone adulteresses – there's no village without one. Let us every seven years have a sabbatical when nobody does any work. Are you in favour of these things, Mr Joyce?

JOYCE: No, no. God gave me reason, and expected me to use it.

LASKI: Me, too.

Mary Stocks could also be a little tart in her comments when she chose. On New Year's Eve, in Bristol, while discussing a question about life beginning at forty, she said: 'I think probably it begins at sixty, at least it did for me, when I retired and started quite a new life, thanks to you, Freddy, going gay on the Light Programme. I'm beginning to wonder whether it may not begin again at seventy-four. Wait and see.'

The next day we understood the significance of this enigmatic remark. Mary's name was included in the New Year's Honours List as a Life Peeress, and Freddy had to get used to calling his beloved Mary 'Baroness Stocks'. In April he rebelled and said, 'Oh, I must say, Mary, it's absurd to keep on saying Baroness Stocks, it's too odd.'

Mary retorted, 'Well, Freddy, I should stick to it, if I were you.'

Freddy was slightly shaken.

Mary always attributed her life peerage to *Any Questions?*, and this encouraged me to reply to complaints that we used too many titled people on the team by saying that we didn't have them on *Any Questions?* because they were lords and ladies – they were lords and ladies because they'd been on *Any Questions?*.

It was in that same April programme that Mary gave her memorable reply to the question: 'The Church promises eternal life after death. Does the team agree that this is in fact a terrifying prospect?'

'Well, it depends in which direction you're going!' That got the longest laugh since 1948 when Ralph Wightman, in answer to the question 'What is the experts' recipe for a happy Christmas?' had replied: 'A large teaspoonful of bicarbonate of soda.'

As we got into 1966 it became increasingly clear that the Government would have to go to the country. A General Election date of 31 March was announced and we went into our teams-of-three-candidates, no-*Any-Answers* routine. But these pre-election programmes were not all politics. In the last of them, a questioner asked: 'Is the theft of a sports trophy of such world-shattering importance that it was necessary for the BBC to interrupt its Sunday afternoon programme to tell us about it?'

Anthony Wedgwood Benn replied, 'In general, I think this sports interruption of programmes is not a very good thing and I love that cartoon in the *New Yorker* which was obviously the musicians' retort to the sportsmen. There was an announcer saying: "We interrupt the sports programme to bring you the last movement of a hitherto unfinished symphony." '

Labour was returned with a greatly increased majority, and Friday evening found us in the Granby Hall, Leicester, as part of a large BBC exhibition, the first of several which were being held to publicize BBC local radio stations. It was all very well for us to help show the flag, but exhibitions are hellish for *Any Questions?*. There is no rapport with the audience, who are casual visitors to the exhibition and not, as we always hope, part of a community who will play an active part in creating the right atmosphere for the broadcast. In fact, the atmosphere was appalling. We were in the centre of this very large hall with the exhibition going on all round us, and a continual, distracting buzz of conversation.

However, the team, which included Bob Boothby, rose above all the difficulties. The first question asked whether opinion polls caused undecided voters to jump on the bandwagon. The team decided unanimously that they didn't. Later on, we got down to the real political nitty-gritty: 'Is there danger that with such a large majority a Socialist Government might go a little too much to the Left and end up with communist tendencies?'

> BOOTHBY: I have very great confidence in Harold Wilson. I think he's the ablest politician in this country and that's why he's Prime Minister today at the head of a great majority. I don't think there's the slightest danger of them going communist. I think that this is the nearest approach to a presidential election that this country has ever seen. The country didn't really vote Labour, Socialist or Tory; it voted Heath versus Wilson and it chose Wilson, and Wilson is in a position of immense power and equal responsibility and it remains to be seen what he makes of it. He's got no more excuses, he's got every single thing that he can ask for. He's really in power, as few Prime Ministers in peacetime in this country have ever been. He's got it, and I believe that he'll use it well.

On 15 April we were at Leigh in Dorset, where a questioner asked for the team's views on music used to soothe highly-strung farm animals. Steve Race contributed this story.

'Music you like is supposed to have a stimulating effect on production. *Music While You Work* was invented during the Second World War, when it did stimulate production by playing fast rhythms – you remember that wonderful Eric Sykes show, when he kept turning down the speed of the gramophone so that he shouldn't have to work so hard. There was one rather funny thing happened during the war. The BBC found it necessary to ban one piece of music; very popular at the time was a song called *Deep in the Heart of Texas* and, if you remember it, the band would play de dah dum dum, be bah bom bom, and twenty-seven thousand workers all over Britain would stop and clap. Thousands of man hours were lost as a result of this.'

That reminded Freddy of a story. 'You remember, about the farmer who put a television screen in front of his animals and they said, "Was it a success?" He said, "An enormous success, they loved it, especially when there was a breakdown and they got the notice Normal Service will Shortly be Resumed." '

But these stories were capped by another in *Any Answers* – about music being played on a farm to soothe the cows, when the prize ram appears in a frenzied state, dashes madly round the yard, charges straight into a wall and drops dead with a broken skull. He had heard Frank Sinatra singing *There'll Never be Another You*.

Three weeks later we were at Devizes in Wiltshire with a team including the opera-singer-turned-broadcaster David Franklin and the Bishop of Crediton. We were very nearly without the Bishop. He arrived late, visibly shaken, with a horrendous story about a road accident on his way to Devizes in which his car had turned over several times. It was a miracle he had escaped with his life. We knew all about the Bishop's driving eccentricities, but this was obviously something out of the ordinary.

Janet Robertson was excellent at dealing with emergencies of this sort. She forced brandy down the Bishop's throat with such a will that he gave the performance of his life and at the end of the broadcast, while being assisted off the platform, he was heard to enquire what the questions had been.

One of the questions had concerned the team's pet economies:

BISHOP: I try to keep up appearances and therefore my main economy is not buying any underwear until I'm compelled to do so.

FRANKLIN: But this is a terrible risk, as the Bishop might have discovered tonight. My mother always used to say, 'Put on clean underwear; you might be knocked down and taken to the hospital, what would they think if you'd got a dirty vest on?' Bishop, have you thought of that?

BISHOP: My archaic underwear is clean.

1966/67

During the summer break of 1966 I had what seemed to be a bright idea that we should tie-up with *The Archers* and take *Any Questions?* to Ambridge.

I got in touch with Godfrey Baseley, who was then the editor of the serial, and we had to decide first of all where Ambridge actually was. He suggested a Worcestershire village called Inkberrow and we went to have a look at it. It filled the bill admirably, with a pleasant hall and a pub which was the very prototype of The Bull. The people of Inkberrow would provide the audience and the questions, but some of the cast of *The Archers* would be infiltrated and their questions might be selected. We also planned that the visit would be mentioned in the serial and I suggested that Freddy Grisewood might appear in one episode, as some real-life characters did from time to time.

Things seemed reasonably set fair for us to open the new *Any Questions?* series from 'Ambridge' until the Controller of the Light Programme, Denis Morris, got to hear about it. Nobody, unfortunately, had thought to tell him, and the first he knew of the plan was on hearing a reference to it in *The Archers* one evening. He objected along the lines of 'great mistake to mix fact and fiction in this way'. There was some fairly rapid back-pedalling. No Freddy Grisewood appearance in the serial and no questions put by any of the Archers characters, though some of them did turn up at the hall and at the pub afterwards, and the rehearsal question was put by Walter

Gabriel.

One of the greatest hazards that I found in producing the programme over many years lay in the team's journey between the hotel and the hall. You would have thought that by booking a taxi we couldn't go wrong but on almost every occasion that one or more of the team were not present when the opening announcement started, it was because some taxi-driver didn't know his own town. Our success ratio was greater when the team drove themselves, guided by maps I scribbled on the back of the menu while we were waiting for the next course.

(DJ: *Michael's maps always frightened me. It is all very well for him as he has been on the journey himself before, but to drive and read a map drawn on the back of a menu at one and the same time is not easy. And very often I have read it upside down and gone completely in the reverse direction. One night, heading for Bluebirds toffee factory in the west midlands, I realized that I was totally lost. Fortunately I saw a man on a bicycle. I hailed him. Not only was he a stranger to the area – aren't they all? – but he didn't even speak English. He was on a cycling tour from France. I eventually got myself on to the right road, but I was determined for the future to have a guide in the shape of some local resident who would be able to lead the team and myself.*)

That autumn, at Bideford in Devon, with Dr David Owen making his début, we went on the air with only one member of the team, Dominic le Foe, sitting on the platform. He had come on from the hotel with Freddy; the others were coming by taxi but had gone astray. Freddy began the programme by letting listeners know we were without our whole team. 'We know they're coming; at any minute they'll be here – I think they're running at the moment into the hall.'

They were indeed. The door at the back burst open, and David Owen, David Price and Dee Wells ran up the centre aisle, taking off their coats as they ran, and clambered on to the platform, to tumultuous applause.

The same sort of thing very nearly happened again at Priddy, a village on the Mendips. Our host at the nearby restaurant had promised to get the team to the hall on time. He only just made it; I heard his car drive up outside, about a minute before 8.15. (We had moved in the New Year from 8.40 but still kept our fifty minutes.)

Another hazard at Priddy – the things the producer of *Any Questions?* has to try to think of! – was that the village hall then had a corrugated iron roof. There was a very heavy rain storm just before the broadcast. If it hadn't stopped in time, the team's words would have been inaudible.

The newcomer on that team was John le Carré, who at that time lived near Wells. His intelligence, fluency, and the way he probed seriously and unpolitically behind every question made him a decided acquisition. He appeared once more, but then moved to Cornwall and politely but firmly rejected my invitations every time we were down that way. He said he no longer had any relish for this sort of public occasion (if indeed he had ever had any). He seemed to me to be an introverted, private sort of man, so I was not surprised, but the programme always needs to attract people of his reputation, mental calibre and integrity outside the well-worn fields of politics and journalism.

On 19 May our thoughts were on the Middle East, where President Nasser had called on U Thant, Secretary-General of the United Nations, to withdraw the UN forces from the borders where they were trying to keep the peace between Egypt and Israel. U Thant obeyed with what the *Any Questions?* team that week regarded as unnecessary speed. The outcome was the Six Days War.

The team which assembled at Woolaston in Gloucestershire on 2 June, while the war was at its height, included Mary Stocks and, making his first appearance, David Frost. Freddy was rather prejudiced against him. 'Do we have to have him?' he asked me. 'Was this wished on you by London?' But when they met, David's charm and the absence of any sort of TV big-time arrogance won Freddy over immediately.

I decided to put the question about the Middle East crisis last instead of first. Around that time I went through a phase of thinking that as there were now so many other programmes commenting on the news perhaps *Any*

Questions? shouldn't depend quite so heavily on topicality. But this particular decision was justifiably critized.

STOCKS: If we can't get the United Nations to act as a United Nations then we've got to, as far as possible, get a consensus among the maritime powers; one hopes that Russia might come in, but I think that's the only hope.

FROST: I think what we should do when this present crisis is over – the situation will go on for ever – is to realize that the reactionary puppets in the Middle East are not our natural allies and that Nasser is not a second Hitler, he is an Arab nationalist, and we've got to come to terms with him.

A week later, for the last programme in the series, a team including Lord Robens and Bernard Levin assembled at Steyning in Sussex. We were listening, as usual, to the six o'clock news, and heard to our astonishment that Nasser had resigned. This time I made no mistake and put a question asking for the team's reactions first on the list. Most of them regretted Nasser's resignation and feared there might be someone more extreme in his place. Bernard Levin pointed out that he had tried to give back to the Arab peoples a pride and self-respect which over the years they'd lost, even though in the end it culminated in total military disaster for him. He added that the forces of Arab nationalism, once released, could not be put back in the bottle 'and by getting rid of Nasser you have not in any way affected that particular problem'.

A prophetic remark came from Lord Robens: 'You've got always to remember that oil is a very important aspect of the whole of the Middle East problem.'

The next day the news came that Nasser wasn't going to resign after all. And so listeners to the repeat on Sunday heard the team solemnly give their reactions to a resignation which now hadn't happened. When I next saw Bernard Levin, he said: 'You made us look a right lot of Charlies.' But I was unrepentent. I merely asked: 'Where do you draw the line?' and he saw the point: once you start deleting things from the repeat because they have been overtaken by events, there's no end to it.

1967/68

During the summer of 1967 we were thinking very hard about Freddy and how long he should continue in the chair. He was then in his eightieth year and there obviously must soon come a time when he would have to give up.

We had a new Controller of the Light Programme, Robin Scott, and new men at the top in Bristol – John Elliot, the man who wrote the successful *Troubleshooters* TV series, was now Head of Programmes and John Tanton was my immediate superior as Talks Editor. While recognizing Freddy's worth to *Any Questions?*, they looked at him with slightly different eyes from those of us who regarded him as occupying the chair almost by divine right.

My own view was unequivocal. I thought we should continue to have him as chairman for just as long as he was prepared to carry on. To a very large number of people he *was Any Questions?*. Robin Scott was on my side. He was not in favour of doing anything about the chairmanship until it became absolutely necessary. He felt that the whole programme would have to be reconsidered if anything happened to Freddy.

And so the new series started on the assumption that Freddy would be there for at least another year. But a below-par edition early on drew a warning salvo from Robin Scott: 'The problem of a bad team is that it exposes Freddy Grisewood. I should be grateful for your views as to the future, particularly in terms of Freddy. I realize this is a recurring problem.' I forget what I replied, but I did make an exploratory visit to see Bamber Gascoigne. We all regarded him as a possible successor to Freddy some time in the future. Bamber not only failed to rise to the bait, but thought we would be quite barmy if we forced Freddy to retire. He, as a team member, had noticed no diminution in Freddy's powers. He liked him and admired his handling of the programme. This, coming from the dynamic chairman of *University Challenge*, was rather impressive. And there, for the moment, the matter rested.

On 3 November we were at Cardiff with a team including Michael Foot, Margaret Thatcher and John Arlott, and one of the questioners asked: 'What is the solution to the problem of unemployed persons who have no intention of earning their living if they can avoid it, as they can often obtain more money by remaining on unemployment pay?'

> FOOT: I don't think this is a problem at all. I think there are very very few people to whom this applies. Most people want to get a job if they can. There may be a few to whom this criticism applies but I think it would be absolutely wrong to reorganize our unemployment pay and our system of arranging in order to deal with this very tiny minority. The vast majority of people who are unemployed are unemployed against their will and it's quite right that when they become unemployed they should be much better treated than they have been in the past; and one of the measures that the Government has introduced is one for increasing the pay that people get when, owing to no fault of their own, they're out of a job. Of course the best solution is to make sure that there is a job for everybody, and the worst feature of what has occurred in the last year, in my opinion, has been the deliberate use of the weapon of unemployment. I was against it when a Tory government used it, I'm against it when a Labour government does it and I think we must concentrate on ensuring that there is

employment for everybody.

THATCHER: It isn't easy to provide a job for everyone in any particular place at any particular time. You can often provide the jobs but they're rather a long way away from where the people are living at the time, so those are two quite separate questions. But to come back to the question which was asked and we've got rather a long way away from, there are some people I know – and the Ministry of Social Security knows pretty well who they are – who don't particularly want a job because they can get quite a lot of money when they're unemployed. They do in fact go after them and interview them and insist that they go for retraining of some kind and from time to time the Ministry has an intensive campaign about this and sorts them out. There are in fact about a hundred prosecutions a year of people who wilfully refuse to support their own families. This is not an easy thing because if you prosecute a person and he has to spend a time in prison his family come on National Assistance or the Ministry of Social Security anyway. In theory, of course, you cannot draw unemployment benefit unless you are ready and available for a suitable job that comes up. If a person has a rather difficult personality he can be so difficult when he goes for an interview that no employer would employ him. So this is a problem. There isn't an easy answer but I think the Ministry does what it can to ensure that people don't just sit around when they could do work which is available.

ARLOTT: There's no solution to this, and that's why no government has ever really set out to produce one. There is no possible solution that would not be likely to make someone suffer who did want to work and better let a few thousand get away with a fiddle – and I don't think many do – than make somebody who honestly wants to work suffer. At any time in this country there's been what is called a hard core of unemployed. It's not that they don't want to work; the fact is, as any employment officer will tell you, many of them are sheerly and simply unemployable. But that's no reason why they should starve.

THATCHER: There's a hard core of unemployed, some people who aren't very talented or are a little bit simple, but this is quite different from people who could do a job of work, but positively don't want to because they can get such a lot on unemployment. I do think that there are a number of people who would quite willingly go to the Ministry of Social Security for supplementary benefit if in their mind they weren't going to be identified with these people who they say are layabouts and people who are lazy and who don't want to work, so it is a problem, but don't mix it up with the hard core who may be subnormal, quite a number of them . . .

The following week, on 10 November, the evening began just as usual. The programme was coming from Yate near Bristol, and we assembled in the usual way at a hotel some four or five miles from the school where the broadcast was taking place.

I did my standard warm-up to the audience and introduced Freddy. As he came on the stage, he muttered to me that he didn't know where the team had got to, one or two of them seemed to have driven off in the wrong direction. However, it was not so much what Freddy said as the way he said it. There was a vagueness about him, a remoteness, which was unnerving. Anyway, the team duly arrived, one or two of them cutting it very fine, and we got on with the programme. It gradually became clear that all was not well with Freddy. He had some difficulty in getting his words out clearly, he called one or two of the team by wrong names, he kept on saying 'all right', and his comments did not always make much sense.

We managed to get through the programme, Freddy thanked the audience and, as we set off on our short journey, I was still not sure whether there was really anything the matter with him. I was giving him a lift to the Royal Hotel in Bristol where he always stayed. I thought his conversation seemed a bit odd, his words somewhat slurred, but Freddy himself was obviously quite unaware of anything wrong. He was his usual courteous, friendly self and I just didn't know what I ought to do. Freddy was the last person to want any fuss made about his health, and he would have laughed at me if I'd suggested he saw a doctor.

With the dilemma still unresolved, we arrived at the hotel and I went in with him. They knew him well there; I asked them to keep an eye on him, said goodnight and left. I rang up the next morning and was told he had left for his train as normal. Then a day or two later we had a telephone call from his wife, saying he had seen his doctor and had been ordered to rest for a week or two. And then after that, a week or two more. We lived on a hand-to-mouth basis, and issued reassuring bulletins to his countless admirers, but it was gradually revealed that the illness which had caused him to miss nine programmes in the summer of 1964 had recurred. After a few more weeks it became clear that Freddy Grisewood would never take the chair of *Any Questions?* again.

Through the rest of that winter of 1967/68 there were five different chairmen all of them from the world of television and appreciably younger than Freddy. One of them was David Jacobs.

(DJ: *I was driving home one evening, listening to the car radio, when I heard the opening announcement for* Any Questions? *with a different chairman. My immediate thought was: 'Something must have happend to Freddy Grisewood – how awful.' My second thought was that there was a very pleasant job there going begging for someone. When I got home, as I opened the front door, the telephone rang. It was Robin Scott, who said, 'How would you like to be the chairman of* Any Questions? *What are you doing next Friday?' 'Nothing,' I said. 'You are going to chair* Any Questions?' *What I didn't know was that he was only offering me a paid audition. I thought he was offering me the job!*)

The first thought that David might be the next chairman of *Any Questions?* came from Bobbie my wife. She heard him doing a *Desert Island Discs* in which he revealed his love of horses, and to Bobbie that is always a prime, indeed an essential, attribute in anyone seeking high office. She was very impressed by the whole broadcast and told me about it. I put the idea forward that we should invite David to be one of the chairmen during the interregnum and Robin Scott, for one, was enthusiastic.

I only knew David as the chairman of *Juke Box Jury* which had recently ended. I had never met him. This omission was rectified in a hotel in Odiham in Hampshire on 15 December.

(DJ: *It was just like I'd imagined. I arrived at a little hotel in the High Street, and waited for the producer to arrive. We got over our introductions, then I said I planned to make a reference to Freddy Grisewood at the beginning and to say how honoured I was to sit in his chair, but would not refer to him again since I had to get on with the programme and do it my way. I was lucky because I had the first-eleven team.*)

This was to have been the occasion of Field-Marshal Montgomery's début on *Any Questions?* Despite his fervent 'Never!' when I broached the subject many years earlier while producing *Command in Battle*, I thought I had at last persuaded him. Odiham was only a few miles from where he lived in his converted mill, and I had chosen the team carefully so that he would approve of his companions: Bob Boothby, who had helped persuade him to appear, together with Mary Stocks and Ralph Wightman, both of whom Monty admired.

But despite all this, he cried off; I was never quite sure why. In his place I invited the considerably less martial Isobel Barnett.

(DJ: *Lucky you didn't have Monty. I'd never have been able to cope; I'd have been too much in awe of him.*)

Even so, David had an awkward initiation. Ralph in later years was apt to imbibe more freely at dinner than was strictly in the best interests of the programme, and Bob had hiccups. In a letter to me afterwards, Bob mentioned that his recently-wedded wife, Wanda, described his performance as being the worst he had ever given on TV or radio. 'My only excuse is that I was fighting against the worst of all human afflictions – an attack of hiccups, not caused by alcohol.'

(DJ: *Bob's hiccups meant that nobody noticed there was a new chairman – it was hysterical.*)

In view of the interest caused by Bob's marriage, I was pretty certain there would be a question about it, so as a gimmick I prepared on tape a short extract from an earlier programme in which he had spoken of women in disparaging terms. Sure enough, a suitable question was submitted, and the engineers had the tape ready to play on a cue from David. Just as we were about to go on the air, I got cold feet and wondered if Bob might take the joke the wrong way and be mortally offended. So I hastily murmured to him what I was going to do, but I don't think he really took it in.

The question asked: 'In view of a recent happy event, have Lord Boothby's views on women changed?' We played the tape: 'Men understand each other, women understand each other, men and women are poles apart. No man has ever understood a woman, perhaps luckily for him. The ideal social situation is to sit in a club from which women are absolutely banished. I spend my life doing that.'

Then Bob gave his new opinion. 'I've sharply changed my views and I do not, to my great surprise and amazement, regret having got married.' Lots of laughter and applause, and all was well.

At the end of the year in Bristol, David Steel made his début. Considering the Abortion Bill he introduced, it may have been rather provocative of me to include him when we had an audience of Roman Catholics. A question was put: 'After the end of Friday abstinence, what reform would the team like to see next in the Roman Church?'

> STEEL: I think that the Church as a whole – not just the Roman Church – ought to accept that there is a new sin and that is the sin of bringing into the world an unwanted child, and I think that if we are going to be far-looking in our attitudes to life and to the future existence of humanity on this planet, we have got to revise our attitude to contraception. During the passage of the Abortion Bill, I had masses of letters from people all over the country, opposed to me, who said, 'Surely the answer is not abortion, but contraception?' All I can say is, I agree.

We were near Bristol early in January when we had a question about the Concorde project and the possibility of cancelling it after five hundred million pounds had been spent. Antony Hopkins remarked, 'I cannot believe that it really matters that much that people should be able to cross the Atlantic in three hours instead of four hours. We are asked to endure a great deal of discomfort, those of us who are not actually going to be flying in the machine, because it's going to break our greenhouse roofs, it's going to shatter our nerves by going bang in the night, and all this we apparently have to accept in the name of progress. I think that is wrong. I think if one could instead go about trying to design more quiet aircraft, and building decent aerodromes away from the centres of civilization and enabling people to get from them swiftly and quietly without getting in everybody else's way, this is a much better way of spending five hundred million pounds.'

On 16 February, in Bournemouth, there was a question about the Asian immigrants then coming into the country. By that time, Enoch Powell had made several of his famous speeches on immigration. Malcolm Muggeridge was in the team that week.

> MUGGERIDGE: I say with the utmost frankness that if I were in power I would totally, as far as was possible, totally stop immigrants into this country from Africa, Asia and the West Indies at this time, and I would not lift that until I was completely satisfied that those who are already here are properly, fairly, justly, equitably incorporated in the population. Now, there's an enormous lot of humbug in this question, and what in fact we pay for in life, collectively and individually, is not so much our viciousness as our humbug. We pretended that the Commonwealth, the old Empire and the Commonwealth, was a multi-racial organization. It never was. It was a piece of complete humbug. We are now paying for that humbug by being confronted with it in the form of these people coming in, and we all know, every single person in this country knows absolutely, that

we are laying up a monstrous, wicked problem for our future people. We know we're doing it, we know that we'll have the same trouble that they've had so gruesomely and horribly in America; the idea that we should voluntarily create it . . . Now, when Enoch Powell, for whom I have a very high respect because he's a truthful man, when he said this the other day, everybody jumped on him – said he's a racialist. He wasn't a racialist, he was trying to prevent racialism poisoning this country.

Now that's what I'd do if it rested with me, but I'm quite sure that our politicians won't do that. They will continue to equivocate and in so doing they will both be cruel to the people coming here because they'll bring them in when there's no proper life for them, no proper accommodation for them, and cruel to posterity, to our people, who will suddenly be confronted in our island, where we had never this trouble, where we incorporated people of all nationalities, of all races into this country, we've never had any trouble of this kind. We shall have it, and we shall have it because of this sentimental piece of humbug, because people will not admit that people, quite apart from race, who have a different economic standard, cannot live peaceably side by side in the same country.

Later in the series there was a question referring to Enoch Powell's speech in Birmingham and to the support he had received from the London dockers, among others: 'Does the team think that there is as much support for Mr Enoch Powell's whims as would appear from the letters, marches and strikes, or are these just the antics of a vociferous, racialist minority?'

Two of the team, at Silverton in Devon, thought it was a minority support, but Philip Haskell had doubts about that ('I think what people object to is finding the character of a community in which they live being persistently changed, and changed progressively more rapidly'), and Russell Braddon also thought the 'minority' was a pretty massive one. ('Ever since he made this speech we have reacted in a way which perhaps isn't Christian or admirable but which is human. We have reacted and shown that there is in us a fear of something strange. A fear of aliens. This is not peculiar to the British.')

(DJ: *At the end of a lively discussion we thought we would carry out our own survey of the support for Enoch Powell. So I asked for lots of letters for* Any Answers, *because the more we got, the more accurate the figure would be. We hoped to attract people who did not normally write to* Any Answers, *and we obviously did: We received about 3,500 letters, of which 2,940 supported Enoch Powell's views, the percentage in favour thus being 84.*)

By the end of February, David had accepted our invitation to become the permanent successor to Freddy, but as we were coming up to a special edition to mark Freddy's eightieth birthday, it was decided that I would take the chair on that occasion and that David's regime would begin the week after.

The birthday programme was held at Liphook, Freddy's own village and, exceptionally, it was recorded, not live, on Freddy's actual birthday, Thursday, 11 April. It was just as well I did decide to record it, because we ended up with well over an hour's material. It was really two programmes: the usual discussion, in which some of Freddy's own favourite panellists took part, the team being Lady Violet Bonham Carter (by then Baroness Asquith), C.A. Joyce, John Arlott and the Bishop of Crediton; and also a series of tributes to Freddy, in person, on tape and by telegram.

The accident-prone Bishop nearly upset the whole schedule by opening the wrong door at the hotel. Instead of the loo as he expected, it was the wine cellar, and in the darkness he fell down a flight of stone steps, and was lucky to escape serious injury. However, it put the timetable back a bit while he was given first aid, with the result that some of the surprise guests arrived at the hotel before the guest of honour, Freddy himself, had left to go to the hall.

Apart from that, all went smoothly. I started the recording with a brief introduction and then Freddy walked on to the stage while the audience sang *Happy Birthday To You*. Freddy came and sat by my side, we had a little chat about his health and then I read out some of the telegrams, including those from Charles Hill, then the BBC's chairman, the Director-General, Sir Hugh Greene and Jim Callaghan.

Freddy then took the chair for the first question, and at the end of it he handed back to me. We recorded five questions, but one of them had to be cut because of time, and the last one asked what would be the most appropriate way of commemorating 'Mr Freddy Grisewood's long and successful broadcasting career', which gave the team the chance to pay their own tribute to Freddy.

Lady Asquith said: 'I think if we took a nationwide Gallup Poll of the best loved voice and the best loved personality on the air today, Freddy would win by an overwhelming majority, hands down.'

Freddy was overcome. 'All I can say is I sit back here and listen to all these wonderful things said to one, and do you know, the extraordinary thing, ladies and gentlemen, is that one hears these things while one's still alive!'

But more was to follow. The three 'surprise' guests turned out to be Anthony Greenwood, the Housing Minister; Quintin Hogg (who had given up his hereditary title as Lord Hailsham); and the Liberal Leader who overcame his inhibitions and performed accurate and amusing impersonations of Ralph Wightman and Bob Boothby. Then we had greetings, on tape, from Isobel Barnett, David Frost and Tony Benn, who had composed a poem in Freddy's honour. It ended:

And now at eighty he is still the same,
Untouched by stardom, modest in his fame.
If only all the worldly wise would
Emulate our Freddy Grisewood.
I hope that on the Judgement Day,
When asked some questions, as we may,
Peter, like Freddy, seeing our unease,
Will murmur quickly, 'Next question, please.'

There was a presentation on behalf of regular contributors to *Any Answers* and then Frank Gillard, by that time

Director of Radio, said, 'I want to salute you, Freddy, with all the affection of a friend and with all the respect that's due to you as a great broadcasting professional, one of the master broadcasters of our time, and to congratulate you on this great career which is so unique and so historic and so memorable and so distinguished.'

And, to the singing of *For he's a jolly good fellow*, the recording ended.

The person Freddy would most have liked to be present was Mary Stocks, but she was recovering from an operation and unable to make the journey. However, I included a contribution from her in the programme *Dear Freddy*, broadcast the previous Sunday; in it Freddy recalled his career, with interjections and tributes from some of the people he had met on the way. This programme was repeated when, four and a half years later, Freddy died.

Well, it was a case of 'The King is dead; long live the King', and the following Friday, David started his reign, at Lyneham in Wiltshire, with a team including Lord Mancroft, whose daughter, Victoria, asked one of the questions: 'Is it right that parents should be allowed to stop their children from smoking even at the age of sixteen?'

Father replied: 'I think one should encourage children to smoke as much as possible and as early as possible in order to discourage them and make them sick and tired of it, so they never come back to it.'

The final question, not for the first time, asked, 'If members of the team suddenly found themselves able to change the shape of the human body, what changes, deletions or additional items would they like to make?'

Lord Mancroft said: 'I should like to have a reserve tank so I can take seven or eight gallons of beer on board, then when the policeman comes around with that blooming breathalyzer, I'd jettison the tank and I'd be perfectly all right.'

(DJ: *After the programme I drove back to London and on the way I was in the unfortunate position of being hit amidships by another car that was coming out of a pub car park. The gentleman immediately said, 'I'm going to have you breathalyzed' and I passed with flying colours and none of them was green. Luckily I had avoided partaking of the RAF hospitality after the broadcast – not an easy thing to do.*)

On 31 May we celebrated the seven hundred and fiftieth edition of *Any Questions?* at Poole Technical College in Dorset. There was a suitably strong team with Mary Stocks, back in action again, Malcolm Muggeridge, Quintin Hogg and William Hardcastle, who were particularly good on the subject of student unrest. It was the time of Danny the Red and the student riots in France. (Bill Hardcastle was then presenting *The World at One* and was always a bit worried that his neutrality would be compromised by appearing on *Any Questions?*.) A questioner asked: 'How is it that although opportunites for further education in this country are today greater than ever before, students are demonstrating against college authorities more than ever before although the latter are more permissive than ever before?'

STOCKS: I think the trouble is that our universities now are a bit over-extended. There are too many of them. They've come too quickly. It means a certain lowering of standards in the staffing of them and the result is that quite a number of people have got into them who ought not to be at universities at all, and that is having a disastrous effect on what you might call the student image, because most students don't do these things. But the trouble is, in certain faculties, it's very easy to get into a subject which doesn't need an intensive intellectual discipline. I would think sociology was one, I would think perhaps English was one, and it's very pleasant if you're mildly interested in those subjects to get the necessary number of A-levels and get a place in a university and then have three years, perhaps more, at the public expense; and I think a lot of people are now doing that and I think there will come a time when the taxpayer will ask why.

HOGG: I agree that the universities in this country are over-extended, but I'm bound to say that student unrest is not confined to this country and some other countries where they are not over-extended show just as much, or more, student unrest. I think that the odd words in the question are 'although the authorities are more permissive than ever before'. If you want to keep discipline in any kind of a body, the thing is not to oscillate between extreme permissiveness, which causes unrest, and extreme discipline, which causes outbreaks, but to keep a fairly tight hand on the rein with firmness throughout, but without extremes in either direction, and I think that the university authorities are in fact very largely to blame for student unrest.

HARDCASTLE: I suspect strongly that the students have a case. I suspect that the authorities have not taken into account the change in overall social patterns, the change in the development of youths at eighteen now as compared with eighteen, twenty years ago and various factors like that. I also think that much more serious consideration should be given to the taxpayer and that some amelioration of this feeling which is going to grow as long as students quite rightly stand for their own rights, that some system of loans and repayments is quite possibly – it's done in other countries – a reasonable way of the taxpayer being told that he's getting a fair return for his money.

MUGGERIDGE: To a great extent what these young people are suffering from in my experience is conceit, because there's such an enormous amount of flattery. They're subjected to flattery as part of this very morbid cult of youth, and also from advertisers and people like that. Now that is very bad for the old, but I think it might be even worse for the young. Another point is that the actual standards of university education are steadily falling, particularly in these bogus subjects, these bogus schools, sociology and things like that, with the result that these students are really not in the proper sense of the word educated at all. We try to persuade ourselves that there are specific causes for their unrest. We say, well, there were two world wars, or we say the society that they're being asked to be members of isn't a suitable one and so on. I think this is largely baloney, that in fact they are simply young yahoos. The truth is that you cannot have order in a society at any level unless you have some sort of moral order; social order, political order, any kind of order is a consequence of moral order. There is no moral order, particularly among these young people, and therefore there can be no social or political order. They are not, in fact, agitating for particular things. They're just disruptive.

Now the big joke to me in this whole student business was when I read, to my great delight, that the students in Sweden had revolted. I thought this was the height of comedy because all the things that are said about students, that Sweden was not in the war, Sweden's not an atomic power, Sweden does not approve of Vietnam, Sweden hands out contraceptives with the morning tea and all the sort of thing they're supposed to be revolting about is available in Sweden.

HOGG: Now, Malcolm, you're not in the Edinburgh pulpit now! I don't think you've produced any evidence for the academic standard falling and I think that was very ill said. I do agree that there is an absence of moral assumptions, for which I don't blame the students, but I would just like to say something about William Hardcastle's suggestion of loans. I think we should be very careful before we accept this. I think that the talented and the qualified are already too heavily burdened with debt in the form of taxation to accept with equanimity a burden of debt in the form of repayment of loans at the end of their qualification.

MUGGERIDGE: Quintin, you're not in the House of Commons now.

HOGG: All I can say is my speech was shorter than yours.

HARDCASTLE: I heard an announcement on the BBC

this morning that there's going to be a new youthful image given to *Any Questions?*. And you know, we are talking like a lot of old codgers. Malcolm, I could write a book *I Was a Teenage Yahoo* and so could you.

MUGGERIDGE: The point is, I'm trying to explain why these young people behave like this.

HARDCASTLE: I'm suggesting you possibly behaved in some similar fashion.

MUGGERIDGE: In fact we didn't. I daresay we might have been better men, we might have enjoyed ourselves more if we had, but in fact we didn't.

STOCKS: What surprises me about the present disorders in universities is the way in which Vice-Chancellors behave. They let them get away with it; they're made of cotton wool. Why don't they send these people down?

MUGGERIDGE: They're a gutless lot.

STOCKS: What are they afraid of?

MUGGERIDGE: They're afraid of the students.

HARDCASTLE: They may think some of the students have a point.

Bill Hardcastle's crack about my piece on the air that morning concerning a new youthful image for *Any Questions?* struck home; it was a pity the piece coincided with a team whose average age must have been over sixty. However, Freddy's retirement had provided us with the opportunity of giving the programme a new look and I wanted to introduce some younger members. I hadn't done too badly three weeks earlier when we had Ann Mallalieu, first woman President of the Cambridge Union, and the writer David Benedictus to represent the younger generation.

Ann, a shade hesitant on her early appearances, blossomed into a fluent, articulate panellist and even on her début showed a pretty wit. In answer to the question at Bruton School for Girls, 'Faced with the choice of music or games owing to the tightness of timetable, which would you advise a girl to do?' she replied: 'After I left school I learned that music and games went together. You had the seductive music put on and it was up to you to run away fast!'

Another aspect of the new look was the attempt to find different audiences. Our new man at the top in Bristol, John Elliot, was horrified by the number of west country villages we still went to, and wanted us to seek more earthy working-class communities in the North. This meant angling for invitations, as earthy, working-class communities in the North tended not to place *Any Questions?* at the top of the list when planning their evening's entertainment. We contacted Butlin's, and suggested we might take the programme to one of their holiday camps. They kindly agreed that we could go to Filey in Yorkshire and off we went, with a team which I thought should attract a holiday camp audience – two TV personalities in Isobel Barnett and Bamber Gascoigne, with the best-known trade union figure of the time, Frank Cousins, and Enoch Powell.

But the hall was by no means full and the audience was tepid. However, there were some good questions, including one which asked for the team's reactions on hearing that Enoch Powell had been advised not to keep a speaking engagement at Birmingham University because of fears for his safety.

Enoch Powell commented: 'To withdraw – and this is what happened – to withdraw an invitation on the allegation of fear for safety when the real reason was disagreement with opinions previously expressed was a disgraceful action and that is the subject for criticism. Now, as regards threats to public figures, I think that the danger very rarely arises from assailants who disagree with the public figure, with his policies or with his views. I think almost always the danger is that if a person's name is in the news, then people who are completely unbalanced, absolutely insane, are liable to associate their own insanity, their own absolutely mindless feelings, with that person, and that is where, my guess is, ninety-five per cent of any danger arises which attaches to public figures. It's quite a mistake to think that the danger comes from people who have thought the thing out, disagreed with the person and want to kill him because they disagree. It's usually somebody who hasn't the slightest idea what the whole thing is about and is far more to be pitied than to be detested.'

Several years later I was to have good cause to recall Enoch Powell's remarks about the safety of public figures.

For the last programme in the series, I managed to lure Peter Ustinov on to the team. Unsuccessful attempts had been made, dating right back to Nicholas Crocker's time, and I only succeeded because he was appearing at Chichester Festival Theatre but happened to be free on the Friday evening we wanted him when we were handily placed at Southwater, near Horsham. The team also included Malcolm Muggeridge, and one of the audience took advantage of the presence of Ustinov and Muggeridge to pose this rather complicated question: 'Mr Ustinov recently asserted that top people are those without sufficient qualifications to be detained at the bottom. Last week Mr Muggeridge wrote that our rulers are fantasy figures in a television western. Could it be that top people are becoming superfluous?'

USTINOV: What I really meant was that as the great advocate stays in the law, some people use it as a stepping stone for something else. I imagine also that the chief of the Hairdressers' Union is very often somebody who didn't get any requests, and no ladies rang up and asked for him by name, so he had more time to devote himself to union matters. And gradually he stopped at the top of that particular tree, and then, of course, his particular talents of that kind exceeded hairdressing.

JACOBS: But now what about top people becoming superfluous?

USTINOV: Well, they can't become superfluous obviously because we can't all be bottom people.

JACOBS: Malcolm, did you in fact say . . . ?

MUGGERIDGE: Yes, yes, I did indeed. I said that as a result of our mass communication media, notably television, the whole of life was becoming a sort of fantasy, and into that fantasy it was necessary for our rulers to fit. What I was thinking of specifically was the start of all the tele-politics when Nixon and Kennedy were standing against each other and Nixon lost the election because he had this afternoon shadow, and in the westerns in which Americans and practically the whole of mankind look for such ideas and values as they have, which isn't saying much, in the westerns the bad guy always has afternoon shadow. And the good guy is properly shaved, and therefore Nixon by not shaving that day deprived himself of the Presidency of the United States.

USTINOV: But by the same process, of course, Makarios got the Presidency of Cyprus.

MUGGERIDGE: Very good, very good. Let me put the same point in a slightly more macabre way. Three weeks ago my eye happened to glance over the TAM ratings, and I saw that two shows had tied for ninth place. One was *The Saint* and the other was the murder of Robert Kennedy. In the minds of the people who draw up the TAM ratings, and in the minds of those who seized upon this medium, those two things in a sense are equated, that is what I'm talking about, our leaders are forced to adjust to that fantasy world.

USTINOV: It's always been clear to me that television would be a much greater threat to politics than it ever was to the theatre or to the movies, that it was supposed to replace. It hasn't done it – it made them more popular. And what you're saying is absolutely brought home to me by the fact that two members of my profession who are not urgently needed by my profession, Mr Ronald Reagan and Mr George Murphy, entered politics, and they've done extremely well. Since there's been no reciprocal tendency in the other direction it suggests to me that our job is still more difficult than their new one.

1968/69

With David firmly in the saddle at the start of his first full series, we took stock of the programme, searching for innovations which had been neglected as long as Freddy was there. One or two minor things – we called David 'chairman' (Freddy had been 'question master'); we changed the opening, so that instead of the audience applauding when the announcement started there was a crisp 'Over to David Jacobs'.

I was also hoping that we might be able to get away from the word-for-word repetition of the question. After a perfectly audible question, it seems time-wasting and even rather patronizing to repeat it exactly, though admittedly this does give the team time to think. I always felt it should be possible to summarize the question, but David found it difficult and when I took the chair myself I realized it certainly wasn't easy to give an accurate summary, reflecting the precise nuances of the question. David usually confines himself to making minor alterations to the preamble.

(DJ: *It might be considered patronizing to re-phrase the question, and I can't always tell whether listeners have heard it clearly or not.*)

Freddy had occasionally brought the questioner into the discussion, but only when there was some doubt about the significance of the question. David sometimes sought the opinion of the questioner, which could pay dividends, especially when the questioner was likely to have some personal experience to illuminate the discussion. We also risked falling flat on our faces. ('Have you any views yourself on how this problem might best be solved?' 'No, that's why I asked the question.') I always regretted not going back to the questioner at Rolls-Royce after the team had emitted a lot of pretentious guff about the honour of working for Rolls-Royce being sufficient reward to compensate for monotonous factory toil – I feel he might have brought the team back to earth.

This questioner certainly brought Ted Leather, Mary Stocks, David Benedictus and Robert Morley back to earth after she had put this question in Bristol: 'Is it necessary to use such abusive language on some of our programmes and so much sex?'

MORLEY: I've never seen people using sex on programmes. Abusive language, I don't know what you mean. Do you mean four-letter words? I suppose you do. Well, everybody uses them in daily life, I can't see any reason why they shouldn't use them when they're doing television programmes or theatre programmes. Of course, this awful prudery of the British has now been broken through and the censor has been abolished and everyone's very much better for it, it's like fetishes which used to be practised only at midnight in secret; now everybody can go about in tight-fitting corduroys, or mackintoshes and everybody's healthy and happy and well. Bring out your inhibitions, bring them out, parade them in front of us and you will feel well, laugh at yourself. Sex is all very funny, don't take it seriously, realize that it's animal and be content to be an animal, don't fuss about it, don't be a prude. It doesn't hurt anyone to have four-letter words shouted in their ears. It may deafen them but it doesn't hurt them. Of course we want more and more licence and then we shall be sensible people and not inhibited, terrible hypocrites. Look at the young people today, happier than they've ever been, and more loved and, I hope, more loving.

STOCKS: Having now got loose on these things it's

become so boring; I mean there's so much of it, you just can't get away from it. To go to a theatre and see a programme about something else, about rather interesting people doing rather interesting things, other than sex, is almost impossible. That's why one goes back to Victorian novels, to get away from the stuff.

MORLEY: I'd say that's the wildest statement I've ever heard, what play on in London today deals exclusively with sex? You can go to *Peter Pan*, you can walk the whole length of Shaftesbury Avenue, you can see P.G. Wodehouse farces, you can see Whitehall farces, they're not plays about sex at all. I don't know any really interesting sex play on in London at the moment.

STOCK: Well, you talk to a psychoanalyst about Peter Pan.

MORLEY: If you see sex in *Peter Pan* then you must never go out at all.

LEATHER: It's difficult after that but I must get back to the question, and I will endeavour to answer it seriously.

JACOBS: Are you suggesting that the others weren't?

MORLEY: What impertinence!

LEATHER: I think it is bad, I do not see any good in it at all; I do not believe, for one moment, that people are better or less inhibited, I think all it does is to set the worst possible example. *The Wednesday Play* is a typical example and I think a disgraceful one. I cannot see what earthly good it does just to hurl in the four-letter words frequently these days when they're quite irrelevant. I don't think this is a good lead, I think it does young people a great deal of harm to hurl four-letter words at them. I'm quite certain, the increases in juvenile delinquency, in breakdowns, in drug-taking, in divorce, in all these things that are wrong, not because I disapprove of them but because they cause human unhappiness, are very much part of this age of licence, and people who have any pretence to guide public opinion ought to have the guts to stand up and say so.

BENEDICTUS: For ten months of my life it was my job to find the scripts for *The WednesdayPlay*; we got letters week after week from people who spoke in almost exactly the same abusive terms as you do, they wanted happy plays about what they called 'ordinary people' . . .

LEATHER: Not abusive terms, they were reasoned terms.

BENEDICTUS: . . . but the whole feature of *The Wednesday Plays* was that they were watched by, on average, nine million people across the country, week in, week out, and I do not believe that nine million people, if what they saw disgusted them, would have watched week in, week out. They might have watched once for the curiosity value. Furthermore, I do believe that those plays were the first plays seen on television in this country which had anything to do with the lives of the people who watched them. That those plays were about the real lives of real people. To take one example, *Cathy Come Home*, which was much vilified when it came out, has led to more positive good than any other television play of our age. It has led to the housing of I don't know how many thousands of homeless people. Well, I won't claim the credit for that . . .

LEATHER: Utterly untrue.

BENEDICTUS: It is not untrue, it led to the foundation of an organization called Shelter.

LEATHER: Indeed it did, and good luck to Shelter and they're very nice people, but there've been dozens of other bodies, notably city councils, rehousing homeless and helpless people for twenty years. There's nothing new about this.

MORLEY: I challenge you to tell me one *Wednesday Play* that has shocked you, and may I ask you, are you going to bring back censorship, would you like to burn the books of the thinkers and the writers and the poets?

LEATHER: Not at all.

MORLEY: This is the typical attitude of the people who don't watch *Wednesday Plays* and don't know what they're talking about.

QUESTIONER: I would like to say that when I put this question I was thinking of us in our homes with our young teenagers. I've got two teenage grandchildren and it becomes very embarrassing for a mother and a grandparent to stay in the same room, and I think when we're trying to set an example and tell the children it's wrong to swear in the home then it's wrong for the programmes to have set this example. You can swear outside, we know, as much as you like but I do think in our homes we should keep it sacred, our homes are sacred.

Robert Morley is a natural for *Any Questions?*; he has style, wit, exuberance and an entertaining manner of airing prejudices. Unfortunately, after his next appearance he was threatened with legal action for defamation and was obliged to make a public apology in an advertisement in the *Observer* and this discouraged him, especially as he considered the BBC failed to support him. ('Mr Morley has decided that it is too expensive for him to appear in your programme more than once in the same financial year,' his agent told me when I issued another invitation.) My successor was more persuasive and Robert Morley has appeared again since my time.

At that stage we could certainly do with the likes of Robert Morley. David's arrival in the chair happened to coincide with the departure of several panellists who had performed outstanding service. Ralph Wightman appeared only once more after the unsatisfactory programme at Odiham; Baroness Asquith's appearance in October 1968 proved to be her last – she died early in 1969; and Bob Boothby was gradually opting out.

We tried to fill the gaps by increasing the number of appearances by Isobel Barnett, Malcolm Muggeridge and Russell Braddon. And Mary Stocks was still going strong. We also decided to increase the number of newcomers, particularly looking to the younger generation to keep the programme going with a fresh vitality into the

Seventies. There had been some devoted followers who suggested that the programme should end with Freddy's retirement and I hope over the following decade they ate their words. At the end of the 1968/69 series, the listening figures indicated that the transition to David had happened with hardly any diminution in the size of the audience, and the figures were to remain pretty steady from then on – television had done its worst.

However, finding new spell-binders remained the most intractable problem, largely because there are ever fewer 'characters' in public life. Look at the House of Commons. For all I know, the MPs may be better as MPs, more conscientious, more hard working, than their predecessors of the Fifties but, regarded purely as characters, they're rather a lacklustre crowd compared with those larger-than-life figures who appeared on *Any Questions?* when I first produced the programme. In public life generally, there is a growing shortage of personalities with that X factor of unpredictability, entertainment value, and even danger. Why?

Lord Robens offered this explanation in answer to a question in Bristol: 'They are disappearing because very largely we're living in a mass-produced society. We all tend not only to use the same sort of things and the same kind of cars, and the same kind of meals prepared from frozen foods, and so on, but our habits are becoming very much tailor made. The colourful characters are disappearing because the varieties of moulds are getting less and we're being driven into this very largely, I think, by branded goods, branded ways of life, and the way in which there's a great deal now of follow-my-leader.'

I have another explanation: whereas people between the wars tended to go to Oxford or Cambridge primarily to enjoy themselves and thus gave themselves a solid grounding in eccentricity which arises out of imaginative self-indulgence, they now go to all sorts of universities primarily to work.

Our efforts to find among people in their twenties and thirties the future Boothbys and Muggeridges were largely unsuccessful. During this series we introduced thirty-five newcomers; fifteen of them could be described as the Younger Generation, but few of them were cutting much ice in public life ten years later.

It is generally believed that David brought with him a new 'showbiz' element, but we had people from the world of show business in Freddy's time – Bernard Braden, for example, and Cyril Fletcher. This element certainly increased after David's arrival but that was largely because, finding that my search for well-known sparkling personalities in the more orthodox current affairs branches of public life was increasingly frustrated, I turned more and more to the entertainment world. For instance, the *Beyond the Fringe* quartet. Jonathan Miller didn't like the standard *Any Questions?* audiences, but was willing to join the team when we visited Pentonville prison; Peter Cook agreed to do the pre-Christmas edition. Both were valuable additions. Dudley Moore, however, seemed unhappy in this setting and only appeared once. Alan Bennett always said firmly he didn't care for this sort of thing.

The most controversial of our recruits that autumn was Paul Foot of *Private Eye*. With the appearance of a Plantagenet Basil Rathbone and politics considerably to the left of his uncle Michael, he turned out to be an amiable young man and an effective panellist – well informed, with a sharp wit and blistering eloquence. Our masters in London were less convinced of his worth, and we in Bristol – John Elliot, John Tanton and I – were to have many struggles with higher authority over his inclusion. There was an occasion when Paul had a go at Dr John Rae, then headmaster of Taunton School, in what London was pleased to call a 'gladiatorial display', though John Rae wrote to me afterwards to say that he had no complaints and would be glad to appear with Paul Foot again.

When we were in Germany (where this confrontation took place) we were being entertained to tea at the home of one of the officers in the army garrison where the broadcast was to be that evening. For some reason, Paul arrived rather late, and it meant finding another chair, making fresh tea and so on. I was amused to note that his public school education and upbringing as the son of the future Lord Caradon suddenly asserted themselves. Said the militant activist, the scourge of the Establishment, 'Oh, please don't bother; I don't want to be a nuisance to anybody.'

His début in Plymouth started us off on the bumpy road to trouble with London. The other members of the team were Malcolm Muggeridge, Dr John Dunwoody, then Labour MP for Falmouth and Camborne, and Margaret Thatcher, who appeared more frequently than any other MP during this series. There was a question: 'Has Harold Wilson regained the confidence of the Labour Party as a result of the recent conference in Blackpool?' Paul had just written a book on Harold Wilson which revealed that he was no great admirer of the Prime Minister.

> FOOT: Harold Wilson – the Labour Party – fought the 1966 election on a series of slogans: full employment, maintenance of the Welfare State, a fair Incomes Policy which applied to prices and dividends as much as it did to wages; and what we've had since then is the highest unemployment since the 1930s, the gradual dismantling of the Welfare State and an Incomes Policy which everyone accepts operates only upon wages and is grossly unfair.
>
> THATCHER: I really don't think he's regained the confidence of the people and I think the basic thing is that what he says really doesn't bear much relation to what he does and one gets the impression that he thinks he can talk his way out of anything.
>
> MUGGERIDGE: Every single figure in our time simply gets into power and does the exact opposite of what he said he was going to do and receives this fantastic applause. The most extraordinary example of course is de Gaulle, but Wilson is running him up.

It was left to Dr Dunwoody to stand up for the Government, which he did sturdily. London reprimanded us, describing him as a not very orthodox Labour MP, which we strenuously denied. They thought the political balance of the team was unsatisfactory, and that we ought not to have accepted the question with Paul Foot on the team. However, there had apparently been no protest from the Labour Party.

There *was* a protest over Dominic le Foe's remarks about the Prime Minister three weeks later. The team had been asked which they would prefer to watch on television, a speech from Mr Wilson or Mr Heath or *Match of the Day*. Dominic le Foe, who had been recommended to me by Jeremy Thorpe as a witty and effective Liberal speaker but who subsequently moved to the Right of the Liberal Party, replied that he would watch Mr Wilson any time.

'Just to see those eyes staring at me with all the sincerity of a family food salesman, to see that pixilated lift of the chin as the lighting takes away that heavy jowl, to see those rabbity teeth flashing over the screen, to hear him saying with that ringing insincerity, "Of course the pound in your pocket won't be worth any less", to hear him give the drama of the ship that was thrown off course and he woke up and found himself clutching a life-belt, all this is something that you'll never get from the open-air sports-minded games player.'

When rebuked by Lord Soper, he came back, 'We have had a Prime Minister who has chosen to use television as his first approach to the nation while things were going well. He has used it and he must be judged as using it, and when I said that his teeth are unphotogenic, I tell you as a television critic his teeth are unphotogenic and I'm staggered he's never had them put right; when I tell you that his eyebrows are blacked in on some occasions and others they're not, this is a matter of record and if you look up the photos you will see it. When you see one week he has a Lloyd George haircut, it's because he wants to look statesmanlike. Mr Wilson is a television performer and as such I would rather watch him than *Match of the Day*, which is the answer to the question.'

Some people thought that the personal attack on the Prime Minister was in poor taste. Lord Hill, in his book *Behind the Screen* (Sidgwick and Jackson), reveals that there was a protest from the Labour Chief Whip (John Silkin) who asked for an assurance that such a thing would never happen again. Lord Hill, then BBC Chairman, pointed out that because of the nature of the programme it was quite impossible to give such an assurance.

In the opening programme of the series, the team were asked whether the MCC should cancel the forthcoming tour to South Africa. Jeremy Thorpe and Mary Stocks, no cricket buff, thought they should. The other two, Lord Mancroft and Peter Jay, concentrated on the difficulty the MCC had got themselves into by not including Basil D'Oliviera in the team, apparently for fear of offending the South Africans, though it was the general opinion that he deserved to be included on merit. In the event, D'Oliviera was selected as a replacement for Tom Cartwright, who had to withdraw, and the tour didn't take place.

The colour question was prominent throughout this series. At Street in Somerset, Jean Rook, the *Daily Express* columnist, reduced the rest of the team to stunned silence in her answer to the question 'Is Powellism nearer to racialism or realism?'

'I am honest enough to say, and I know there are millions like me, I should loathe to live next door to a black man, I should loathe to live in a black district, I should loathe my children, had I children, to go to a black school. I know it's shameful, I know it's horrible, but I feel this and I believe that there are millions of British people who feel it; and I do think that if one lived in Bradford or Wolverhampton where the immigrant problem is so concentrated and so agonizing, I'm sure that it must be very terrible for them and that strong feelings must be aroused. I agree that we cannot sweep Powell's views under the carpet. He's gone too far, he's been too extreme. He's wrecked his case unfortunately because I think that part of what he was saying made very good sense.'

When he had recovered his breath, John le Carré said, 'What Jean Rook presumably objects to is not the content of what he said but the style in which he said it. I object very much to the content, which I think is racialist. I also object to the style, because, alas, as Jean Rook has demonstrated, it's realistic. At a time of doubt, when we are confused, when the state of alienation exists, we reach from our confusion towards simple absolutes, just as the Germans in the Thirties were quick to identify the Jews as the people responsible for economic loss, as the hyenas of a corrupt society, so we very easily reach for similar formulas and that is made much easier by the English standards of excellence, the secret standard of superiority which we know we nurse. But only one thing matters to me and that's this. We gave promises to these people; long ago we said, "You are the same as us; we colonize you, we give you our status." By what right can we conceivably withdraw these promises?'

The originator of Powellism was on the team the following week. This edition presented me with considerable problems, some of them of my own making. I had the daft idea of teaming up Enoch Powell and Tariq Ali, one of the leaders of the militant student movement, and I wrote to Enoch Powell in the normal way, as I wrote to all teams, telling him who else would be with him. He reacted strongly, as I might have expected, and sent a copy of his reply to the other two members of the team. Everyone has a perfect right to object to appearing with someone and normally the person objecting is the one to withdraw, but somewhat disingenuously I had not at that time issued the invitation to Tariq Ali, so it seemed sensible to abandon the idea of inviting him.

Private Eye got hold of the story, and I was criticized for having asked Enoch Powell if he would be prepared to appear with Tariq Ali. But I was in the business of building teams for the education, information and entertainment of the listeners and not of making an issue on matters of principle. I could hardly keep from Enoch Powell the fact that Tariq Ali was on the team. I couldn't forbid him to read *Radio Times*. And then on finding out, if he withdraws, we are left with a team of three.

That having been settled, fortunately before *Radio Times* went to press, we then had another problem. The programme was due to be broadcast from the Pressed Steel Sports and Social Club at Cowley at their invitation.

However, the club committee got to hear of unrest among some Oxford undergraduates over the presence of Enoch Powell on the team and they feared demonstrations. The geography of the club premises was such that demonstrations were only too easy. They got cold feet and told me they couldn't guarantee our safety, therefore would we kindly take our custom elsewhere.

In great secrecy, I moved the whole thing to the concert hall of Broadcasting House, London. We assembled an audience by writing to some of the regular contributors to *Any Answers* who lived in London, and the most elaborate precautions were taken to guard against any demonstrators following us to Portland Place. I was therefore somewhat alarmed to hear it mentioned on the *PM* programme that afternoon. (DJ: *A good example of the way the left hand of the BBC often doesn't know what the right hand is up to.*)

Feelings were high at that time, so I decided to abandon the usual formal dinner party and instead had a stand-up buffet to avoid any confrontation before the programme. The other members of the team were Marghanita Laski, Lord Wigg, a former Labour Minister, and Auberon Waugh, the writer. (DJ: *In fact, Marghanita Laski told me she would sit on the platform with Enoch Powell but not at the dinner table with him.*)

As was so often the case when I was full of anxious foreboding, nothing whatever happened. The broadcast passed off without incident. Our *Any Answers* people did not disappoint us as far as questions or audience reaction were concerned. We plunged straight into the question of the evening. 'Does the team think that immigrants damage our national and traditional way of life?'

> WIGG: No, I don't.
>
> WAUGH: I think it's bringing about a certain amount of change in our traditional way of life. I wouldn't have said necessarily this was for the worse. I think that the presence of a large immigrant population will help eventually to create a more diverse, less egalitarian society, and that is one which I personally will welcome. There may be tensions inside that society;

I won't even mind them much. But then, I am not a democratic politician and I don't have to survive on the approval of the populace. I am a middle-class person, living delicately by myself, and I don't suppose that there's an immigrant living within ten miles of me. The ones I see I quite like, and I welcome their presence.

POWELL: Surely, it must depend how many. Clearly, if the number is relatively small – especially if they are relatively dispersed – then they can probably contribute a net benefit to the community. If their numbers are large, and particularly if they are concentrated, then they may place strains upon the community and may alter its character, in a way which the community itself feels – whether it ought to or not – is intolerable. So I say this is a question of numbers.

WIGG: We mustn't let Mr Powell get away with this. You see, he said, 'Immigrants – it all depends upon numbers.' But it also depends on what kind of immigrants. You see, I have a suspicion about Mr Powell. I don't think he would have said anything about immigrants if they had come from the white Commonwealth, or if they'd been Irish. He's only raised the question because he has discovered that talking about immigrants in relation to colour is a popular thing to do, from a political point of view.

POWELL: It depends indeed on whether the immigrants are different, and different in important respects from the existing population. Clearly, if they are identical, then no change for the good or the bad can be brought about by the immigration. But if they are different, and to the extent that they are different, then numbers clearly are of the essence and this is not wholly – nor mainly – necessarily a matter of colour. For example, if the immigrants were Germans or Russians, their colour would be approximately the same as ours, but the problems which would be created and the change which could be brought about by the introduction of a large bloc of Germans or Russians into five areas in this country would be as serious – and in some respects more serious – than could follow from an introduction of a similar number of West Indians or Pakistanis.

LASKI: Of course we have had these large and overwhelming blocs in the past, such as Anglo-Saxons and Danes and Normans, or Huguenots and German Jews and Russians. But I want to go back to the original question – our traditional way of life. I'm the descendant of immigrants, and the thing I've always been most glad to live in this country for is that I thought that its prime virtue was a tolerant liberalism. Now, if we had a country in which Mr Powell and people who agree with him attacked and exacerbated that traditional liberal decency and changed it into a dislike, a distrust of the stranger and the foreigner who's always added and contributed, it's not a traditional way of life that I myself would care to share any more. I find that the trouble with English life – perhaps because we're an island – is that it tends perpetually to stagnate and become dull. And history shows that every time we've had immigrants, we've had Mr Powells agitating against them. In every case I think it can be said that the immigrants have added to and enriched our national way of life.

As to the question of colour, I think I'm a poor person to speak on this simply because I don't understand it. I regard myself as coloured, in so far as I'm a Jew – I'm a Semite, and coloured as Arabs are. I've had coloured people living in my house, since my children left home; I live next door to coloured people. In fact, I'm perhaps prejudiced; I wouldn't now have anybody but coloured people living in my house, because they are so much cleaner, quieter and more decent than any white person I could conceive of having.

WAUGH: When you stress about tolerant liberalism as a virtue, I think you're now dealing a little bit in western middle-class virtues. I don't think that it's ever been a particularly working-class virtue, this tolerant liberalism. I think it's an entirely middle-class convention. I think that the main opposition to the coloured invasion is a working-class one, not entirely but very nearly entirely. And I think that if one has to generalize about the English working-class – well, you'd have to say that it is no less unintelligent and no less ungenerous and the only true generalization you could make is that perhaps it's a tiny bit idler, but I don't think that you can say that it has ever consistently shown great liberalism.

POWELL: I'm prepared to say that the tolerance which has been shown by the British people – and it is mainly the working-class people – towards this enormous influx over the last ten years in certain specific areas, has been beyond all praise. The people of those areas have seen the towns which they knew utterly altered, they have seen themselves more or less literally driven from one area after another, and the way in which they have tolerated this thing is incredible and, as I say, it does them immense credit. But this again turns on a matter of numbers. There is always a limit to toleration of any – you used the word 'invasion', Auberon, you used the words 'coloured invasion', and I was reminded of Marghanita Laski's reference in her list to the Danes. Now, we were invaded by the Danes, they did alter the country and we fought them for two hundred years. Is that what is meant to be allowed to happen?

LASKI: Were we wise to do so? Didn't they add to us in the end?

POWELL: Only because we fought them and eventually subjugated and Christianized them.

LASKI: You've often spoken of the danger that this coloured immigration can bring.

POWELL: Yes, I have.

LASKI: What specifically is this danger?

POWELL: The danger that if there is a large and increasing concentration of unassimilated immigrants in certain areas in the country, tolerance will break down and there will be violence. That is the danger which I foresee, unless we take steps to ensure that the numbers do not increase as is foreseeable, and that the concentration does not continue.

LASKI: Would you call orthodox Jews, who stay in their own communities and practise their own ways of life, unassimilated immigrants?

POWELL: The numbers are relatively small compared with those of the Commonwealth immigrants already here – again and again and again I come back to the fact that this is a matter of numbers. Almost any unassimilated element can be tolerated and can live in the community if it is sufficiently small in proportion, both generally and in a particular area.

Another aspect of the *Any Questions?* new look was to visit more adventurous locations, and with the object of embracing John Elliot's coveted working-class audience we got ourselves invited to a Working Men's Club in Sunderland. I found it a daunting experience. The audience were seated at little tables, crowded with pint mugs of beer, and at regular intervals they would rise from the table, either to replenish their mug or to dispose of some of the beer already consumed. It was like doing the programme in the middle of Waterloo station.

Afterwards we were led up to the most lavish buffet I have ever seen. Their hospitality was sensational and they were polite about the programme but they had a job to conceal their feeling that we were rather a tiresome prologue to the serious business of the evening, which was bingo.

A still more traumatic experience was provided by our visit to Pentonville Jail. The only stipulations made by the Home Office were that we should not select any questions on crime and punishment and that their representative should scrutinize the chosen questions before we went on the air. There was also to be a censor key under my control. We only installed this on very special occasions. Normally, I had no electronic control over the live broadcast. There was really no point, because if anyone said anything dreadful it would already be heard by millions before I could operate the key, but the Home Office seemed to feel happier if we had one, and, just before the broadcast started, the Governor pointed to it and muttered, 'My career is in your hands.' I hope his career didn't suffer. It shouldn't have done. We had an excellent programme, with an intelligent and responsive audience. John Arlott was especially popular.

(DJ: *I think that when John spoke, his voice conjured up pictures for them – it was the English summer, green fields, in fact, freedom. Every time he spoke they warmed to him. So much so that I believe he became intoxicated by a feeling of power. To those chaps he was everything that meant life outside. Most of them had no idea he'd been a policeman!*)

On 14 March we persuaded Honor Blackman to appear – a big draw because of her role in *The Avengers* and a James Bond film. She was also by no means uninterested in politics. Lord Robens gave her and David a lift up to Yorkshire in his National Coal Board aircraft. (He usually combined an *Any Questions?* appearance with a visit to a coal-field.)

(DJ: *We drove in NCB1 from Hobart House, the Coal Board headquarters, to Luton Airport, where the Coal Board 'Dove' aircraft was waiting for us, and as there was fog about, Lord Robens was rather bothered that we might be diverted from the original landing point so he had NCB2 at Barnsley and NCB3 was standing by at another airport. Honor Blackman thought it was more James Bond than James Bond. She looked magical, and Lord Robens entered into the spirit of things with gusto. On arrival at the airport he glanced apprehensively over his shoulder and said, 'I think we've shaken them off all right.'*)

The following week at Hayle in Cornwall, Paul Foot had a spirited exchange with Sir Gerald Nabarro on a question about public schools: 'What does the team think of a statement made by a politician that you're wasting your money sending your children to a public school when a comprehensive school is just as good?'

> NABARRO: Ninety-five per cent of all the children of this country are educated at state schools. Five per cent are educated at private fee-paying schools. The parents of those children pay large sums of money for their private education; it is their personal choice and I defend absolutely their personal choice. If they wish to spend their net income after paying heavily

through taxes and rates for the education of the other ninety-five children in every hundred, if they still prefer to spend their own money on private education for their own children they should be allowed to do so. Now Mr Anthony Wedgwood Benn made this statement, the Minister of Technology, a most able politician, a most likeable man. He himself was educated at Westminster, one of our great public schools, as Paul Foot here was educated at one of our great public schools, at Shrewsbury, good luck to them both, I mean look what it's produced here in this case. You see I am the odd man out in the Tory Party, Paul Foot, I was educated at a London County Council School through fourteen years.

FOOT: That's the best argument for public schools I've ever heard.

NABARRO: Well, you may think so, but you are not an argument for state education, my friend. All I defend this evening is the right of parents to use their own money as they desire. I neither drink nor smoke and if I like to use my money, my income that I earn by the sweat of my brow, on educating my children at a public school, with the full consent of my wife, I defend that as the inalienable right of any free British citizen irrespective of what Mr Anthony Wedgwood Benn may think.

FOOT: That was a magnificent speech – on behalf of those people who are free, who have two thousand pounds a year spare to spend on their children's education. It's like the Ritz. The Ritz is free to everybody who's got the money to go in and spend the money there and public schools are free to everyone with the money to send their children there, which is a very small percentage of the population. That's the first point. The question is whether or not it's a waste of money to send your children to public schools and I think it is a waste of money because I think that the public schools are masculine, disciplinarian, worst of all, they're elitist. They bring people up to think that there is no one in the world who matters except themselves, that's the worst thing that they do. They don't tell people about what's going on outside, about the poverty and misery in which large numbers of people are living, they don't tell people about that. They tell them that they are important, they are the leaders of the future, they are the only people who will matter and they produce arrogant snobs. Maybe I'm one of them but that doesn't argue against it, at least I've seen through it and argue against it now.

(DJ: After the programme when we got back to the hotel, I went to the bar and asked Gerald what he was going to have. He replied: 'I'll have a large Scotch.' I said jokingly, 'I didn't ask you what size, and anyway I thought you said on the programme you didn't drink!' And with the usual engaging twinkle in his eye, he said, 'I didn't drink on the programme; I'm going to now!' How I miss him – we got on terribly well. I think our backgrounds were much the same. I had him on a television programme, when he said, 'I'm like you, David; I had my education in the market-place of life.')

One thing about Gerald, he really did his homework. He would always come with a large file, with details of the questions discussed the previous week (on the assumption they wouldn't come up again), full biographical details of the other members of the team, and background information about every possible question which might be asked that week. And he was a real character. In Jack Longland's phrase, one of Nature's Etonians.

1969/70

On 5 September, at the beginning of the new series, the newcomer was Cecil King, former chairman of the *Daily Mirror* group. The team also included Quintin Hogg and Robert Morley, making his second appearance. One of the questioners, at Twyford in Berkshire, asked: 'What aims and ideals would the members of the team attempt to achieve if they had the opportunity to take control of the *Sun* newspaper?'

KING: I had control of the *Sun* for about eight years; I'm afraid I had no success and I don't anticipate that anybody else will have any more success than we've had. If we could have transferred half a million buyers from the *Mirror* to the *Sun*, the *Sun* would have been saved and the *Mirror* would not have been damaged. But we found no way of doing it.

MORLEY: I hope if Mr Murdoch comes here, he will run the paper amusingly, he will run it cheerfully, he will not always be denigrating the party in power and he will turn his attention to the humour, the wit, the culture and the pleasure, the abiding pleasure, of living in this country.

KING: If he follows your advice, he will lose more money than I did.

Another questioner asked: 'How much farther can certain civil rights leaders go before they commit sedition?'

KING: The Irish Nationalists who, of course, are aiming at abolishing the border, have found that civil rights agitation gets them more sympathy than an agitation for the abolition of the border, so very wisely they are concentrating on civil rights. Whether this leads them to the edge of sedition or not I wouldn't know, but I should have thought politically it's a good line for them to take.

HOGG: It's all very well for you to say that, Cecil King, but there are pictures of people with stones and petrol bombs and out of, I think, the three thousand members of the Ulster Constabulary, six hundred are already casualties. So that you can't just talk of it as if it was a kind of public relations exercise in the *Daily Mirror*.

KING: But this is a state of feeling which has existed since the invasion of Ireland by Strongbow in 1215. It's not a temporary or casual event, it's a continuation of a state of agitation which has gone on for many centuries.

HOGG: Yes, I think you're doing an injustice both to the civil rights people, and to the people who don't like the border. They are really quite separate issues. There are plenty of, for instance, Roman Catholics in Northern Ireland, or so they write to me and tell me and I accept it to be true, who don't particularly mind being part of the United Kingdom. But they do particularly mind having a secondary position as regards jobs or houses or local votes and so on, and I have no doubt at all where I stand on this matter. I'm against any sort of violence, I'm against most sorts of demonstration, but I am in favour of the border, and I am in favour of civil rights.

KING: But surely the British Government established long ago that the only way of getting anything done is to use violence. Rational argument gets you nowhere, it may get you as far as a campaign pledge, but it certainly won't get you any further, whereas if you break a few windows or frighten a few ministers' wives, things begin to happen. And the Irish have long ago learned this lesson, and after a period of quiescence are bringing it into use again. That's exactly, of course, why Hitler invaded Czechoslovakia. He thought the only way you could get anything done was by using violence, but the trouble about violence is that you've got no guarantee who is going to win. There are still some people in this world who want the right side to win, but possession of force, or the use of violence, is no guarantee that the right side won't lose, and this is why I'm against it.

MORLEY: I think everybody knows that the Irish enjoy a punch-up. But I think that anyone reading the papers realizes that there has been a tremendous lack of efficiency, to say the least of it, with the civil authorities in Ireland. They've allowed a state of affairs to continue in the 'B' force – they've obviously been a mob of Fascist brutes, and they've behaved very badly to the Catholics, who are in a minority, one's sympathy is very much with dear Miss Devlin, who said, 'I tried to get the British Parliament recalled.' It's the last thing the British Parliament want to do. They want always to shelve the issue, to leave things as they are, to hope things will get better. With the people who run the Ulster Government today, things are not going to get better. Now, at last, as Shaw has pointed out, nothing is ever done until people are prepared to die and things are now beginning to happen in Ireland.

Things are going to get better for the Irish. The Catholics are not going to be discriminated against and this has been achieved by violence, and violence very often achieves what Parliament doesn't achieve and it's nonsense to talk about sedition and 'it's better to do things by the Parliamentary way', because we all know that the British Parliament wash their hands of the Irish question whenever possible, because it's political dynamite and this is something that they don't like touching.

HOGG: I've never heard such clotted nonsense. To begin with, things are not getting better, they are getting worse. Let's get that absolutely clear. What has happened has been that eight people have lost their lives of whom one was a child. Many, many people have been injured, whole rows of houses have been burnt, they have been Roman Catholic houses no less than Protestant houses. The feeling between the two communities has burst and erupted into hatred and if anybody thinks that this is something that in the comfort of an English Thames-side constituency one can say, 'Well it's a bit of all right because so-and-so is in the minority and so-and-so is in the majority,' all I can say is he has no human heart at all.

MORLEY: I hope you're not speaking about me.

HOGG: I am speaking about you, Robert Morley.

MORLEY: You don't listen to a thing I say, which of course is your natural profession. There have been grave miscarriages of justice in Ireland which have now been brought to the attention of people in this country and things will be put right. First of all, we've got the army going in and dealing with something which the police in Ireland don't deal with because they're hopelessly biased and have lost the support of the public. Now the British have got to once more pull the chestnuts out of the fire. But we weren't prepared to do this until the riots occurred in Bogside.

HOGG: If you have any idea that the British are either going to put things right in Ireland, or have ever succeeded in doing so, or are going to now either under a Labour government or a Conservative government or any other government, you're making a mistake. It is the Irish people of both communities who have got to learn to live together as neighbours and the most the British can hope to do is to get a little breathing space, perhaps for six weeks if they are extremely lucky, perhaps for a few hours, in which passions can be allowed to reduce.

We paid our second visit to Northern Ireland, to Belfast, in November. It was all very different from our first visit three years earlier. There still hadn't been much in the way of bombing, but the British troops were very much in evidence – steel-helmeted and carrying rifles at the ready. It was to be quite a long time before we visited the Province again.

The eight-hundredth edition of the programme coincided with its twenty-first birthday. We'd rather run out of meaningful locations, so we went to Sutton in Surrey, which was handy for the top brass from London and for the chief guest of the evening – Freddy Grisewood.

(DJ: *We'd been to have lunch with him the previous week and I had recorded an interview which we used at the beginning of the programme. Freddy, who had always made much play of the fact that he didn't own a television set, revealed that he had become a television addict, and was a great fan of* Z Cars. *I recorded the interview for safety's sake, but Freddy was in such good form on the night that I was sorry we hadn't done the interview live.*

He took his place in the front row and I remember looking down at his dear face – that and his voice never altered, no matter how crippled his body had become. After giving the usual introduction, I said that the guest of honour was the man who had occupied the chair for so long. Then the audience applauded – I'm not sure they didn't cheer – and it went on a very long time. It was one of the most moving moments of my career. He was such a generous man that he wasn't saddened by the fact that he sat where he did and I sat where I did. He said afterwards he had enjoyed the evening more than he expected – he didn't listen now and had forgotten what a good programme it was!)

We included the two main regulars of that time, Mary Stocks and Malcolm Muggeridge, together with founder member John Arlott and a distinguished newcomer, Bryan Forbes, then Head of Production of Associated British Pictures Corporation. He made a very promising début, but like so many people, was somewhat less effective on his second appearance. He referred to it afterwards, from his experience as an actor, as 'second night nerves'. People who were poor on their first appearance might have been better next time. But we shall never know.

On 12 December we were at the Harborne and Quinton Community Centre on the outskirts of Birmingham. The announcer cued over to David as usual. He said where we were and who we had on the team: Lord Soper, Jeremy Thorpe, Iain Macleod and a newcomer, Lady Rachel Billington. There was a dutiful burst of applause.

(DJ: *I continued: 'Now, you may have wondered why my voice was sounding a little more nervous that it does as a rule at the start of this programme. And I have to tell you that I'm exceptionally nervous indeed because I sit here – on the stage of this Harborne and Quinton Community Centre, on the outskirts of Birmingham – completely alone. We have a dinner party before the programme, and when I came out – and I leave a little earlier than the team – I said to the taxi driver who was about to bring me: "Off we go." And he said, "Where to?" So I said, "The Harborne and Quinton Community Centre." He said, "Where's that?" "Well," I said, "I really don't know." So he said, "You must know where you're going." And I said, "I've absolutely no idea at all."*

However, I had managed to persuade the driver to find the Community Centre and arrived at more or less the usual time, but I warned Michael that the team, all coming in one taxi, might not fare so well, so a message was sent to the announcer to say that he might have to delay handing over to us. He apparently never got the message and handed over to us just the same.)

While David was making this unorthodox introduction, I went out of the hall to have another look to see if the team were in sight. It started to snow. Standing there, hatless and coatless, I felt like a minor character in a Victorian melodrama. There was no sign of the team, so I trudged back into the hall and walked dejectedly up the aisle, dripping with snow, and called out to David, 'We'll go back to the studio.'

Soothing music was then played for the listeners, while I resumed my lonely vigil outside. After about five minutes, a taxi drew up and disgorged Soper, Thorpe, Macleod and Billington. They were hustled into the hall and on to the stage, and the programme started again. I was too unnerved by the crisis to think of changing the first question, so the unfortunate team, still breathless, were pitchforked into a weighty discussion on capital punishment.

(DJ: *I seem to remember Jeremy saying if it was for the taxi driver, his answer might be different!*)

A later question asked the team whether the MCC was wise to invite the South African cricket team to this country next summer, in spite of the incidents surrounding the Springboks' visit. Lord Soper was on the team with Margaret Thatcher, when a similar question was asked in Northampton on 30 January.

SOPER: I'm quite convinced that South Africa has brought politics, and evil politics, into sport, and I want to make the clearest denunciation of that evil as I can.

THATCHER: I think it will be a tremendous tragedy if the tour is put off because of a minority of demonstrators stopping the majority of people who I think wish to look at cricket, which is a very good game to look at, anyway. We don't in fact stop the Bolshoi Ballet coming, or any other cultural exchanges between East and West because we disapprove most strongly of some of the regimes beyond the Iron Curtain. I think we can learn a great deal from one another, and in particular the South African team could probably learn a very great deal from the amicable way in which we conduct our affairs over here.

A minority certainly has a right to demonstrate here – that's what part of our politics are about. But I doubt very much whether minorities, by constantly demonstrating, have the right to frustrate the wishes of the majority. And if a small minority stops tours of this kind taking place, then any minority in future, by a violent or non-violent protest, can stop many activities which most of the people in England enjoy.

SOPER: I'm sure Margaret Thatcher forgets that it's only because minorities have the chance of turning themselves into majorities that true democracy has a chance of survival. I've no use for sowing tintacks on the pitch, and I wouldn't walk behind the bowler's arm and that sort of thing. But I'm determined myself to believe, and to act on the belief, that we have to create a public opinion on a wicked thing called apartheid.

THATCHER: Yes, look, the time for a minority to turn itself into a majority is at the time provided in a democratic country at election time.

SOPER: I believe we've got to set a standard, and I think we've got to stick by it, and here is a matter of absolute principle.

THATCHER: Well, in that case you're not going to allow anyone over here from Russia so long as the Jews are treated in Russia as they are, because you disapprove of the treatment of a minority.

SOPER: All right. I believe consistency is a virtue where you can find it, but there's no such thing as total consistency, and certainly I would be very chary of accepting the typical Conservative view of what's happening to the Jews in Russia. I have plenty of evidence to the contrary, but even if it were so, the professed policy of Russia, even if it falls well below that policy, is equality. The professed policy in South Africa is inequality, and that's the difference.

THATCHER: So it's the theory that matters more than the practice!

Early in 1970 the BBC's new plans for radio were announced. This was the *Broadcasting in the Seventies* plan which caused much controversy, largely directed against the proposals to truncate the Third Programme. But the main provisions concerned local radio, which was to replace regional radio, and generic programming, which was to replace mixed programming, so that by switching to Radio 1, 2, 3 or 4 listeners could feel confident that they were going to get pop, light music, serious music and the spoken word respectively.

John Elliot decided to resume his writing career, and John Tanton emigrated to the United States. I applied for his job, which carried new duties and a new title, Network Editor, Radio.

Any Questions? and *Any Answers* were to move from Radio 2 to Radio 4. The changes, due to start in April, were discussed in the programme at Newent in Gloucestershire on 20 February, with the playwright, Dennis Potter, putting the case against generic programming.

'I think the changes are in general based on the proposition that people know what they like, whereas I believe that people don't perhaps know what they like until they hear it. And it does seem to me to be an abdication, a reversal, of all that the BBC over the years has stood for: that mixed programming – variety, the chance of stumbling across something you didn't know before, the chance of being entranced, maybe while the kettle is boiling, maybe in mid-stride, as you were about to switch off; whereas if it is now all channelled, all separated, it is an instant, canned kind of thing in its concept. Now, I myself find it easier to cross the road than to switch stations, for some peculiar reason. Lots of people are like this. They tend to switch the thing on. After a while they don't like it, off it goes maybe. But if there were that element, as there always used to be, of surprise: a play, some music that you haven't heard, a discussion which rivets, catches your attention – you have all the ideal ingredients of a vital intelligent radio broadcasting system. And this is being almost wantonly – and, it seems, against the wishes of many senior BBC producers – thrown out of the window.'

Our first live broadcast on Radio 4 was on Friday, 10 April 1970, at 8 p.m. – it meant a very hasty dinner. (Six months later we moved back to 8.30.) It was the end of an association with the Light Programme (from 1967, Radio 2) dating back very nearly twenty years. I regretted the move because I thought we should lose listeners. Radio 2 got a bigger evening audience than Radio 4, and I thought Dennis Potter's point about people being reluctant to switch stations was a valid one. However, my fears were not justified. Most of our loyal Friday evening listeners followed us over to Radio 4.

The Controller of Radio 4 was Tony Whitby, a fellow-Bristolian, for whom I had the very greatest admiration and affection. His early death from cancer was a grievous loss to his friends and to the BBC. Immediately after that first live Radio 4 broadcast he telephone me at Banbury. But it was not to register his delight at having *Any Questions?* on Radio 4. He ordered that two words should be deleted from the repeat.

The offender was Marghanita Laski. In a question about litter, she made use of two rather short words to describe human excreta and Tony said these must come out of the repeat. I made the necessary arrangements. Predictably, there were a lot of letters – half of them complaining about the words having been uttered, the other half complaining about the words having been deleted from the repeat.

A few weeks later, Harold Wilson decided to go to the country and the election was fixed for 18 June. My wife, who has her psychic moments, though less frequently than one would wish when waiting at the Tote window, was quite convinced that E. Heath and M. Bowen would both triumph. Sure enough, after the election Ted Heath became Prime Minister and on the 19th I heard that I had got the Network Radio Editor job.

A week later, in the last programme in the series, at Hastings, Lord Kearton then chairman of Courtaulds, said that the whole question of industrial relations was the single most important worry for this country. 'Unless we can get a new and more meaningful dialogue between employers, the unions and the Government – I think mainly between the employers and the unions, and the unions with their own members – within a very short time indeed, then I think this country is poised on the edge of an absolute catastrophe.'

The future, with a new Government pledged to reform industrial relations, was indeed full of ominous interest, with consequent fascinating prospects for *Any Questions?*.

I remember Frank Kearton saying before the programme that he didn't expect to be asked again because I was leaving it. But I wasn't in a great hurry to leave. I was by no means certain how viable this new post was. To continue as producer would mean being away from the office once a week, and the travelling was now more extensive than ever, but it might help to save my sanity to have an escape route from the interminable round of meetings and being incessantly at the receiving end of tiresome complaints from above and below.

Above all, *Any Questions?* was just about the most pleasant programme, radio or television, for any BBC man (or woman) to be associated with, and to give it up seemed to me to be the most bizarre act of self-deprivation since Arthur Miller gave up being married to Marilyn Monroe.

I decided to sit tight.

1970/71

Thus I began the 1970/71 series resolved to remain producer for the time being. London seemed perfectly happy with the arrangement.

It was a challenging time for the programme. Many of those who had helped to make it what it was had departed for varying reasons, but we were able to welcome back the stars of the Labour Party, lost to us for the past six years when they were Government ministers. Denis Healey, Tony Benn, Barbara Castle, Jim Callaghan, Tony Greenwood, Roy Jenkins, Shirley Williams, Dick Crossman, Dick Marsh and Tony Crosland were all back in the fold within a few months. Of our star Conservatives we lost only two – Margaret Thatcher and Quintin Hogg – to the Government.

However, in the opening programme at Folkestone, there were no MPs. Manny Shinwell was now Lord Shinwell and the others were the Countess of Longford, Alastair Burnet and Russell Braddon.

(DJ: *We had to rush for the train back to London afterwards, and any thought that Manny Shinwell was getting a bit old for the hurly-burly of* Any Questions? *was immediately crushed. He ran faster than any of us!*)

In that first programme there was, inevitably, a question about industrial relations. The subject dominated *Any Questions?* at that time, with particular reference to the Heath Government's proposed legislation. That week they were discussing strikes affecting the motor-car industry.

BRADDON: Wage inflation necessarily leads to a panic that one's money is not going to be worth what one hoped when one got it, therefore you strike for more immediately, particularly since the Tory Government has said that it proposes laying down legislation which will perhaps inhibit these strikes in the future, and therefore inhibit the possibility of gaining quick rises by quick strikes.

LONGFORD: It's no good stopping it by legal action, they'll simply strike against the law against the strike. That won't settle it. There must be a change of heart, and a realization throughout the whole country that we are a community and that we stand or fall together, and that personal, individual greed is going to lead us nowhere.

BURNET: I don't honestly think that is going to come as quickly as a situation in which some employer – and it will have to be the Government – says: 'Actually we have too many dockers in this country. Actually we have too many miners in this country. Actually we protect the mining industry in this country; we don't allow oil imports to come in to compete with coal over certain sectors in this country. We have too many railwaymen running too many railways in this country for it to be economically viable.'

Now, these are very hard things to say to people who have worked all their lives in these industries. But I do hope that people will realize that when it comes in the end to some closures one of the reasons why there have had to be men and women turned off at Singer's in Glasgow, and at other factories there, is simply that in part they have struck and argued their way into wage increases which have made their firms uneconomic, and now they feel the result.

On 9 October we were at Bedford College in London. As always with a student audience, I had at the back of my mind the possibility of demonstrations, though there had been some student audiences in the past whose failing had been apathy. The students of the Union Society, who were looking after the local organization, had assured me that none of the tickets would get into the hands of the political activists. It was therefore somewhat unnerving, when I was selecting the questions in an ante-room, to have one of the students rush in and reveal in alarm that 'There are 24 members of Soc Soc in the fourth row!'.

I gathered that these were members of the Socialist Society. The impression was that they were up to something. The impression was strengthened when I did my warm-up and brought the questioners forward to the front row. There was a certain amount of to-ing and fro-ing between the fourth and front rows, like a sinister game of musical chairs, a lot of muttering, scraps of paper changing hands. I tried to rise above it, but it was lucky I knew my spontaneous preliminary remarks by heart – my mind was elsewhere.

The team was Lord Mancroft, Bryan Forbes, Shirley Williams and Bernard Williams, formerly Professor of Philosophy at Bedford College. It was the first time we'd had a husband and wife together on the team. Unfortunately it didn't turn out to be a very good idea: I didn't know they were on the point of separating.

For a while there was a deceptive calm among the audience. The first two questions went by peacefully. The third question was about political kidnapping. There was one person who barracked Bryan Forbes when he said we were living in an age of near-anarchy in many areas. The barracking intensified when Bernard Williams spoke. David issued a mild rebuke.

We had another question, and another, in the course of which the Voice broke out again. David got rather fed up and said to him, 'Oh, do you know, sir, you are a very boring gentleman!' The prolonged applause made it clear that the audience shared this view. Then David did something which made the small hairs on the back of my neck start to rise. He directed Alison to take the microphone to where the man was sitting to hear what he was on about. Somewhat reluctantly, Alison went. Oh Lord, I thought, what ever shall we get now – a string of expletives which cannot be deleted? Oh, for a censor key!

But all was well. The Voice mildly revealed itself as belonging to an ex-student who had failed his exams and merely wanting to make comments as the speeches went along. David's initiative served its purpose and we reached the end of that question without any further interruption. But with the next question, the Soc Soc ploy became clear.

Instead of a question about football which we had accepted and Alison had typed out in the usual way for the questioner to read, a different one was substituted: 'At the recent Labour Party Conference, no post-mortem was made on why the Party lost the election. Is it not because when in power the Labour Party totally betrayed the workers' cause and inevitably became the tool of big business and American industry? And are they not totally discredited in their traditional role of the Party of the less favoured members of this society?'

(DJ: *This took us by surprise. We had no copy of the question, so I asked the questioner to hand it up to us. I explained that the normal drill was for questions to be handed in when the audience came into the hall and the producer decided which questions would be most suitable for the programme. 'Censors them!' called out a voice from the fourth row. 'No, he doesn't censor them,' I said. 'He doesn't let questions come through that we had last week or the week before.'*)

David could have added, 'Or questions involving matters which are sub-judice, questions of purely local interest, questions which, in the producer's view, are unlikely to stimulate an interesting or entertaining discussion, or questions, like the one submitted, which are not really questions at all, but lengthy statements of opinion.'

However, we were quite willing to accept the question now that it had been put. Shirley Williams replied first. 'The poorest group in society – that's to say, the ten per cent of people on supplementary benefits – did in fact increase their situation in real terms by eighteen per cent over these five years, and my own belief is that one of the things that defeated the Labour Party was that a great many people resented the fact that they had to pay high taxes for this purpose, and that a great many people resented the fact that there was a claw-back system under which family allowances went to the worst off.'

Then followed quite a lot of barracking from the fourth row as well as the questioner. Mancroft couldn't get a word in. Bryan Forbes said to the questioner, 'You really are a more definitive bore than your companion.' Further prolonged applause from the long-suffering majority, in the course of which a voice called out a word to describe Bryan Forbes which the transcript tactfully calls '(Unintelligible)' but which I heard distinctly and recognized from my army days.

(DJ: *I was furious. I said I didn't intend to allow them to muck up the programme for a whole lot of people by their obscenity. I added, 'Hands up all those of you who want the programme taken off the air.' It was a bit of a gamble. Fortunately, no one put their hand up.*)

Bryan Forbes then harangued the barrackers, who barracked back. Then followed a lull in which Lord Mancroft was at last able to put the Tory view: 'By and large, the electorate, which is an educated and sophisticated electorate, looked at the causes put forward by both parties – there was no one issue, there were about twenty issues on both sides – added them up and came to a decision. And the two issues put down in this question would, I think, be the last in most people's mind when they voted.'

Bernard Williams shared the views of his wife and Mancroft. 'It is untrue that the reason why the Labour Party was defeated last time was because it pursued insufficiently left-wing policies.' He added that he didn't think a revolutionary basis existed in this country and that seemed to him one of the fundamental errors of certain kinds of militant policy. End of discussion. And end of demonstration. Two more placid questions. End of programme. Start of post-mortem.

Tony Whitby was with us that night and the only immediate problem was whether the rude word should be cut out of the repeat. A practical man, Tony rang the Duty Officer at Broadcasting House. Had anyone rung up to complain about bad language? No one had. So the repeat went out the next day without any editing. No one complained. But listening recently to the recording preserved in the BBC archives, I heard the word quite clearly.

(DJ: *I remember Mary Stocks calling on me on Saturday morning and asking what the word was. I didn't tell her. Oddly enough Lord Mancroft, despite his distinguished military service, had never heard the word before!*)

Mancroft was with us again on 22 January. With the chilling description of 'the best after-dinner speaker in London' hanging round his neck, he could nevertheless be relied on for two or three *bons mots* per programme. (On an earlier appearance, when asked for a collective noun for bishops he had suggested a surplice of bishops.) Giving advice to enable middle-aged husbands to remain attractive to their wives, he said, 'Well, as the poet Mancroft once movingly put it –

To keep your marriage happy,
With love in the loving cup,
Whenever you're wrong, admit it,
Whenever you're right, shut up!'

He also produced this aphorism on the subject of women's fashions (hot pants were in vogue just then): 'Women don't dress to please. Very few women dress to please their menfolk. Very few women dress to please themselves. But the vast majority of women dress to annoy other women.'

The following week we were in London again, at the Chartered Insurance Institute in the City, and we welcomed back Roy Jenkins. I was asked by BBC television if we would let them film the whole programme as they wished to include Roy Jenkins in a documentary they were producing about the Labour leaders in opposition. I agreed. I learned afterwards that the programme was called *Yesterday's Men*.

I thus found myself on the outer fringes of a controversial production which is always said to have been the cause of considerable friction between the BBC and the

Labour Party. In any case, I learned the hard way that it was a mistake to allow the programme to become involved with television, because television people regard their own needs as paramount; the needs of a live radio broadcast which they happen to be filming are negligible by comparison.

However, the television crew turned out to be the least of my problems that evening, because just as we were about to go on the air, I learned that there were no Post Office lines and therefore no live broadcast. It was a mistake on the part of the Post Office engineers, not ours – the Post Office provides the lines between the outside broadcast point and the BBC Control Room, which means that we are affected if there is a dispute involving the Post Office engineers. This wasn't a dispute, just an error.

The audience warm-up that evening was being handled for the first time by the BBC's Director-General, Charles Curran. He was very understanding about the hiccup in the arrangements. I decided, mistakenly, to go ahead at around the proper time, recording on site, so that the repeat would at any rate be complete. It involved keeping in close touch with the engineers, walking back and forth between the stage and their room, much to the annoyance of the television people because I walked in front of one of the cameras each time.

In the end we got on the air only about five minutes late and it would have been better to have waited. With considerable ingenuity, our engineers borrowed a radio car from Radio London, connected it up to the output from our equipment in the hall, and transmitted the programme from the car to the control room at Broadcasting House.

February marked the début of Hugh Scanlon, President of the Engineering Workers' Union. I had never met him, but the Tory Press had prepared me for a testy, aggressive, blunt character and I awaited his arrival at the hotel with some trepidation. On my way out to look for him, I stumbled across a small, mild, bespectacled man, looking rather like a benign bishop, who asked me humbly, in a soft, north country voice, if I could direct him to the room where the *Any Questions?* team were meeting. It was the ogre himself. Hugh Scanlon proved to be an undoubted acquisition and to have a keen sense of humour. When I last met him he was Lord Scanlon, and he gleefully passed on the comment of an erstwhile comrade that 'it takes Hugh to Quango'.

Three weeks later the newcomer was Robin Day. For some time I had been steadily increasing the ration of TV anchor-men. The attributes which had led them to be chosen to present TV current affairs programmes like *Panorama* and *Twenty-four Hours* were much the same as those which led them to be attractive propositions for *Any Questions?*. They were intelligent, articulate, knowledgeable, accustomed to the cut and thrust of live controversial broadcasting. They were also well known to the public, an attraction to the audience in the hall and to the listeners who were interested to hear what their opinions were after being accustomed to watch them eliciting other people's. And so men like Ludovic Kennedy, Kenneth Allsop, Julian Pettifer and now Robin Day began to appear more frequently on *Any Questions?*. The Television Current Affairs hierarchy began to be concerned about it. They were worried that their star presenters' reputation for impartiality might be threatened if they were heard expressing political opinions in another programme – and they wouldn't be a lot of use to *Any Questions?* if they failed to express personal opinions on political matters.

But television producers tended not to worry very much what was happening on radio, and when the policy was laid down that I should approach the editor of the programme concerned each time I wanted to invite one of these anchor-men, I didn't anticipate a restrictive attitude. Nor was there.

Robin Day was particularly useful to us. He had an instinctive ability to 'play the programme', to sense what was needed at any particular moment and to supply it vigorously. Also he revealed, what he had had no opportunity of displaying to viewers at that time, that he had a sense of humour.

After one of his appearances, I told him, rather incautiously, that he was 'another Ralph Wightman'. He did not appear to regard this as a compliment. 'I shall not appear in your programme again,' he said coldly. The next day I wrote to him, spelling out in detail and with the utmost sincerity, the ways in which he displayed all the attributes of an *Any Questions?* regular. I would gladly have had him on the team just as often as he was willing to appear. He softened, and did appear once or twice more but before long I got the impression that he felt the fears expressed by the current affairs hierarchy were valid, and he was lost to us.

He later told me he disliked having to make instant answers on topics on which he had no detailed knowledge because this tempted him into sweeping generalizations in order to be provocative. He had reacted unfavourably to the comparison with Ralph Wightman because he didn't want to become a performing 'character'.

Ralph Wightman died in May that year, and David paid a short tribute to him at the beginning of that week's programme. Arthur Street had died in the summer of 1968 when the programme was off the air, but on the first anniversary of his death I had produced a memorial programme, *Portrait of a Countryman*, in which some of Arthur's most pungent contributions to *Any Questions?* were interspersed with appropriate tributes. It was one of the few productions in my career that I felt really satisfied with. A lot of affection and admiration went into the making of it.

One thing is certain – no matter how long *Any Questions?* lasts, no one will ever exceed the number of appearances by Ralph Wightman (213) and Arthur Street (165).

People appear far less frequently nowadays, seldom more than twice a year, and nobody on the current lists is even approaching their century.

Robin Day put in a second appearance before the end of the series. Also on the team was Jim Callaghan, returning to the programme after his years in Government. I was able to persuade him because the programme coming from Seaford in Sussex, near his farm. They were involved in an animated discussion on unemployment. A questioner asked: '815,000 unemployed at the latest count – what would members of the team advise the Government to do about it?'

DAY: I think that the problem is a very, very serious one. If the Government expands the economy too much, puts too much money back into the economy in order to reduce the number of unemployed, which everybody wants to see reduced, then you run a danger of worse inflation than we have at the moment and risk to that balance of payments, which the Government of which Jim Callaghan was a member can claim credit for having raised to a very high level. If, on the other hand, you don't put some money back into the economy then you get a slump and even worse unemployment. Therefore it's the old business of how the Government really knows how much to do and when, and no government has found the secret of this fine economic tuning. I think we've got to wait and see and this is obviously what the Government is doing, to wait and see whether the measures which the Budget introduced, which put 350 million pounds' worth of consumption back into the economy, are going to be enough to put the situation in the direction of less unemployment. To the trades unions and the TUC I would say: 'Remember what the Labour Government was urging you, that the only alternative to unemployment on a large scale is to work for an incomes policy.'

CALLAGHAN: Ever since the days of Keynes and certainly since the days of the Coalition Government, during the war, it has been accepted that the Government iself can control the level of employment or unemployment and it is not sufficient to try to slide away from that and say 'We are ushering in a new dispensation in which you're all going to stand on your own feet'. Let us be quite clear: if the level of unemployment is going up, it is because the Government is not taking measures or making an effort to reduce it, because they put other priorities higher.

It is obscene when people cannot get jobs who are willing to work, and we've seen enough of this in Durham and in Wales and in Scotland, and there are people today out of work who could begin work if the Government were ready to take other decisions. Now, the other decisions that they take may mean that prices will go up, they may mean that the balance of payments will in the end begin to deteriorate, but democracy has to make the choice. The Government has to make the choice on our behalf, and this Government has made, in my view, the wrong choice: it's to say, 'We will destroy the investment grants in the development areas; we will destroy the Investment Reconstruction Corporation; we will use monetary policy in such a way as to squeeze firms large and small; we will remove the grants from the shipbuilders; we will undermine the steel investment programme. We as the Government will create unemployment.' That's wrong, and everybody in this country ought to say so.

DAY: I think a good many people would like to be reminded that in the Budget the Government did also take a number of measures which were designed to make for bigger investment, to relieve the companies of some Corporation Tax, to abolish SET, which should put three or four hundred million pounds back into the economy. But I think Jim was a little simplistic, because after all, unemployment was quite high, not quite as high as this, but it was quite high when his party left office, I forget the exact figure, but it was the highest for thirty years then. And the same arguments about it being wrong were used by his own left wing and by a lot of other people who thought it was far too high then, and it really is no good talking about Keynes now and 'We must all be in charge of our economic destiny'.

CALLAGHAN: I'm horrified when I hear members of the audience shout 'rubbish' when I allege that it is within the power of a government to control the level of employment, because if we don't accept that, we really are going back to the 1930s and I promise you that there are millions of people in this country who have lived through it who don't intend to do that.

The Robin Day–Jim Callaghan dialogue was on a lighter basis in response to the question: 'When an aggressive approach as in politics or interviewing is required in public, does the team find this attitude creeps into one's daily personal life?'

DAY: I think that if you can't argue heatedly and vigorously – not violently in the sense of punching one another, but vigorously – then you can't maintain a friendship. I'm not sure that I'd apply that doctrine to married life, particularly with my wife in the hall. But what the questioner is saying is that in politics and television journalism, people have to, he thinks, appear aggressive or hostile, and whether this rubs off in their ordinary conversation. I hope he'll believe me when I say that I've never come across the distinction. I've interviewed Jim Callaghan many times on the television – in and out of office – sometimes there've been quite vigorous exchanges, but no more or less vigorous than I might have with him afterwards over a drink, or if I met him in his own house. It would be a slightly different kind of conversation, because it would be limited by time and so on and so forth, but the nature of it – no, it wouldn't be any different at all.

CALLAGHAN: Well, I often used to say to the BBC when they wanted me to have an interview – could it be Robin Day?

DAY: Oh, don't go too far, Jim.

CALLAGHAN: I don't want to destroy your future career – you're a promising young man – but I always felt that Robin Day's questions were pertinent, they were pointed, they were certainly never aggressive in that sense, but I think we must try and bring out this distinction. The questioner talks about an aggressive approach being required. It is not required at all. I, on the whole, like to be pretty peaceable, but there are certain things that bring out a 'gut' reaction in me. If anybody talks to me about unemployment, I see red straight away, and I think there are plenty of people of my generation who do, and we can't help it, the adrenalin is going to flow. But if afterwards I'm extremely polite to a political opponent and have a drink with him, that doesn't mean I was insincere in the approach I made when we were discussing this particular problem. I felt it extremely strongly at the time. As to being interviewed, I've no objection to the pointed questioner, and indeed when I used to be interviewed when I was a minister, on the whole I rather liked a rude interviewer. It wasn't why I asked for Robin! I used to rather like a rude interviewer because the public sympathy would then be on the side of the man who was being heckled rather than on the side of the chap who's doing the heckling.

DAY: Could I just make one brief confession, having said what I said, I think it would only be honest to say that occasionally my wife says to me as a supreme rebuke, 'You're not on television now!'

On Good Friday we were at a Community Centre on the outskirts of Coventry, with Isobel Barnett, Ted Leather, Antony Hopkins and Des Wilson of 'Shelter'. We went on the air as usual, and apart from a howling draught coming from the wings, everything seemed to be as normal. After we had been broadcasting for a few minutes, I heard the voice of one of our engineers on the headphones I always wore during the programme. He said, 'You'd better come outside. The police are here, and want to talk to you.'

I left the stage as nonchalantly as possible and went to the room at the back where the engineers had their control point. There were two policemen there; also the warden of the Community Centre. Apparently, as soon as we had gone on the air, there had been a telephone call to the police from an anonymous caller, saying that there was a bomb in the Community Centre, timed to go off at nine o'clock.

'Do you think it's a hoax? What do you advise?' I asked one of the policemen.

'Up to you, sir,' he said unhelpfully.

I consulted the warden. It was really his decision. If he insisted that we stopped the broadcast and cleared the hall there was nothing we could do about it. It was his hall, the audience were his members.

He didn't hesitate. 'I'm sure it's a hoax,' he said stoutly. 'We'll carry on.'

I drifted somewhat less nonchalantly back on to the stage. One or two eyebrows were raised in my direction. Isobel Barnett thought I had been taken ill and was prepared to put her knowledge and experience as a former GP at my disposal.

Someone was talking amusingly about hot pants as I resumed my seat and began scribbling a note. It read: 'The police have received a message that there is a bomb in the hall timed to go off at nine o'clock. We think it is a hoax. Are you willing to continue?' I then passed the note round the team, each one reading it in intervals of thinking and talking about hot pants. They were very British – if that is a suitable phrase to use about a team which included a Canadian and a New Zealander – and each gave me the thumbs-up sign in turn.

As nine o'clock approached, I fought against the temptation to have a look under the table cloth. Of *course* it was a hoax. All the same, ought I to have given the audience a chance to scarper if they wanted to? Did I give Alison the option of making an orderly withdrawal? I forget.

Nine o'clock came and went. Nothing whatever happened, other than the calm, measured tones of the splendid *Any Questions?* team carrying on regardless.

However, the incident made me realize how very vulnerable we were to this sort of thing. If we went off the air because of a hoax telephone call there would be no end to it. And there came a time, after the bombing of a coach on the M62 in Yorkshire, when one could not automatically assume with impunity that any telephone call about a bomb was a hoax.

On the advice of Stuart Wyton, Head of the Network Production Centre in Bristol and a former Controller of the BBC in Northern Ireland, we ceased putting the exact location of *Any Questions?* in *Radio Times*, just the county. I also made a nuisance of myself to the police and to the hall authorities wherever we visited by asking for a search of the hall to be carried out before the audience assembled, so that if there was a telephone call while we were on the air we could be confident it was a hoax. An offer by the police to search the hall if there *was* a telephone call during the broadcast was no good – it would mean going off the air and encouraging other nutcases to make telephone calls in the future. In fact, I made rather a meal of the whole thing. But we never needed to go off the air – at any rate for that reason.

1971/72

Questions on Northern Ireland, ever more frequent, always made me feel anxious. I feared that inflammatory remarks, with tempers high in a live discussion, might possibly have unfortunate, even tragic repercussions.

One evening, I was so alarmed by the reactions of some of the team when listening to the latest news from Northern Ireland at six o'clock that I went straight out into the hotel lobby and put a telephone call through to the Director-General. Charles Curran and I discussed the team, and came to the conclusion that it would be better not to accept any question on Northern Ireland that evening.

However, on the opening programme of the 1971/72 series, I had no particular cause for concern, because a team including Elizabeth Longford and Denis Healey spoke calmly enough on a question about partition.

> HEALEY: Ireland was partitioned after the First World War because a lot of Protestants in the North said they would fight – and they had support from a lot of people in the British army at the time – unless they had a place to live. I think partition at that time was inevitable. I think the tragedy was that the line along which the partition was drawn deliberately included a large number of areas which were almost solid Catholic, because the Protestants said they couldn't run a bit of Ireland unless they brought in Tyrone and Fermanagh and Derry and areas like that.

LONGFORD: It's bad enough to partition a country, but when you have unwilling people living in one partitioned part and then you treat them as second-rate citizens, when you give the jobs to the majority – even though the minority are a third of the whole – when you have twelve to fifteen per cent unemployment in Ulster, very tragic, we're all sorry, but you have forty-six per cent unemployment in many Catholic areas, then that cauldron is going to blow its lid off the moment something comes to start up the explosion – as it has come.
HEALEY: That, like most statements about Ireland, is a very eloquent one, but the fact of the matter surely is that in the last three or four years a great deal has been done to remove these discriminations of which Lady Longford talks and it's not when the discriminations are worst that the trouble comes, it is now when every practical measure has been taken to remove them. What you are left with now is a minority within the Catholic minority who say, 'We have the guns, we are prepared to use them, to shoot innocent people, and therefore you have to treat us as if we were the majority,' and that I think is an intolerable demand to make of any British government.
LONGFORD: I agree with you but it's too little and too late. All these things should have been done fifty years ago; now, of course, the extremists get control of the situation; I think it's terrible, as you do, that children are shot in the streets, it's ghastly and one weeps to think of it. But why has it happened? It needn't have happened. History does speak in these dreadful action and we've got to listen.
HEALEY: Surely the answer now is – you can't solve this problem by force. You can hope, with the presence of the British army – and I don't think any army in the world could have stood up to the sort of provocation they've had from both sides – you can hope to buy time for a political solution, but the use of the army isn't a solution in itself, and the beginning of a solution is to recognize that the parliamentary

system, the party system, as we know it in Britain, cannot work in a country where the communities are so deeply divided; you can only, therefore, satisfy the legitimate demand of the minority to feel that it's equally treated by building it into the organs of government in Northern Ireland at every level. And this is what Mr Wilson was suggesting when he suggested introducing proportional representation there and I hope very much that the Government in the next few weeks will take active steps to remove this fifty-year-old grievance from the minority in Ulster.

I remember the programme on 8 October primarily for the tussle I had with the local radio man who was doing the warm-up, over his T-bone steak at dinner beforehand. My doggy-bag was by then an established *Any Questions?* joke. As my ration strength of dogs steadily increased – at one point the total reached eight – I became more and more frustrated by the spectacle of tender morsels – and sometimes much more than morsels – of steak left on their plates by nervous members of the team, being carted out to the kitchens. So I took to bringing a doggy-bag with me, and the dogs eagerly anticipated Friday evenings and my return after the broadcast. If everybody had had fish for dinner, their chagrin was harrowing to witness.

(DJ: *The local radio man was supposed to leave for the hall with Michael, who put his fork into the steak prior to whisking it away into his doggy-bag and the unfortunate fellow cried out: 'I haven't finished yet!' The present producer, Carole Stone, has no animals at home and generally eats fish, so I'm happy to be able to report that the doggy-bag days are now over!*)

On 3 December, we had the habitual question about the inequality of the sexes in the *Any Questions?* teams and Bernard Levin challenged me to provide the answer there and then on the air. I simply said: '(a) I will write a letter to *Any Answers* and (b) there will be two women on the team on New Year's Eve' and got myself off the hook that way.

The two women on New Year's Eve were Isobel Barnett and Glenda Jackson. Later in the series another team included two women, Gwyneth Dunwoody and Beryl Reid. You will note that in each case the 'other woman' was an actress. I was inviting quite a number of actresses around that time – Eleanor Summerfield, Irene Handl and Patricia Hayes also appeared, as well as two actors, Jack Hedley and Colin Welland. Sylvia Syms and Sheila Hancock were already featured, as were Bryan Forbes and Rosamund John, who had retired from acting.

It was beginning to show. A correspondent took me to task for inviting show-biz names on to the programme, presumably in an effort to boost audiences. He wanted more politicians, as the programme was surely basically a political programme; more intellectuals from whatever walk of life, and a generally more informed and informative outlook. I replied that we'd always aimed to include at least one non-political member of the team and denied that it was basically a political programme – its function was just as much to entertain as to inform. But he had a point.

There are many actresses, accustomed to a script, who become inarticulate when deprived of one. However, there are others, with strong opinions and a deeply-felt community sense, who are able to express themselves persuasively – and always in a well-produced musical voice which is pleasant to listen to. They are also well known. 'Oh, I'd love to meet them' was the reaction I wanted from our listeners on hearing who was to be on the team. When reading the names to the local organizer over the telephone, I was depressed if the response was '*Who*?'

I recruited from the theatrical profession and television in order to arouse this sense of expectancy. In trying to find new women, especially, there seemed few other fields which could give me quite what I was looking for, apart from literature and journalism, already quite closely explored. Politics, yes, of course; but you had to be selective. There was a distressing tendency for Labour women to sound like viragos and Conservative women to sound as if they were perpetually opening bazaars. I don't deny that there would have been many other women, perhaps among academics or the social services, who would have been intellectually superior and more articulate than my show-biz recruits. You could certainly mount a much more searching, intelligent and informative discussion programme than *Any Questions?* but you would almost certainly lose much of the entertainment value and the glamour.

In June 1972, the opposition to the Heath Government's Industrial Relations Act reached a climax in the case of the dockers who were sent to prison for defying the ruling of the Industrial Relations Court, only to be rescued by the Official Solicitor. The team at Hastings that week included David Price, Conservative MP for Eastleigh, Malcolm Muggeridge and Lord George-Brown, and they were asked: 'Can the Industrial Relations Act work, after considering the events which have occurred this week?'

> PRICE: The answer is 'Yes', but it depends what people mean by working. I've never held the view that this Act was going to deal with the real teeth and guts of industrial relations; and I think anyone who pretended it did doesn't know what industrial relations are all about. But I believe as a long-stop – rather in the same way as nobody pretends that the law really regulates the relationships between husband and wife, but it's still necessary to have a certain background of law, not least when marriages break up – this is where I think the Industrial Relations Act is useful. I think it's also useful in respect to getting some concept of contract into our affairs.

> MUGGERIDGE: The point is, if people realized it – which of course they don't – the whole system of law is in the process of breaking down, because our society's breaking down. And therefore this particular law, which was duly passed by Parliament, has become completely farcical. A shop steward says, 'I'm not going to take any notice of this law,' and then another court says that in saying that he hasn't put himself into contempt, and therefore one way and another I think it has become a total farce. But

it's not alone in that. You'll find that more and more laws, as we go on, become both unobserved and farcical. That's how things break down.

GEORGE-BROWN: It's not farcical, it's tragic, because workers, trade unionists, managers, whoever we are, we all know that there is something gone wrong with the industrial situation of Britain. Now, I never thought bringing in the law was going to help. But, somehow, somebody has got to bring back some order into our industrial situation. The better paid workers have really got to accept that it's time they stood back and allowed the lesser paid workers to come up a little bit nearer to them. And if what happened as a result of this week is that we're going to get anarchy, and that the stronger are going to speak more powerfully, then I think it's a tragic week, and I think it's up to everybody here – everybody, whatever side of the outfit they're on – to try to use a bit of sense about it. But the law won't do it.

MUGGERIDGE: But, George, if the law can't do it, who is going to do it? Parliament obviously isn't, because Parliament's passed a Bill, and the Bill by universal consent has produced a farcical situation.

GEORGE-BROWN: At the end of the day, it's whether people will do it, and passing a law which says they must do it, and in default of doing it, you will send them to prison, doesn't work. And this is why a democracy is different from a dictatorship. It's very, very tough trying to persuade the people – individuals – that they have the responsibility, they must act sensibly.

I remember Vic Feather, by then General Secretary of the TUC, telling me, on our train journey back from the programme at Hull, that he thought the Government was wrong to bring in such a controversial Bill as the Industrial Relations Act without having had a very large majority at the General Election. The implication being that a government with a comparatively small majority should confine itself to legislation about which there was a consensus.

I thought that when we were in Hull we would at any rate be assured of strong audience support for Vic Feather when he was defending picketing. I was wrong. Here was a large audience, in Hull of all places, with every opportunity for anyone who wanted to attend *Any Questions?* to get a ticket, and yet we might have still been at Hove, where Barbara Castle had been booed by the audience for saying that the Industrial Relations Act was intended to damage and weaken the trade unions. Vic battled bravely, but he not only had the audience but also the other members of the team against him – Isobel Barnett, Alan Whicker and Patrick Moore. Patrick played to the gallery and muttered and gesticulated while Vic was trying to make a rather difficult case. As I told Patrick afterwards, using his favourite metaphor, it wasn't cricket, and he agreed. Nice man that he is, he went to the station bookstall the following morning while we were waiting to catch our train and bought a copy of his latest book and presented it to Vic, suitably inscribed, as a peace-offering.

Our visit to Hull was one of several coinciding with BBC Weeks organized by local radio. At two of them, Hove and Liverpool, despite my protests, we performed in a tent. Senior engineers soothed me by saying there were no technical reasons why *Any Questions?* shouldn't be broadcast from a tent. Maybe there were no technical reasons, but it appeared to have escaped their notice that canvas does not keep out extraneous noises in the way that walls do. It wasn't too bad at Hove, though we suffered from a certain amount of traffic noise, but at Liverpool it was sheer hell.

We were adjoining an area where helicopter flights were taking place, and every so often the team's words would be drowned as another helicopter took off. We were just a small part of the large Liverpool Show, and the audience drifted in and out of the tent throughout the broadcast. Some of them didn't know the programme and, after a bit, clearly didn't want to know it, either. Alison, who has a keen sense of humour, fell about at the spectacle of me trying to cope during my warm-up with a far less genteel audience than I was accustomed to in the villages down south.

It was at another BBC Week, in Nottingham, that I ran into some internal trouble over remarks made by Paul Foot in answer to a question about the resignation of the Home Secretary, Reginald Maudling, owing to his involvement in matters which were the subject of police investigations. Paul, as was his wont, was outspoken, but I don't remember it occurring to me that I ought to consider whether any of his remarks should be cut out of the Saturday repeat for legal reasons.

On Monday morning, London was on the phone. Had I taken legal advice? I pointed out that I had driven back from Nottingham all the way home after the broadcast and got up rather late on Saturday morning. How was it possible to get legal advice – our legal department would need more than the summary I could give them? They would want to know precisely what was said, by all the members of the team; it wasn't just a question of quoting one sentence.

In the event, nothing was heard from Reginald Maudling, and in conversations held on my next visit to London, it was clear that members of the Legal Department were by no means unanimous over whether some of the remarks should have been deleted. If lawyers couldn't agree, what hope had I? Anyway, one always has to bear in mind that to delete something may be an admission that it was defamatory – and the person whose remarks are deleted may object.

As a result of this uncertainty, a new procedure was set up. The programme was recorded on the site of the broadcast by our engineers on a cassette, which I took home with me and if there was anything I was doubtful about, I could play it over the telephone to someone in the Legal Department. Life was made easier after I discovered that one of the lawyers habitually listened to *Any Questions?* on Friday evenings, so he knew what I was talking about. In fact, sometimes when I rang up he would greet me: 'Yes. I thought I'd be hearing from you!'.

1972/73

At the start of our new series there were just three months to go before this country's entry into the EEC. The team at Birmingham – it was another of those BBC Radio Weeks – included Ludovic Kennedy, Russell Braddon and Richard Marsh, and they didn't seem overjoyed at the prospect of joining the Common Market.

KENNEDY: My real fear is that when we go into the Common Market, people will go on thinking things are just the same, and the unions will go on asking for outrageous demands, and employers will go on in the way they do, and nobody will change anything at all, and if this happens we really will be in a very precarious state indeed.

BRADDON: How much homework have you done for this thing which is about to happen to you next January? I suspect – not enough. I think you're going to be clobbered.

MARSH: If we go in thinking it's going to be an easy ride, this country will get clobbered so hard it will really wonder what's happened, we certainly won't get big benefits within five years. Our job is to ensure that we have our role in the future.

Any Questions? teams had been talking about whether or not to enter the EEC for something like twenty years. The fact that we were now in didn't discourage people from putting exactly the same sort of questions about the advantages and disadvantages. In the edition of 22 June

1973, at Ludlow, Denis Healey spoke out in answer to this question: 'After six months, does the panel consider that the Common Market agricultural policy is working as intended, and what alternatives would they like to make?'

'It certainly isn't working as it was intended by anybody except the French Government; it's doing them very well and it's doing the Dutch very well. But the real trouble with it is that it's making housewives all over Europe, not only in Britain, pay a lot more for their food in order to make the rich farmers richer without really helping the poor farmers; and it's producing idiocies like pushing up the price of butter all over western Europe and then selling it at a fifth of that price to the housewife in the Soviet Union. I think that the thing that needs changing if you have a common agricultural policy – and I've a strong suspicion that probably it would be more sensible at this stage for each country to deal with its own farmers in the way that suits it best – but if you've got to have a common policy, the sensible thing is not try to help a small section of farmers by increasing the price of food but to help the farmers who really need it by increasing their incomes. And that, in a way, is what we used to do with the sensible old agricultural policy we had in Britain.'

Denis Healey was in the team on 17 November 1972, the week Freddy Grisewood died, and he paid this warm tribute to Freddy: 'I think he was one of the kindest and most friendly people that it's ever been my privilege to meet. For a young man, as I was when I first met him appearing on this terrifying programme, where any word misplaced could produce a thousand letters of protest, he was the most helpful chairman one could ever hope to meet, and underneath this immense kindness and gentlemanliness, if that isn't an old-fashioned word, there was enough steel to push me in the way I ought to be going.'

And then, as Freddy would have wished, we got on with the programme, and a very good programme it turned out to be. I remember one particular exchange between Robin Ray, star of the TV programme, *Face the Music*, and Edward du Cann on the subject of keeping diaries.

RAY: I think there's something incredibly squalid

about keeping a diary. It's very much like keeping press cuttings. I mean, imagine going home after you've had a perfectly good evening and meal – instead of going to bed drunk or happy or however one does go to bed, you sit down at your little desk and you start scribbling down what everybody said and who said what about whom. I think that's a dreary way of living one's life.

DU CANN: What bothers me is Robin Ray's habits. I want to know why he goes to bed either drunk or happy. Why don't you go to bed drunk *and* happy?

It was in November that the BBC celebrated its fiftieth anniversary and, as our contribution to the festive spirit we wallowed in nostalgia, going back yet again to Winchester and having two members of the original team with us, John Arlott and Jack Longland. John Arlott hadn't been on the team for nearly eighteen months, and in answer to my letter of invitation, he replied sardonically that his solicitor had agreed to the exhumation. The other two were almost as long serving – Mary Stocks and Ted Leather. It was here that I had my second brush with television, when BBC at Southampton decided to produce a programme featuring the Hampshire-born John Arlott, and including part of the *Any Questions?* discussion at Winchester. However, compared with the *Yesterday's Men* outfit, the Southampton boys were surreptitious and the only real hardship was seeing in the final programme what appeared to be an overdrawn amateur performance in a minor role in *Charley's Aunt* who turned out to be me doing my warm-up.

Television again invaded us at the end of the year. One of the current affairs programmes was doing a feature on Jeremy Thorpe and wanted to include film of him taking part in *Any Questions?*. We were at Teignmouth in Devon. The film crew arrived in the afternoon just as I was leaving the hall to go to the hotel to meet the team; I left under the impression that agreement had been reached that the film camera would remain unobtrusively at the back of the hall. When I returned in the evening, I found the camera installed on the stage on a tripod just by the end of one of the tables. I bowed to the inevitable, as graciously as possible, and the live broadcast started.

We had just about got used to the camera's baleful presence, when the cameraman lifted it off the tripod and started wandering around the stage, between the team and the audience, taking shots from every conceivable angle. The team bore it all with remarkable equanimity, though Arthur Marshall, making his first appearance, found it disconcerting to have to talk with a camera pointing up his left nostril, and rather hoped this didn't happen every time.

(DJ: *Absolutely typical of people with cameras. They do believe they're more important than anyone else. Stills cameramen are just the same. You must wait for them; they put you in stupid poses; but if you don't do what they want they make you feel you are being obstructive.*)

Jeremy was on the team again at Peterborough on 16 February, an occasion when my mind must have gone blank as I was considering the questions, because I stupidly chose one about a judge's recent decision to reduce the compensation of a car accident victim who wasn't wearing a seat belt. What I had overlooked was that Jeremy's wife had been killed in a car accident. David avoided bringing Jeremy into the discussion and I apologized to Jeremy afterwards, but it was a disagreeable few moments when I realized what I had done.

A fortnight later I was taking the chair myself, under tragic circumstances. David's son had been killed in a road accident in Israel and when Friday came, David was still in Israel. That programme, from Appleton, near Warrington, was understandably subdued.

Driving up in the car with Alison that day, we heard an item on the news about an act of cannibalism, in which a pilot whose plane crashed in the Arctic ate human flesh to survive. We turned to each other and said: 'Well, *that's* something we shan't have a question on this evening.' And yet, for some reason which I cannot explain, I changed my mind, and when a question was submitted, asking how the panel felt they would react in a similar situation, I accepted it.

When I say I cannot explain, I *had* to explain in answer to letters of protest which reached me the following week. I replied that a current affairs programme with the title *Any Questions?* should not accept the premise that any topical issue which might offend any listener should necessarily be excluded, though the producer should consider what was and was not in good taste. Exactly. It was a mistake to have accepted the question.

This programme also gave rise to ructions of a political nature. It was a matter of balance. I had Tony Greenwood, former Labour minister; Lord Robens, also a former Labour minister, but who had, in my view, moved discernibly to the Right; a young leftish journalist, Anna Coote, and Russell Braddon, certainly of the Right, but not an orthodox supporter of the Heath Government. A mild protest came from the Conservatives, perhaps sparked off by a discussion about Dick Taverne's victory in defiance of the official Labour Party in a by-election in Lincoln:

> BRADDON: There seems to be nobody in any party in this country, left, centre, middle, right, whatever, who speaks to us in words we can understand; who convinces us that he has a policy to which he will adhere; who gives us a policy about which we've been previously consulted; who doesn't in fact treat us with contempt once he's got to the place that he wants to, which is Westminster.
>
> ROBENS (in answer to a point made by Anna Coote): I wouldn't agree that the Labour Party is a centre party. In my years of experience in the Party I've seen it infiltrated by all the left-wingers – Marxist, Maoists, Trotskyists, the lot – and today the Labour Party is a federation of the most amazing ideas and has ceased really to be in my opinion a coherently thinking party. And for my money I would like to see a clean sweep and I would like to see a new democratic party in this country which was composed of the centre and right wing of the Labour Party and the centre and the left wing of the Conservative Party and, if they were to run the show for about five years, we may get some common sense. There can be no

doubt that the trade union movement is certainly being very much infiltrated by the Left – by Marxists – and that they have now got virtual control over the Labour Party and the Parliamentary Party.

On 30 March at the Open University, Milton Keynes, Lord Hill returned to the programme after an absence of ten years – he had been lost to us by reason of being Chairman of the ITA and then of the BBC. (I had wanted to invite him in the former capacity, but London vetoed the idea.) The former Radio Doctor was in very good form; it brought back memories to hear what Jeremy Thorpe once described as 'that rich, bed-pan voice'. A true professional, he picked up the technique again just as if he had never been away, especially in answer to the question 'Does the team think that zero population growth is a necessary aim for this country and if so, what legislation is required to achieve it?'

'What the hell's "zero population growth"?' he demanded. 'All you young people go home tonight and say to yourselves, "We've agreed on zero population growth." I think that we're in danger of being bamboozled. I remember twenty to twenty-five years ago, when I used to offer advice on the air that nobody ever took, and I once said in a misguided moment, "Britain needs more babies." The statisticians were telling us by forward projection of their figures that the population was declining and I thought I must encourage a little joyous exercise. I never had a more hostile post, and the tenor of it was this: "That's our business. To hell with the State telling us what we're going to have by way of family. It's our business." But in those days, the statisticians told us population was declining. Now they tell us it's rising; now they speak to us if you've got five children, as I have, as if you've been engaged in a life of obscenity and indecency! What rubbish it all is! People will have the families they want. The statisticians may be right but, my goodness, they may equally well be wrong.'

On 4 May we were at Thornbury in Gloucestershire and the team, including Anthony Wedgwood Benn, Nicholas Scott, then Conservative MP for Paddington South, and

Bernard Levin, were faced by this pertinent question: 'What does the team think about MPs who advocate comprehensive education, yet send their own children to selective schools?'

BENN: I think it's a matter for them. I wouldn't want to comment.

SCOTT: I've never been a particular advocate of one hundred per cent comprehensive secondary education , although I can see that a gradual extension of comprehensive education has a very great deal to be said for it. But I do think that public men have a right to distinguish between the advocacy of a policy which they believe can bring results for the people they represent and the personal decisions they have to make about things that affect their children. And I think it would be very wrong if we sought to impose the consequences of their public statements on members of their family in every single case.

BENN: Well, now we've moved on from commenting on other MPs to comprehensive education – which is what I hoped we could talk about as far as the question is concerned – of course, the truth is we haven't got comprehensive education. If you take London, for example, or Birmingham: the selective system lies side-by-side with the comprehensives so that the grammar schools cream off a certain group and the comprehensive schools are not wholly comprehensive. Now, I am strongly in favour of every child having access to the mainstream of education, and the effrontery of education is to select at eleven by examination or in any other way those children they think worth educating and then shunt the rest off to the labour market as quickly and as conveniently as can be done. This is an outrage and denies this country and its children the opportunity to which they're all entitled, to be able to go to a school where they have got access to all that schools can today offer. And that is the case for comprehensive education, and I deeply believe in it.

LEVIN: Ah, but the question isn't about whether the

team is in favour of comprehensive education or not. It's about: what do we think of MPs who advocate comprehensive education yet send their own children to selective schools? And this is a very important problem, and Nicholas Scott giving in effect the answer that Wedgwood Benn ducked, I think disgracefully, is nonetheless wrong. He said – and it is a fine liberal principle – that we should not seek to impose on public men certain standards of behaviour in how they have their children educated. Well, as a principle as stated, of course I agree. But the fact is that in this particular situation the public men in question are actually seeking to impose on the rest of the country the standards in which they believe.

There is, as Benn has just given, the case for comprehensive education and nobody suggests they're hypocrites and don't really believe in it; they do believe in it. But it's all very well to say: we mustn't impose it upon them because that inhibits their freedom of choice. The fact is that if the policy itself inhibits the freedom of choice for other people, they then have got a very important moral dilemma. As a matter of fact, there is an answer to it, and it is this – which in fact is from time to time given, albeit in a rather shamefaced way: that a man may say, a Labour MP who sends his children to a selective school while advocating comprehensive education, 'It's all very well for me to make sacrifices for myself in furtherance of my principles; am I entitled to make sacrifices of my children in furtherance of my principles?'

But there is another point even beyond that one, which is we all know damn well if in fact a law was passed saying that all Cabinet Ministers of a party advocating comprehensive education – or indeed, any party, actually, now I come to think of it – should send their children to State schools; if that law was enacted on, let us say, a Thursday afternoon, not later than the following Tuesday morning £500 million would be voted to improve the State education of this country. And that seems to me to be the essence of the scandal and the hypocrisy, not people who honestly want the best for their children while advocating something else for everybody else's.

BENN: Well, first of all, I won't criticize colleagues – I'm sorry if that's ducking the question, but I won't. I don't think the idea of comprehensive education is to impose anything on anybody, but to remove a barrier on thousands of children every year who are denied access to education. It's the removal of something that's imposed. But secondly, of course, there's no sacrifice because comprehensive education is the best education available and any sensible parent would send their child to a comprehensive school.

SCOTT: But, you know, that really is an assertion that you're making well in advance of any concrete evidence. Of course secondary modern schools were in many cases inferior, and they could only be brought up to a reasonable standard by a spread of the concept of comprehensive education. But there are as many different paths to comprehensive education as there are paths to Heaven, and to suddenly say that in 1966 or '70 or '76, we are going to impose this and remove the choice and remove the traditions of excellence that exist inside the selective system seems to me certain to dilute the quality of education and that is not something this country can afford.

On 1 June at Cookham, Berkshire, just after the announcement of Princess Anne's engagement, a team consisting of Robin Ray, Alex Jarratt, then Managing Director of the *Daily Mirror* group, Michael Parkinson and Katharine Whitehorn, were asked if they envied Mark Phillips the life he would lead from then on.

JARRATT: Without any disrespect to Princess Anne, I can't think of a worse fate. Think of the public occasions that he's going to have to attend in future – every fête, every sort of public meeting, every flower show that goes on during the course of the year – and think of my colleagues in the Press for the rest of his life on his tail. It's nice to marry into that sort of money right from scratch, but I don't think it's worth it.

PARKINSON: Speak for yourself.

RAY: I've just been totting up what I think Mark Phillips can reasonably expect to get: possibly a house in Hyde Park, £100,000 a year, instant promotion to Brigadier; whereas, looking back on my own relationship with my own dear wife, whom I love as Mark Phillips obviously loves Princess Anne, I got an electric toaster, a stone hot-water bottle and a copy of the *Kama Sutra*. I would just like to say I would be more than happy, and if the engagement is off I'm open to proposals.

JARRATT: You can't ride, Robin.

PARKINSON: I always feel on an occasion like this that it brings out the worst in fellow members of my craft. This absurd daily regurgitation of what is, after all, a very ordinary story: two people fall in love and want to get married. Why this awful nonsense that goes on incessantly? We're all of us in television wanting more money to do programmes about important things, and yet the other morning the BBC sent down – at huge expense, I've no doubt – an outside broadcast unit to King's Cross station to see a perfectly ordinary puffing train arrive on platform twelve. What happened is that the train arrived and the reporter said, 'Well, the train's arrived.' As it had. And the only conceivable news story would have been if he had got off wearing her dress and she had sprouted another head. None of which is likely to happen.

RAY: I don't want to be uncharitable, Michael, but will you go on record now that if you're offered Princess Anne and Mark Phillips for your programme, you'll turn them down?

PARKINSON: I'll have to refer you to Artists Bookings.

WHITEHORN: Well, they won't offer them enough money, so *that* will be all right. But I take your point about how trying it is for the Press. My husband went on one of the royal tours to India, and it was a very deadly journalistic assignment simply because here was something about which you can't say anything but good. And when you work it out, most bits of journalism that are any fun are saying something fairly – shall we say? – two-edged about somebody. How can you ever make happiness news? Well, actually, I don't mind them making this particular sort of happiness news. I think it's a welcome antidote to some crumbling old lord who has to buy sex leaping up and down in bed with a couple of call girls. I think it's rather nice to have the other side stated and you can probably only ever print happiness if it's got a crown on it.

1973/74

During the summer break I presented six programmes under the title *25 Years of Any Questions?*, extracts from some of the outstanding editions since 1948. These were popular and led up towards the climax of our twenty-fifth birthday on Friday, 12 October, when once again the broadcast came from Bristol.

The climax itself was a bit of a let-down. I had thought we might mark the auspicious occasion by including some people we would not normally be able to include – a Government minister or the Leader of the Opposition – as well as some international star of the magnitude of David Niven or Alistair Cooke, who might conceivably be more impressed by the thought of a twenty-fifth birthday gala than by an ordinary edition of a radio series. But no such luck. In the end I settled quite happily for the seasoned and valued contributors Mary Stocks, Isobel Barnett and Richard Marsh, with Kenneth Williams as a prestigious and unpredictable newcomer. Probably due to inadequate briefing on my part, he did not appear very happy with the role in which I had cast him, and, all in all, it was not one of our better programmes.

Mary caused some consternation among the London contingent by making some very tart references to the Arabs in general and the Syrians in particular, apparently based on a disagreeable experience at a Syrian border post. The general feeling, not only inspired by this outburst, was that Mary, then over eighty, was understandably coming to the end of her broadcasting career. I was determined that she should not be allowed to drift away, in the way that Ralph Wightman and Arthur Street had disappeared from the programme without any formal recognition of their services to it over so many years.

Of course, it's not quite as easy as it may sound, because one seldom knows at the time that a particular appearance is to be the final one. People are invited less frequently as they grow older and inevitably lose some of their freshness and vitality, and become more repetitive; gradually they make way for others who bring a new spontaneity and dynamism to the programme. It's a mistake to allow the listeners' happy memories of their younger selves to become tarnished.

I didn't want this to happen to Mary. I doubted whether listeners would yet have noticed any reduction in her high standards of performance, but they soon would. So I wrote her what I fondly imagined to be a very tactful letter, thanking her for all she had done for the programme and suggesting a small farewell dinner party. There was clearly no diminution in her powers of invective. She appeared to find the parallel I had drawn with Street and Wightman an unattractive one, and she rejected the invitation. However, she later relented, as Frank Gillard, with whom she had a very close friendship, was going to be there, and the party took place, pleasant but subdued. I came to the conclusion that there just isn't any tactful way of going about this.

The following week's edition had some lingering repercussions, and at one time looked like involving the programme in its third legal action. We had this question: 'Sir John Stratton, chairman of Britain's biggest meat marketing group, has received a pay rise of £16,416. The workers in one of his factories are restricted to a pay rise of £2.26 per week. Is this likely to encourage the trade unions to co-operate with the working of Phase Three?'

In the course of the discussion, Lord Robens and Lady Howe, wife of Sir Geoffrey Howe, were critical of Sir John Stratton's pay rise, coming at the time of the Heath Government's rigid pay restraint. Lord Robens referred to 'getting round the rules' and Lady Howe spoke of him having made a song and dance about the salary increase. There had been a great deal of criticism in the Press that week, and I looked upon it as fair comment on a matter of public interest and didn't delete anything from the repeat. We broadcast a few letters in *Any Answers*, evenly divided for and against Sir John Stratton.

The next day a letter arrived from Sir John to the Director-General, asking for an apology to be broadcast, and with the sinister final sentence: 'Meanwhile my solicitors are obtaining the opinion of leading counsel.' At first our legal department advised against making an apology. They thought a jury would hardly be likely to be very sympathetic towards Sir John. Then, a week later, the situation changed. Sir John announced that he was intending to give away his bonus. A jury might now regard him as a good guy after all. At a press conference, Sir John stated: 'I am advised by leading counsel that some of the statements made in public are libellous and I shall be taking steps accordingly.'

We had to move fast, to get our apology in before a writ for libel was issued. But we had to obtain the agreement of Lady Howe and Lord Robens. This took time. However, we were all set to broadcast the apology at the beginning of the programme on 14 December, which was coming from Carlisle, and I got on the train armed with the agreed wording.

Reading all the newspapers, I found them full of stories of pay restraint, of miniscule rises, everyone screwed down to the last penny, and I suddenly got cold feet. On Crewe station I rushed to the telephone and rang our Legal Department. 'If we solemnly read out this statement, about a pay rise of £16,416 being permitted by the Pay Code, the audience are just going to fall about,' I said. But they were adamant. It had to be done.

That evening I prepared the ground very carefully. I warned the audience what was going to happen; begged them not to react in a way which would defeat the object of the exercise. In the event, they were as good as gold, and the apology, the explanation that the sum was paid under a profit-sharing agreement made with the company in 1962, that it had not been intended to imply that Sir John had circumvented the pay code, was received in complete silence.

A year later John Stratton appeared on *Any Questions?* at Charles Curran's suggestion. He was an effective broadcaster; there was a touch of Montgomery about his style. But, as often happens, his second appearance didn't live up to the promise of his first, and there was no opportunity of trying again because he died not long afterwards.

Early in November, the programme was affected by industrial action for the first time. There was a dispute in the Post Office which meant that there were no land lines to carry the broadcast from Harston, near Cambridge, to the BBC Control Room. However, we got round the difficulty. The programme was recorded on site about ninety minutes earlier than usual, and then the tape was taken to a BBC studio in Cambridge, where there were permanent lines to London, and played from there.

In October that year fighting had broken out in the Middle East again – the Yom Kippur War, with the Arabs flexing their muscles over the oil weapon and British motorists feeling the pinch. Concurrently, there was industrial action by the power workers and a proposed overtime ban by the coal miners which developed into the confrontation which finally brought down the Heath Government.

A questioner at Winsford, Cheshire, on 9 November asked for the team's reactions to these disputes in view of the oil shortage. The team included the writer and broadcaster Jacky Gillott and Alastair Burnet.

> GILLOTT: The oil shortage is not the responsibility either of the power engineers or the coal miners; the responsibility in the short and immediate term is that of the Arabs who are withholding supplies, but more importantly and in the long term it is the fault of governments who pursue a particular form of economic strategy which is insanely voracious of oil – people who have over the years geared our entire

economic system to a very large degree to a single fuel source; and, of course, have made us vulnerable as a result. Now we really mustn't mix these two questions up; we must criticize our governments for having secured us like alcoholics on to the bottle of oil and we must consider quite separately the situation of the miners and the power strikers.

BURNET: I think if there is an oil shortage – and there isn't one yet in this country, it depends on how the flow of oil goes – plainly if one is a trade union leader and one does want higher wages, it's extremely sensible to take action at such a time. And one of the reasons why the miners are taking action is that strikes in this country do normally succeed in getting a better award than was offered before the strike began.

GILLOTT: Mr Joe Gormley has advanced the argument, and it may appear superficially to be specious, that it is actually in the nation's interest for the miners to have an overtime ban at this moment and to thereby increase the money which is paid to them. Because, he says, in view of the likely oil shortage we need men in the mines.

The following week, in Barry, Glamorgan, we were talking about inflation. A questioner asked, 'How can we overcome our present difficulties and ensure a stable economy?' The team included Enoch Powell, John Cole, then deputy editor of the *Guardian*, and Brian Morris, Professor of English at the University of Sheffield.

POWELL: Oh, dear. Oh, dear, oh, dear, oh, dear. Not on my night off, surely? I have to tell the Government the answer to this day in and day out. It's a bit hard on a Friday night. But just a caveat to the questioner. He said 'ensure a stable economy'. Now, nothing that's known to man can ensure a stable economy, if by economy we mean the total productive, economic experience of a nation, because the nature of the world is such that there is constant change and fluctuation and it's no good imagining that you're going to walk out of history into some sort of stable economic regime. That just doesn't exist; but governments can provide some approximate stabilities, and the stable value of money, in my opinion, is one that they ought to do their best to provide and, in modern times, commonly fail to. To sum up a long story as briefly as I can, it is really governments that cause inflation because they find it convenient to inflate. They find it an easy way of financing their extra expenditure from which they very often hope electoral benefit, and they find that it gets them out of the problems of matching expenditure with taxation which, after all, lies at the heart of democracy. The essence is, you have to say to the people, if you want this, then, at the same time, you have got to pay for it. Inflation is really a way of fluffing that and of fudging the question. So the answer is that governments have got to manage their taxation and their expenditure so that they match one another and that they do not find themselves pouring out the flood of additional money which has swept the rise in prices in this country up to ten per cent per annum and more.

COLE: I'm afraid Enoch Powell and I, as I anticipated, are not going to agree on much of this. I think ordinary people have a lot more to do with it than he is prepared to admit. We're never going to get a perfectly stable economy without a prices and incomes policy. I'm not very happy about the present Government's Prices and Incomes Policy. In my experience a voluntary one is the only one that is likely to last over a long period, because this is the most intimate area of a man's economic life, what he is paid, and he will do it if there is some form of social contract between Government, employers and trade unions and he feels he is getting a square deal in the tax system, in the way the Government treats him in the social services, he will be prepared to exercise some restraint, to have some regard for the common good, but only if the social contract is there.

MORRIS: I've been reading the newspapers today and

in one of them I read how Mr Enoch Powell would solve this particular problem, and in another of them I read how Professor Nicholas Kaldor would solve this particular problem, and one of the surprising things to me was that both Mr Powell and Professor Kaldor said that the answer was to cut government spending and to increase the level of taxation. Mr Powell did, at least, have the grace to say that this would be an unpopular measure. When I find both Professor Kaldor and Mr Powell in agreement I am sure that they are bound to be right. I am equally sure that what they suggest is not going to take place, because what could be electorally less popular? What government, beset as this one is by every accident of fate and fortune, is going, at this stage, to raise taxation and thereby break the last of the promises that Mr Heath made at the last election and leave him with a score of absolutely zero?

POWELL: I'd like to offer Professor Morris a little encouragement in return for his brilliant demonstration of logic, and I understand he isn't a professor of logic. He says, what could be less popular than the Kaldor/Powell solution? I'll suggest an answer to that question. The continuance of inflation at the present rate or faster. I think after another year or two of this rate of inflation, that could well be more unpopular than anything which might be done to cure it, and in that I hope that there is reason for less than his total pessimism. I'd just like to come back on one point with Mr Cole who says that the people are to blame. Right, I'll take this head on and I'll select those people that are most thought to blame, the unions – the rapacious, monopolistic unions who demand outrageous increases in wages and get them. Ah, you cheer! No, no, no, no, no, no; you cheered too soon. Please imitate Professor Morris. Take it logically, take it coolly. Why is it possible for a union, which demands fifteen, twenty, twenty-five per cent to be paid fifteen, twenty, twenty-five per cent when only two or three years ago, let alone ten years ago, whatever they demanded they would've only got – what? Three, four or five per cent. It must be that there is more money going around, which enables the employer, and forces the employer if he wants any men, to pay fifteen, twenty and twenty-five per cent and renders it impossible for any union leadership not to demand fifteen, twenty and twenty-five per cent. So I still say, and I invite you to consider this calmly, that the cause of it must lie with the Government which provides the additional flood of money without which the strongest and most wicked unions in the world could never cause a spot of inflation.

COLE: I don't think that one ought to let Mr Powell on a programme like this without reminding him that he is a backbencher of a Government which was elected on the promise of keeping taxes down, of reducing taxes, and if you ask me for the single act of this Government which made a stable economy more difficult to achieve, it was the early budgets in which direct taxation was cut to the benefit of the better off members of the population and to the detriment of the less well off. This made it much more difficult to convince trade union leaders, and ordinary trade unionists, and housewives, who've seen their food prices going up by forty per cent since the Government came to power, it made it more difficult to convince them that they should be the only people to exercise restraint.

MORRIS: Let me go back to one absolute, basic central essential. Get rid of greed.

POWELL: Act of Parliament?

MORRIS: Certainly not by Act of Parliament – they've never got rid of greed in their lives since Simon de Montfort's date. When I found that my own little trade union, which is a harmless little affair, was negotiating fiercely and eventually successfully to get us a pay rise, I remember sitting back and thinking, 'Good, splendid, high time, too, quite right! Professors are the most underpaid and overworked crowd of people in this nation.' But as soon as somebody else, as soon as the Amalgamated Engineers or the miners or somebody else wanted a pay rise, I found myself saying, 'Good gracious me, these people – greed, that's all it is, give them an inch they take a mile.' The way to solve our present difficulties, the way to ensure a stable economy, is to get rid of personal greed and let those of us who are without sin cast the first stone at the Government.

In the last programme of 1973, a team including Richard Crossman and Reginald Maudling were faced by this question at Charlbury in Oxfordshire: 'Will it ever be possible in a free society to organize wages, salaries and profits on a just basis, avoiding the conflict which exists now?'

CROSSMAN: All the evidence so far, first from us and now from the mess which is being made by the Heath Government, shows that if you go on trying to impose these elaborate norms, forcing them on people, you achieve the most appalling confrontation and I don't think that this is really a very good way of managing things.

MAUDLING: Could I just ask Dick how he proposes to solve the problem, in that case?

CROSSMAN: There is only one way to solve it and Reg knows the answer very well. If you don't do this, it solves itself. It solves itself, of course, by heavy unemployment and that's a fact. All these are elaborate devices to try and maintain full employment, and I want to maintain full employment, but there comes a point where the elaborate mechanisms for maintaining full employment which are bringing confrontations between miners and the City and the Prime Minister make one wonder whether Enoch Powell might not possibly be right. That's all I will say. Makes me wonder.

MAUDLING: Shocked to hear Mr Crossman, one of the intellectuals of the Labour Party, advocating a policy of substantial unemployment in order to deal with an inflationary problem which that policy would only make worse rather than better. If we had massive unemployment it would merely mean that people who had strong bargaining power would continue to get large wage increases whereas hundreds of thousands of other people would get no wages at all. Is that his policy, really?

CROSSMAN: No, it is not. I didn't, of course, advocate it. I wasn't talking as a politician to another politician, but as a member of this team thinking aloud.

MAUDLING: But I asked you what you'd do.

CROSSMAN: All I'm saying to you is, that there is this fact that if we don't introduce these elaborate mechanisms, it will in a sense solve itself. That's all I was saying.

MAUDLING: At whose expense?

CROSSMAN: At the expense of those who cannot discipline ourselves in this particular way. I mean, I don't think a modern community can be expected suddenly to sit down and have all this abracadabra about norms laid upon them and what they're allowed in Phase One, Phase Two and Phase Three. I can't see how you can ask people, and they won't, of course, in the last resort. They get damned angry and then all these rows occur. This mechanism which Mr Maudling and all his colleagues went to the country in 1970 saying was totally improper, totally impracticable, wholly useless, proven useless by ourselves – and I agreed with them, because we tried it and I agree with every word they said about it – and then, blow me, if they aren't at it again, another damn U-turn and there they are busily doing exactly what they said was useless.

Early in February a General Election was announced, with Ted Heath fighting it on the theme 'Who governs the country, the Government or the Unions?' I was a bit peeved about the election, if only because I had at last managed to persuade the actress, Diana Rigg, to take part in the programme on 8 February, and as this came within the three-week campaigning period I had to ask her to withdraw and be replaced by a candidate, though neither

Norman St John-Stevas, Roy Hattersley nor Emlyn Hooson were, in my view, an entirely satisfactory substitute for the delectable Miss Rigg.

The election also interfered with another milestone in the history of *Any Questions?*. Our thousandth edition fell on 15 February and the star-studded, non-political team I had selected had to be replaced by Denis Healey, Sir Geoffrey Howe and Des Wilson.

The election was a real cliff-hanger, and we went on the air from Wolverton in Buckinghamshire on 1 March, the day after polling day, uncertain who would be Prime Minister by the time the programme was repeated again on Monday morning (by that time, Tony Whitby had given us a second repeat). Ted Heath was still in Downing Street, taking soundings with the Liberal Party.

Dorian Williams thought the crisis called for a national government and suggested that the Queen should send for someone quite independent like Lord Robens to form a government with the best brains of all parties. Russell Braddon sardonically suggested that it might be better for the Queen to send for Joe Gormley.

In fact, the man heading the new government turned out to be Harold Wilson, and I found myself with a team for 8 March whose right wing consisted of the two men the Conservative Party seemed to blame for their having lost the election – Enoch Powell, who had not stood in the election but had recommended the country to vote Labour, and Campbell Adamson, Director-General of the CBI, who in *Panorama* had apparently been critical of the Industrial Relations Act.

In the course of the week, I received a telegram from Campbell Adamson saying he was unable to appear. I decided to strengthen the Conservative representation by inviting Norman St John-Stevas again, to replace him. I then learned from Enoch Powell's secretary that he did not think Mr Powell would be very happy about sharing the platform with a Conservative MP. By the time I had done a great deal of soothing telephoning, I knew just how Henry Kissinger must have felt.

The team was completed by Baroness Wootton and

John Cole – also recruited at short notice for reasons which escape me now – and it was a lively programme, at Nantyglo in South Wales. There was a question about the situation where no party had a majority for its policies.

> ST JOHN-STEVAS: I think in that electoral situation you have got to look at those parts of your policy which command the widest support in the House of Commons. That you must do, because if you don't do it, then in fact you will find the country plunged into another election. Enoch looks at it quite calmly. Perhaps, Enoch, you wouldn't look at it quite so calmly if you'd just fought an election, as I have.
>
> POWELL: I did and I won it.
>
> ST JOHN-STEVAS: I don't think that you won it, Enoch. You caused perhaps someone else to lose it, and that is a very different thing.

An answer to the final question was headline news the next morning. The question was: 'Do the members of the panel have any unfulfilled ambitions, and if so what are they?'

> POWELL: I have the unfulfilled ambition, but not an ignoble one, of leading the Tory Party.
>
> ST JOHN-STEVAS: There are worse things than an electoral defeat, I see!

It was difficult from then on to know where precisely to place Enoch Powell from the point of view of a team's political balance. On his next appearance he was accompanied by a Tory peer, a Labour MP and Liberal peeress. In that programme, we were still talking about the minority Government and whether a coalition was desirable. Enoch Powell commented: 'What is absurd, surely, is to say that the electorate wants a coalition because the result of an election is a dead heat. I would be very surprised if any elector went into the polling booth saying, "Now, I am going to cast my vote in such a way that the total outcome will be a deadlock." He can't do it.'

The team was also asked what they thought of their Christian names. Enoch Powell said: 'I'm thoroughly satisfied with both of mine. People look me up in the telephone directory and they say, "Oh, he's ex-directory."

I'm not ex-directory at all; the simple fact is that they don't know I was christened John. What's more, I have a great affection for my second name, which is perhaps more familiar. Now, people think that I write my name J. Enoch Powell and that the Enoch is emphasized for political and publicity purposes. This is not at all so. When I was a boy at grammar school and was hoping to be a distinguished classical scholar, there was a very elderly classical scholar of the name of J.U. Powell, who actually had the temerity to write articles on the subjects which I had decided to make my own speciality. This was terrible, it seemed to me, and therefore to avoid the possibility of his inferior work being mistaken for mine, I called myself J. Enoch Powell; that's how it started.'

We visited Penge, in Kent, on 24 May, the day the Prime Minister raised to the peerage his political secretary Marcia Williams, to the accompaniment of a certain amount of criticism. Over drinks, the team said firmly that they did not see how the subject could be avoided, and I tried to crush any cowardly thoughts about failing to select a question which might give rise to some uninhibited, even dangerous comments. I remained true to the title of the programme by accepting a general question on the honours system, so that the team could comment on the news of the day if they wanted to but weren't obliged to.

As the question was repeated, I felt a slight queasiness in the pit of my stomach. Glenda Jackson spoke first. 'I think it is an absolutely splendid award and I applaud Mr Wilson's absurd bravery in according it.'

Marghanita Laski referred to 'today's astonishing and perhaps rather devaluing news' and Malcolm Muggeridge confined his remarks to the comment, 'a rather interesting example'. And that was all. I breathed again.

Later on, I tried to persuade Baroness Falkender to appear on the programme. She replied most courteously to my invitations and even finally accepted one of them but then had to withdraw, much to my disappointment.

1974/75

We began our new series in the middle of another General Election campaign. Harold Wilson, beset by all the problems of a minority government for six months, had decided to go to the country. In the first of our special election editions, with the usual three candidates, the Liberal candidate was Christopher Mayhew, who had been the Labour candidate in one of the 1964 election editions, and the Labour candidate was David Owen. One of the audience in Bristol put this pertinent question: 'Why do politicians label themselves Tory, Labour or Liberal, when they change their coats so many times?'

MAYHEW: Let me explain that it's quite wrong to say that I left the Labour Party. I've always been a moderate member of the Labour Party, indeed on the right of the Labour Party, for more years than I care to say; and of course the Labour Party has suddenly in the last few years gone sharply left. It is the Labour Party that has left me, it is not I who have left the Labour Party. Furthermore, I still feel profoundly proud of having for many, many years actively supported the old Labour Party of Clem Attlee and Hugh Gaitskell. I think that party served the country splendidly, but today all the old opponents of Hugh Gaitskell have moved in. All the people against whom Hugh Gaitskell warned us when he made his famous speech, 'We must fight and fight again to save the party from the left-wing extremists' – and we did while he was there and we won; but under the new leadership, in spite of our great efforts, this no longer became possible and today the very people against whom Hugh Gaitskell warned moderate Labour people have moved in and entrenched themselves in the constituency parties and in the unions. If I felt there was a real chance of the moderates in the Labour Party getting together and really reinstating the old ideals and the old principles of the Labour Party I'd never have left, but I do think that I took the right course.

OWEN: Chris, it's too arrogant to assume unto yourself the sole mantle of moderation in the Labour Party. There are many other people who knew Hugh Gaitskell and loved Hugh Gaitskell and the speech you quote from the 1962 conference was not as you said it. He didn't say he'd fight and fight again to save the party from the left wing. He said he'd fight and fight again to save the party he loved and Hugh Gaitskell loved the Labour Party and for all you say about the Labour Party I don't think you ever did love it. It's a strange party. Of course we have differences, but it's a great party, it's a party that embraces a very large number of people with different views and different backgrounds. It's a party that I love and I'll stay in it and I'll fight for it, and it's a party that allows you to hold different opinions and I personally regret your leaving the party. You were a friend of mine on many issues. I think you made the wrong choice. Your position should be to stay with the party; and the fact that you can now say that none of your basic positions have changed – remember this, one of Hugh Gaitskell's great passions was fighting against injustice and inequality and that's the cement of the Labour Party and that's the cement that will always keep us together.

The following week's election edition, in Southampton, included Margaret Thatcher and Roy Hattersley who were asked: 'If, as a result of the outcome of the election, either one of the present party Leaders resigns, would the team like to see a woman as party Leader and therefore as a prospective future Prime Minister?'

HATTERSLEY: It rather depends who the woman is, doesn't it? It's very clear, isn't it, that the leader of the Labour Party who is going to be Prime Minister a week today, is as secure in his leadership of that party and the leadership of this country as he's been for the last ten years, which is very secure indeed and, therefore, I think this is what politicians call a hypothetical question, but despite the wild hypothesis I do think one thing, that there is one woman in this country, and Mrs Thatcher will forgive me for saying this, who seems to me to be a paragon of all the political virtues and that is Mrs Shirley Williams, who over the last fortnight as well as over the last ten years has demonstrated some of the highest qualities of political talent, ability and integrity, and if I was one day lucky enough to serve in a government which was led by Mrs Williams, I'd be very proud to be a member of that administration, very proud indeed.

THATCHER: Well, I wouldn't be overjoyed at the prospect of being leader of a party at the moment. Nor do I think somehow that the country is ready to have a woman leader. I remember watching the scenes at Cowley very carefully on television and, after all, a woman took a very courageous part in trying to end that strike. She said a lot of things so sensible that men hadn't thought of saying them, but then in fact some of the men, as they came out of those works, were jolly glad that the women had taken a part; others said, 'No, they should jolly well not poke their noses into it, it's our business,' and there really is a very great deal of prejudice still in this country against women and whatever you do by way of legislation, whatever you do by way of publicity, I don't somehow think that the country is ready for it, unless there really clearly is no alternative man available. I just don't see that there will therefore be a woman Prime Minister in the next ten years. Now, let's not think beyond that.

(DJ: *I went back to London afterwards from Southampton in a train without a buffet car and was looking forward to a drink. I managed to buy half a bottle of Scotch. In our compartment Margaret Thatcher sat in one corner opposite her secretary and I sat in another corner. We were drinking from the bottle – in great moderation, I hasten to say. Margaret Thatcher had taken her shoes off and undone the bow on the top of her blouse and she had her feet up. She was very tired with the campaigning, but very relaxed. She said, 'Thank heaven my constituents can't see me now.' And I said: 'It's a pity they can't.' Because, for once, she looked vulnerable and they would have loved her.*)

Roy Hattersley was right; Labour won the election with an increased majority, and therefore Harold Wilson remained as Prime Minister. The loser, Edward Heath, found his leadership challenged and just before the election of the Conservative Party Leader, with Margaret Thatcher as one of the candidates, the team at Impington, Cambridgeshire, were again asked for their views on a possible woman Prime Minister. Norman St John-Stevas said, 'Margaret has shown very great courage in coming forward and we have always been a party that appreciated courage, and I think a lot of people would feel extremely disappointed if that courage which she has shown didn't achieve its appropriate rewards.'

Shortly afterwards, Margaret Thatcher's courage did achieve the appropriate rewards. Some time earlier, I had booked her for an *Any Questions?* several months ahead, and to my delight, she indicated that she would keep the engagement.

Alas, the evening did not live up to expectations. It began badly, with the BBC staff car driver losing the way to Wotton-under-Edge in Avon. Margaret Thatcher thus arrived somewhat late at the hotel after a tiresome journey, but didn't hold it against me, beyond suggesting rather firmly that BBC drivers should be issued with maps and trained in their use.

What she may have held against me was the composition of the team. I had done my best to provide appropriate opposition, but the people I most wanted were not available, and admirably and forcefully as Sheila Hancock expressed a radical point of view, an actress could not be expected to be authoritative in the political sense, and that pleasant veteran of politics and broadcasting, Lord Houghton, was unexpectedly subdued.

Margaret Thatcher certainly held against me – and made it clear at the time in no uncertain manner – the selection of questions, and we sat together on the stage after everyone else had departed while I tried to explain the reasons for my choice. In particular, she thought it a mistake not to have included a question on education.

However, afterwards she went round the school where we were, met a lot of local people, admired the rose garden, and was very charming to everybody in a natural and unaffected way. You would have sworn there was nowhere she would rather have been at that moment than admiring the roses outside a school 120 miles from home – assuming the driver could find the way back.

On 22 November, attentive listeners might have noticed that David, in his introduction, didn't actually say where we were. A clue might have been provided by the first question: 'What steps should the Government take to curb the activities of the IRA?' The notorious bombing in the Birmingham pub had just taken place and I suppose I thought that if we kept quiet about the location until the end of the programme there was less chance of our being pestered by telephone bomb hoaxes. We kept this up until the end of the year, when we were in Holmer Green, a village near High Wycombe, and the festive spirit gave me the courage to reveal the fact to the listeners.

We had the usual sort of question about Christmas – whether the younger generation enjoyed Christmas as much as the grandparents of today did in their youth. Lord Hill's memory went back to early days – 'When, before broadcasting made us the lovable and law-abiding people we are today, we actually made our own fun at Christmas time. Aunts recited, uncles played the fiddle, there was a bowl of tangerine oranges on the piano, muscatels and almonds – and you whipped an almond every time you passed and left the muscatels. Aunts used to lift veils and plant moist but insanitary kisses on the heads of small boys. They carried with them a strange aroma. When I was a boy I thought it was the aroma of a Parisian scent. It was only later in life that I discovered it was the flavour of Halliton's oatmeal soap. In those days we made our own fun; we didn't sit glossy eyed in front of the television set, with the longest speech 'Ssh!' to the children. They were great days. Broadcasting may be the most marvellous way of doing damn all that's ever been devised but there was fun when we made our own games in our own way at Christmas time.'

We took the programme to the Bath Festival on 23 May and I managed at last to persuade Sir Arnold Weinstock, the boss of GEC, to join us. I also lured back Bernard Levin – he had gone into purdah as far as broadcasting was concerned, much to our misfortune. Both Bernard and Sir Arnold were horrified to discover that the broadcast coincided with a performance of Bach's B Minor Mass in Bath that night, and at one point I gravely feared that we should go on the air with a team of only two people. In all my future invitations to Sir Arnold I was careful to specify that intensive investigation had failed to reveal any performance of the Bach B Minor Mass within fifty miles of the *Any Questions?* location, but he still didn't accept again.

The other two members of the team, the two apparently untempted by Bach, were Norman St John-Stevas and Ann Mallalieu and one of the questioners asked whether the Americans would be justified in using armed force to secure her oil supplies or would they just make conflict between the NATO and the Warsaw Pact countries more likely.

> LEVIN: The two things are not, in fact, incompatible. She might be justified and yet cause conflict between NATO and the Warsaw Pact countries. The fact that some course of action might lead to conflict, or any other unpleasant or untoward consequence, should not in itself be a reason for not adopting it. There are worse things, after all, than conflict. And I suspect

that what would happen in practice if there were another global oil conflict, starting from another Middle East situation, if it came to the crisis, the Americans would in fact use force and Britain, while tut-tutting, would be glad that they were doing so because it would at any rate safeguard our supplies. You see, you can't answer a question like this in general terms. You can't say yes they would be justified, or no they would not be justified. There are different circumstances in different cases. I certainly would not say that there are no circumstances in which this could be justified. I can certainly envisage circumstances in which it would be and in which, despite the clamour which would instantly be raised against it, I would have to support it.

WEINSTOCK: Presumably the questioner means armed force in the sense of sending troops into the Middle East, invading Saudi Arabia and Iran and so on. I don't think there's ever been any such threat of the use of armed force. Everything would depend on the circumstances. One can imagine that if the lives and livelihoods of Americans depended absolutely on securing oil supplies, and oil supplies were unreasonably and impossibly cut off from perhaps not just the United States but the whole of Europe and the civilized world, they might be justified, in whatever sense you like to use the word, in using force.

But what would certainly be rather better than that is if all the users of oil would have a common policy *vis-à-vis* the producers of oil, and the American Secretary of State at the time of the great oil crisis suggested a Confederation of Oil Users to deal collectively with the oil suppliers. And I'm afraid the British and French were the two principal parties to scupper that plan. We and the French ran off to the Saudis and tried to make separate arrangements, which will turn out in the end not to be in our interests.

MALLALIEU: America, like most of the industrialized countries of the world, has for years enjoyed the right to obtain primary products, like food supplies, from the underdeveloped countries at a cut rate. Americans are now being asked to pay what is for those countries a more favourable rate. Those countries are at last saying, 'This is the only asset we have and we're going to make sure we get a fair price for it.' And I should like Bernard Levin to tell me under what circumstances he could possibly justify a country like America going in, intervening, either in the Far East or in any other country which supplied it with a raw material, and forcing that country to sell it at the price that America requires. I can see no justification for armed force under those circumstances at all.

LEVIN: No, but you would if people in this country were literally starving to death. Which, after all, if our enormously oil-based economy had come to a total stop because there was no oil, would literally be the case. Now, of course, I don't say that if the Arabs put the price of oil up another X dollars a barrel that would be a justification for seizing the oil by force. That's not what I'm talking about. What I'm talking about is a wholly unreasonable – I'm not talking about price now – cutting off a supply which is literally necessary for the life of advanced industrialized nations. There is a point in those circumstances where that old and, alas much abused maxim, necessity knows no law, operates.

ST JOHN-STEVAS: What the questioner is asking is really, is it ever justified to use force to defend your vital interests. I think one would give a limited assent to that. On the other hand, the possible consequences of using force in the nuclear world of today might well be that you trigger off a general war which would destroy everyone and which would make the attainment of that limited objective unjustifiable. So you first have to answer the question on that moral plane and then you have to go on to the practical considerations of whether, in a particular case of a Middle East or another country, you would in fact be successful in using force. All we could say, being British, is that our own attempt to do so, at Suez, wasn't markedly successful and therefore it would be wise to be rather prudent before rushing to the use of force in the Middle East in such a case.

WEINSTOCK: The avoidance of the use of force in international affairs, or in national affairs if it comes to that, depends upon reasonable behaviour. While there is a great deal in what Ann says, that the industrialized countries had cheap raw materials for a very long time, implying too cheap – and one doesn't know exactly what that fair price is – if the whole of the economy of the West is based on oil or raw materials at a given level of prices, any attempt to make a violent change, very suddenly, to that level of prices, will have consequences which are not reasonable because the act is itself unreasonable. And, if people behave in a reasonable way, you will get to a reasonable balance between the price of raw materials and the price of manufactured goods.If not, you get chaos in international trade, which can lead to all sorts of things.

At the beginning of the edition of 11 July 1975, David sadly commented on the death of Mary Stocks, some eighteen months after her last appearance in the programme.

(DJ: *It was particularly sad for me as she was on the very first programme I chaired. I also lost a neighbour; she lived round the corner and used to pop in and see me. I always have this picture of her, looking like a Dr Barnardo's boy orphan, with short-cropped hair brushed back, wearing a pullover with a turn-over collar. She thought of fashion not at all, except that she regretted mini skirts were not fashionable in her earlier days because she considered she had rather good legs – remember her answer to the bikini question!*)

Any Questions? owed a very great deal to Mary, and she always stressed that the debt worked in the other direction as well. I can still see her head nodding and her mouth working with relish whenever she felt she had said something outrageous, which was far from seldom. She was one of the few exceptions to another *Any Questions?*

rule that panellists tend to become less amusing as they grow older. In particular, her sense of comedy timing persisted undimmed.

For the last programme in the series we met on a very hot, thundery evening at Littlehampton, Sussex. Elizabeth Longford was a member of the team, and at that time one of her daughters, Lady Antonia Fraser, was the subject of comment in some newspaper gossip columns, so we asked Elizabeth, in our normal, courteous, thoughtful way, whether she would feel embarrassed by a question on gossip columns. She said she would welcome one. With public figures like Malcolm Muggeridge, Lord George-Brown and Lord Hailsham (who had been made a life peer and had thus reverted to his former title) comprising the rest of the team, we decided that this would be a rattling good question. Unfortunately, nobody submitted it.

What was submitted, and accepted, was this question: 'What does the team think are the reasons for the apparent inability of the middle class in this country to assert themselves or to be seen to assert themselves?'

> **GEORGE-BROWN**: I don't know what we mean nowadays by the middle class. When I started out as a trade union official, an awful long time ago it seems, I knew the working class, I was one of them, and I didn't live in Littlehampton, I lived in Peabody Buildings, Blackfriars. And when I began, one knew the working class, one knew the middle class, one knew other people were richer. The problem has changed. Most of my friends, happily because of our efforts, and you – and that's why you're sitting there like that – because of our efforts you now live a middle-class life. And I'll tell you something else, too, a lot of chaps who think they are working class because they are on wages, have a very comfortable, cosseted life, with redundancy pay, with security of employment, whereas my kids, and a lot of other kids of working-class people who now have what you are pleased to call middle-class jobs, have no security at all and these are the people who are beginning to assert

themselves, they are the children of working-class people. And with great respect, that's what we set out to do. We set out to make our children into middle-class children, we've done it, but they are a jolly sight less well off than some of you who think you've got trade union protection from here to the end of time. And I would suggest to you, it's time we stopped the class war; we fought it, we won it a long time ago, and now – can't we just talk as colleagues and friends who face much the same problems? And my kids face it a damned sight less well placed than some of you do who, in the docks, for example, in the pits, for example, walk off with hundreds of pounds a night for a one-night damned shift. Tell me a middle-class person who does that. (*Applause and boos*)

LONGFORD: I feel a sympathy for people who have acquired skills at great cost, and for a long time, perhaps seven years' training, and then in the end the salaries that they can pull down are far less than that of a sturdy able-bodied labourer. But I wouldn't encourage them to go on thinking along those lines because history doesn't stand still and the middle class, as George says, has got to merge itself into the country, it's got to forget its identity, as this one professional educated class, and it's got to believe in itself as permeating the whole country and helping it in the ways that are needed.

MUGGERIDGE: The reasons that the middle classes of this country don't assert themselves is because they have no power. The power in this country has been moved from them to, specifically, organized labour. And the middle classes cannot, through the ballot box or in any other way, assert themselves. They are in fact licked and they've got to accept it.

HAILSHAM: Well, I don't feel licked at all. I'm a professional man, I'm the son of a professional man, and I'm the father of professional children, and I'm going to fight for my continuing existence and so are they. We're not going to be licked and we're going to win, because there are two sorts of people in this country. There are those who want everybody to be like everybody else, the friends of uniformity; and there are those who think people have got a right to be different – different because they may be Roman Catholics, different because they may be Jews, different because they may want to be self employed, different because they want different standards of education, or intellectual or social amenities, different because they want to be different, and those who want to be different have got to assert themselves. And as the universality and the uniformity of society is one of the great evils of our time, we're going to win, because we're going to see that as each one of us is attacked, each minority as it is attacked by one of these great juggernauts, the great Trade Union Congress, the Labour Party, or what have you, we're going to stand together and we're going to beat them. (*Applause*)

MUGGERIDGE: I knew he'd get a colossal hand for that, and it is utter rubbish. I'll tell you why, very briefly. Throw his mind back to when his Government was in power and he was a member of it. A moment arose when there was a strike, and the power stations were picketed by trade unionists. His party is predominantly a middle-class party, none the worse for that; but when it was in power and it was confronted by that situation, there was nothing it could do, and it, in effect, capitulated. That is the proof, that is the answer to the question. If ever there was a time when, if they had any fight in them, they should have fought, that was it and they capitulated, and they capitulated because they did not dispose of power sufficient to deal with the pickets at the power stations.

HAILSHAM: Look what has happened since, the people will have more sense next time, they'll back us.

MUGGERIDGE: Next time, next time, when are you going to get a next time?

HAILSHAM: Oh yes, there'll be a next time, and it's

coming sooner than you think. (*Applause and cheers*)

GEORGE-BROWN: I have just one simple point I want to put, and I want to put it especially to those who were trying to shout me down. Please remember, the trade unions were born because people were oppressed, and because those who had the power were corrupted by the power. I just want to say to some of you, to my friends, power corrupts, absolute power corrupts absolutely, and our trade union machines are showing the proof of that now.

1975/76

In August 1975, David and his wife Caroline were on holiday in Spain with Richard Marsh and his wife. The car in which they were travelling was hit from behind by a lorry and the two girls in the back were killed.

The new series was to open at Darlington with a railway audience. That weekend marked the hundred and fiftieth anniversary of the Stockton to Darlington railway and we had been invited to provide part of the celebrations. It had been fixed several months in advance, as had some of the team. As it was a British Rail occasion, what more natural than to invite the chairman of British Rail, a frequent member of the *Any Questions?* team for many years, Richard Marsh.

His presence on the very first programme of the new series only four weeks after the tragedy was an unhappy coincidence. I imagined that everyone would realize that the invitation had gone out and been accepted well in advance (though, to my horror, I later met one or two friends who seemed to think I had done it deliberately as some sort of grisly gimmick – they must have had a very low opinion of me). So it was purely a matter of whether Dick himself wished to withdraw or appear as arranged. There were heart-searchings about it in London – I gather Peter Hardiman Scott, then Chief Assistant to the Director-General, was sent round to British Rail Headquarters to discuss the matter. Dick thought about it, and then said, 'Why not?'

(DJ: *If you've got to get to grips with something, you might as well jump in the deep end. Michael did us a good service. It got it over and done with. Both Dick and I were glad that we were able to jump in the deep end together.*)

The expected question on British Rail coupled it with the Post Office: 'Does the team consider that the increase in rail fares and forthcoming increases in postal charges will in any way solve the problem of ever-increasing deficit?'

Richard Marsh said: 'No. Increases in fares won't solve the problem; the main problem is that no government has ever yet made up its mind what it wants with either the Post Office or the railways. If it makes up its mind what it wants, the people in both those industries are capable of providing it. Whether you pay in taxes or fares you have to pay the price at the end.'

We had another question involving the nationalized industries at Nantymoel, mid-Glamorgan, on 21 November, when Sir Monty Finniston, British Steel chairman, drew attention to the fact that the Minister of Technology, Tony Benn, with whom he had had some disagreements, had been moved to another ministry while he himself remained at the head of British Steel. But his triumph was short lived.

It was a bad time for the *Any Questions?* tycoons. There had never been much problem over building up a strong team of top people from the trade union side – having been brought up the hard way, many of them were effective, if rather long-winded, debaters. But it had been a long and laborious process to acquire ten or more top people from the leading private companies and nationalized industries with some spell-binding ability, who became, recognizably, the *Any Questions?* tycoons.

In the end, we achieved a pretty impressive cast list, but then within a period of a few months it crumbled before our very eyes. Graham Dowson, a forceful advocate of private enterprise, ceased to be the Chief Executive of the Rank Organization. Lord Stokes ceased to be top man at British Leyland. Before long, Richard Marsh would cease to be chairman of British Rail and Sir Monty

Finniston, chairman of British Steel. Campbell Adamson ceased to be Director-General of the CBI. It was all very disheartening for us – and no doubt for them as well. However, Lord Kearton went on to even greater heights as boss of the new British National Oil Corporation, and the perennial Lord Robens had remained very much a top person by going from the National Coal Board to Vickers.

At Christmas, David took a much needed holiday. His neck had been badly jarred in the accident, and he was in considerable pain. I was in the chair for a couple of editions, including a very frivolous Boxing Day programme at a hospital in Bath. Arthur Marshall, not unusually, strayed entertainingly from the strict terms of a question about receiving retirement pensions at sixty. 'All sorts of jolly things happen to you when you're sixty-five, all sorts of benefits. I haven't actually got my hearing aid and I'm rather in need of it, because I'm getting a little bit hard of hearing, and the other day I was listening to the wireless with half an ear, and the news came on and I suddenly heard him say, "Severe fighting has broken out again in Debenhams." And I thought how absolutely extraordinary . . . I only hope it doesn't spread to Harrods! And I had a terrible picture of ladies lashing at each other with handbags and so on. But, of course, it turns out to be the Lebanon.'

In January, David received the Variety Club award as Radio Personality of the Year (the same award that Freddy had received in 1961).

On 9 January, at Bromley, there was a question involving Margaret Thatcher as the new Conservative Leader: 'In view of the relatively poor performance of the Opposition in Parliament recently and the seeming lack of shadow MPs having much ministerial calibre, how do the team feel Mrs Thatcher must act to create a real alternative government which would be popular with the electorate?'

The team included Lord Jacobson, former editor of the *Daily Herald* and the *Sun*, and Malcolm Muggeridge.

> JACOBSON: The one thing that is quite clear about the Opposition under Mrs Thatcher at the moment is that they don't want an election now, they don't

want to bring down the Government. I can understand why; she's relatively new to the job, but I think the problem is that we all know very well what Mrs Thatcher is against, we know that she's against everything that the Wilson Government proposes, but who knows what she is for? The fundamental problem facing the Government at the moment is an economic one. We know that certain people in the Conservative Opposition, Keith Joseph and so on, produce one set of remedies, the monetarist remedy; there are some who want a compulsory incomes policy and some who want a voluntary incomes policy. I don't know where Mrs Thatcher stands. I doubt whether anybody else does.

MUGGERIDGE: My true opinion is that the Conservative Party no longer wants power because it hasn't the faintest idea what to do about the only really important issue that arises, that is to say, how to deal with the trade unions; and therefore I think Mr Wilson's Government is perfectly safe unless they come to grief within themselves or by finally alienating the Scottish Nationalists who may well, before very long, hold the balance of power.

Within a few weeks, of course, the Labour and Liberal Parties were to have new leaders as well.

On 13 February, we were at Bedworth in South Wales and the team included Jeremy Thorpe. It was one of the producer's most spectacular anticipations of events. Jeremy was very much in the news. Allegations of a homosexual relationship, which he strenuously denied, had been made in open court by Norman Scott in a case in which it had no conceivable relevance and the Press were making a great deal of it. When Jeremy arrived at the hotel, it was clear that he was feeling the strain. I had a private talk with him. He was obviously expecting a question about the Press publicity, and had virtually memorized his reply. He was keyed up to it. It was merely a matter of deciding whereabouts in the programme to place the question.

We had the usual pleasant dinner party, and I went off

to choose the questions. To my consternation, no question was submitted either on Jeremy Thorpe or on the Press campaign, nothing that even remotely touched on the subject which must have been in the forefront of everybody's mind. This put me in a difficult position. Everybody listening to the programme would be expecting a question on this. If, as the programme went on and on, we still didn't reach it, people would assume that I had censored it. It would also be a let-down for Jeremy himself. He had a point he wanted to make; he knew exactly what he was going to say. It would be an anti-climax if he were not given the opportunity.

Rightly or wrongly, I decided that *Any Questions?* that evening must include this topic. As with the Norwich Union affair, it was a matter of persuading our hosts that their fears of causing embarrassment were unfounded. When we reached the third question in the broadcast, this is what listeners heard: 'What does the panel think about the way some of the popular Press have been hounding public figures?'

David went straight to Jeremy, who began with a historical survey of some restrictions on press reporting. Then he continued: 'The real problem, and I think this is what the questioner has in mind, is that we do allow people absolute privilege in a court of law; anyone can go into a court of law and say anything he likes, and the person who may or may not be named has no right to reply. I could, for example, go into a magistrates' court and say I plead guilty to speeding but I did it because at the time my mind was so horrified by the fact that I happen to know, and nobody else does, that the Archbishop of Canterbury has committed bigamy. Now, if I were to say that, it would be perfectly legal, and there is nothing the Archbishop of Canterbury could do about it except to say it wasn't true! In fact, usually the Press would ignore it, and they would think it was the vapourings of some lunatic, unless they thought, of course, there was a scurrilous story and they'd had a hand-out in advance, and by some miracle of chance, found themselves in this tiny magistrate's court, knowing I was going to say something about the Archbishop of Canterbury.

'I think this is an aspect of our law that we've got to look very carefully at. I believe a magistrate or a judge should be able to say to an accused, "Now, look, I don't happen to think that is relevant to the charge and I rule it out of order. If you want to repeat it, you can, and if you do repeat it I have warned you that in my view it is not relevant, it is attacking a third party who is not here, it is nothing to do with the case; if you do repeat it, the Press will be entitled to print it, but you must render yourself liable to defamation if the person involved wishes to take that action."

'That can't be done, and therefore I think that basically if you're going to keep a free Press, there has to be a little give and take on both sides. I think, for example, of the Poulson bankruptcy proceedings where counsel, perfectly properly, asked questons relating to Mr Crosland and a Mr George Brown, and of course the Press said, "Ah, George Brown's had a free holiday." It wasn't that George Brown at all, it was another George Brown – there are a lot of George Browns in this country – but none of them had any right of reply in the courts, all they could do was put out a rejoinder. It's happened with Dick Taverne, when he likewise was attacked, and therefore I think we've got to look at this.

'I can't think of any immediate cases, of course! I'm merely thinking of previous politicians who have been affected, but it does seem to me that if someone is going to abuse the right of absolute privilege, then I think there ought to be some control.

'The only other place where there is the right of absolute privilege is in the House of Commons, but of course if somebody says, "I know that the Archbishop of Canterbury has committed bigamy," there are 634 MPs who can get up and say "Prove it or withdraw, and I challenge you to say it outside the House of Commons," so that even in Parliament there is some restriction; in the courts there is none. It seems to me that this is a basic liberty which might well be protected.'

With his cautious legal mind, Jeremy concluded by

saying he was quite certain the Archbishop of Canterbury had *not* committed bigamy!

Another member of the team, Jacky Gillott, said she deeply admired the way Jeremy had conducted himself with fortitude and dignity and a resilient humour over the past few weeks. What made her really sick was that after splashing this story all over the front page, the editorials questioned Jeremy's suitability to remain in leadership of the Liberal Party. 'I think, in fact, the publicity has had quite the reverse effect, and if I may say so, I think it will not have affected your political chances adversely.'

However, when Jeremy next appeared on *Any Questions?* he was no longer the Liberal leader.

Meanwhile Harold Wilson had resigned as Prime Minister in March; that week, at Chesham, Buckinghamshire, we didn't have a question about his qualities as Prime Minister, but about the qualities most needed in the next one. Enoch Powell said, 'Of course, the incumbent who's going out had some remarkable qualities, and we can't hope that his successor will have the same infinite adaptability, the same infinite suppleness of approach to the changing circumstances. Perhaps it would be a change . . . no, I was going to say it would be a change if we went to the opposite extreme and had something completely rigid. But we had that before, didn't we? So that won't do. No, I want something as different as possible from both of them.'

The following week's team were asked, more specifically, whom they would choose as the next Prime Minister. Lord Kearton chose Tony Benn. 'A man of great ability, great courage, and in fact he was the only one of the candidates who put forward a clear, defined and definite programme. He's a man of considerable intellect and he's got a great many things going for him, but as he has dropped out I suppose I'll go for the man that Tony's going for, Michael Foot.'

Tom Jackson chose Jim Callaghan who, he believed, would inherit most of the qualities of Harold Wilson in relation to the party and to the nation.

On 14 May we had a very pleasant visit to the Dorset

village of Stalbridge, best known, at any rate among National Hunt racing people, for the gallant little grey, Stalbridge Colonist, who beat Arkle in the Hennessy Gold Cup in 1966. He had been bred there by the farmer and breeder Harry Dufosee, who, when the old horse was at the end of his distinguished career and was put up in Ascot sales as being 'ideal for point-to-points' (it was like expecting an ageing Nureyev to dance in village halls), went to the sales and bought his old favourite so that he could spend a dignified retirement in the village where he was born.

Some of this story David told to the listeners in his introduction. What he didn't mention was that Stalbridge Colonist was no longer there, because less than a month previously Harry Dufosee had given him to my wife, a long-time admirer of the grey, described by his former jockey, Stan Mellor, as the sweetest and bravest horse he had ever known. On the Sunday after the broadcast, Harry came to lunch with us, to see his beloved Colonist happily installed in his new home. When he left, he stopped the car half-way down the drive and the old horse put his head in the window to say goodbye. Four days later Harry died.

At the age of eighty-six he had been surely one of our oldest questioners when he had asked the team at Stalbridge if they thought doing away with the tied cottage would help agriculture. But two of the team – Ann Mallalieu, a former racehorse owner and keen hunter, and Lord Oaksey, who rode Stalbridge Colonist in his last race – were more at home with this question: 'Does the team think that in view of the recent tragic events at horse trials and race meetings it is time these events and others such as the Grand National were banned because of the unnecessary suffering caused to the horses involved?'

OAKSEY: I imagine that the questioner is referring to the dreadful tragedy which ended the Badminton Three Day Event when Lucinda Prior Palmer's horse fell dead after competing in the show jumping. I don't think anybody who's ever been fond of animals will doubt how Lucinda must have felt about the horse that had carried her through that admittedly severe test, so that no words can be too bad for the quite large number of people who have written to her, believe it or not, accusing her of cruelty. I have ridden in the Grand National and I admit that horses do get hurt in it; on the other hand, if there weren't racing and steeplechasing, the thoroughbred would not exist in such very large numbers and he certainly wouldn't be looked after with such loving care as he is. I believe that horses who achieve any success in steeplechasing, like Stalbridge Colonist, although he never ran at Aintree, love to jump and love to gallop. If you're going to have any test at all you've got to have a supreme test and the Grand National is the supreme test of a horse. I believe that the small number who get hurt in it are more than justified by the happy lives which a very large number lead.

MALLALIEU: When an accident happens which affects an animal or a person it is, of course, a tragedy, but anyone who has anything to do with horses will know perfectly well that if a horse doesn't want to jump it doesn't jump and, as I know to my cost, if a horse doesn't want to race it doesn't race. It's a mistake to think that by banning events such as these, which give enormous pleasure to countless numbers of people, you're going to cut down totally on suffering to horses. Looking round the countryside one sees over and over again fields with not a blade of grass in, containing one or two ponies which someone has bought thinking their child's going to enjoy riding, which are then thrown out during the winter, fed inadequately, their hooves are never trimmed – there's an enormous amount of quite unwitting suffering that goes on, caused to horses often by people who are desperately fond of them but simply don't know how to cope with them. This is where we ought to be directing our energies, not at the Grand National, not at horse trials like Badminton, which are examples of how horses should be brought up and should be cared for.

Another aspect of cruelty to animals came up at Hereford on 6 August. A questioner pointed out that the Victorian Cruelty to Animals Act was a hundred years old that month. Under it, five and a half million animals were used annually by British laboratories, two-thirds for non-medical profit, and eighty per cent without anaesthetics. 'Does the panel not consider it is time Parliament reviewed this Act?' he asked.

The team included Dennis Potter, a sufferer from a severe form of arthritis, who said, 'I exist because I take weekly a drug which is highly poisonous. One of the consequences of that drug, one of the things I was advised in taking it, is that I cannot have any more children. Now they discovered this by tests upon animals, you couldn't have a volunteer to test whether a monster would be born because of this drug. This drug is very necessary to very many people, it's used in cancer, it's used in a group of diseases, but that doesn't absolve the responsibility of us in animal experiments to make sure that these experiments are only those that are absolutely necessary for human health and survival. For example, rabbits are strapped down and new shampoos are tested by dropping into their eyes chemicals which cause immense pain, the animal is strapped, there is no anaesthetic. A whole range of cosmetics, of skin lotions, of minor medicines, of the beauty industry, a whole proliferating commercial enterprise which this Act of a hundred years ago could not possibly have anticipated, is now being called into existence and millions of animals for no good reason whatsoever are subject to quite callous torture; and I think certainly the Act needs the very closest attention so that the meaningless and obscene cruelties in the name of profit can be removed and that is not to say that I don't think, alas, that some animal experimentation is not necessary, but certainly a review of the Act.'

That programme marked the first appearance of our new secretary, Sue Harris – in her home town of Hereford. She had the sunniest disposition I have ever come across; it was impossible to be moody or bad-tempered in her presence and everyone loved her. Tragically, she died from cancer at the age of twenty-six.

(DJ: *It's often easy, because of the sadness of such a tragedy when a young person dies, to imagine that they possessed some extra special quality, but in the case of Sue Harris, from the moment she joined us, it was obvious that she* was *special. We were all captivated by her. She was rosy cheeked, slim-waisted, bright eyed and in the first flush of the excitement of love, marriage, the setting-up of a new home and taking on us at the same time. She had a very slight Hereford accent, and referred to* Any Questions? *as 'the progrum'. I see her sweet smile and her cheeky face whenever her name is mentioned, and the 'progrum' will never be the same without her.*)

1976/77

In the summer recess of 1976 I went to America. Before I left, I did the usual recce of future locations. One of them was Basingstoke, where we had been invited by the London Street United Reformed Church as part of their festival. In due course I fixed up the team. It included Enoch Powell.

When I returned to the office at the end of October, I heard there was trouble at Basingstoke. I telephoned the church people and was told that, after the team had been announced in the local Press, an organization in Basingstoke stated that Enoch Powell would not be permitted to speak in the town. The church people were not unduly concerned. They were confident that none of the tickets would get into the hands of anyone likely to cause a disturbance and in any case their stewards would be able to handle any situation which might arise.

But then the police contacted me. They had information that some of the tickets had indeed got into the hands of people who would try to prevent Enoch Powell speaking. They suggested that I might consider changing the venue – or the team. My normally quiescent personality flared up. I was *not* going to change the team. But what about the location? After all, the church festival people were our hosts, their church might be at risk. It must be their decision.

Unlike our hosts at Cowley, the church stood firm. They were anxious for *Any Questions?* to be included in their festival. They thought the police were being alarmist.

So there we left it. I notified the team that we might run into trouble, and I discussed with our engineers whether it would be a good idea to fit each member of the team with a personal microphone so that less extraneous noise would be picked up – if there was any extraneous noise. They decided that our usual microphones, placed on the tables in front of the team, were sufficiently directional – that they largely picked up sound from the direction in which they were pointing. There was one microphone for each member, plus one for David, one for Sue to hold for the questioners, live only at the moment they put their question, and one on the stage facing the audience as an effects microphone which could be switched off if necessary. According to the engineers, we should be able to carry on even if all hell broke loose.

I set out for Basingstoke on 12 November in some trepidation but still far from sure that anything was really going to happen. As soon as I arrived, I knew for certain that something *was* going to happen. In the lobby of the hotel where we were meeting I came across a BBC television film crew. They had come down after a tip-off. The threats were undoubtedly going to be fulfilled. I begged the crew not to show themselves in the church until any demonstrations started – I felt if they were visible from the start of the broadcast, they would trigger off trouble which otherwise might not occur.

There was no particular tension among the team – the others were the Labour MP Judith Hart, Lord Robens and the Bishop of Winchester – over drinks and dinner, but after I had left to go to the church to choose the questions, they had visitors.

(DJ: *Two young men came into the dining-room followed by two high-ranking police officers who threw them out, but not before Enoch Powell had spoken to them. He answered their questions and every reply seemed far more sensible than the questions warranted. It was amazing that he could reply to their shouts so calmly and not altogether without relish.*)

Outside, on the short walk to the church, Sue Harris and I had to pass through a large, though orderly and good-humoured, crowd of student demonstrators. Then, when we entered the ante-room which had been set aside for us to sort the questions, we had a shock. It was full of uniformed policemen. There must have been about fifty of them. I was told they would only show themselves if there was violence. I didn't know whether to find this reassuring or not.

I did my usual warm-up, with somewhat less concentration than usual, to an ominously quiet audience. David and the team arrived, and the broadcast began.

The first question was about Mr Powell's recent statement of support for the continuance of the Labour Government. Enoch Powell spoke. Then Judith Hart. Then David called on Lord Robens and at that point a man stood up in the middle of a pew near the back and called on Judith Hart to leave the platform and join the demonstrators outside (who were by now giving tongue – presumably they were listening to the proceedings on portable radios).

Judith Hart replied that, if there were questions concerning racialism, she would rather be there to argue with Mr Powell so that listeners could hear the other side. It was important to preserve free speech. The heckler at the back was not satisfied. The chanting outside continued. And when Lord Robens tried to answer the original question, other demonstrators inside the church got to their feet and started shouting. To be near the receiving end of the sheer hatred in those hoarse, raucous voices was a very unpleasant experience. 'Don't do your own cause such damage!' called out Judith Hart. David asked the Bishop to say some soothing words, after which the noise abated somewhat, and Lord Robens was able to give his reply to the question and we moved on to the next – one about the proposed amendments to the marriage service.

The Bishop spoke first and, while he was speaking, there was the sound of tinkling glass as a stone came through one of the windows. David asked the Bishop to comment on that, and he did, but by now the noise had resumed, louder than before, there was shouting from different parts of the church and drumming of feet. The demonstration was well organized and very effective.

At this point, I decided that it was impossible to continue, now that people's safety seemed to be endangered (those who organized the demonstration afterwards denied responsibility for the stone-throwing). I also thought listeners at home would be unable to hear the team. (In fact, the microphones picked up remarkably little of what appeared to be an overwhelming racket in the church.)

By this time the television crew had hurried in and were busy filming the scene. They had kept out of sight until the demonstration started in earnest. I discreetly left the stage and went to a room behind, where our engineers were operating beside a very large window. They reported that stones had been rattling against it and they didn't argue when I said we must take the programme off the air.

After my departure from the scene, David rightly decided not to leave the team exposed and led them off into the ante-room, the one with all the police in it. The forces of law and order were still maintaining a low profile. The team, David and I reviewed the situation. The politicians, accustomed to the hustings, were calm, Enoch Powell calmest of all.

The minutes passed. I went back into the church. The stewards had ejected all the demonstrators. So David led the team back on to the stage, and I sent a message through to the announcer.

Very soon we were on the air again. The demonstrators outside must have heard it on their radios, because they started chanting again, rather half heartedly. But this time there were no demonstrators inside and so we were able to continue fairly normally. I calculated how long we had been off the air and therefore how much more we would need to record in order to have a full programme for the repeat.

Needless to say, I did not in any way edit the earlier part, so listeners, intrigued by the coverage on the television news that night and in the national Press the following morning, were able to hear for themselves exactly what had happened. It did get the programme a tremendous amount of publicity and a very large listening audience on Saturday.

(DJ: *It was one of the saddest occasions in the whole of my broadcasting career. I couldn't believe that in a church, in a town in Britain, you could see ordinary people who had come to their favourite programme, having to sit there with fear in their eyes.*)

The following May I wrote to Enoch Powell to offer him another *Any Questions?* date. With inadvisable jocularity, I excused the delay by using some such phrase as 'I have been looking for somewhere where I could guarantee your safety (not to mention mine!)'. It was clearly a matter upon which he was sensitive, as I might have guessed had I recalled his remarks at Filey about Birmingham University's withdrawal of their invitation to him to speak there. He pointed out in his reply that he had been taking part in the programme on average three times a year without any incident of the kind which had interrupted the programme at Basingstoke. 'It was, in fact, not merely exceptional but unique; and I cannot accept the implication of your letter that your safety or mine would be at risk at any of the normal venues of this programme,' he wrote.

In my reply I elaborated on the problems as they appeared to me and offered two dates later in the year but he did not feel able to accept them or the opinion that 'secure premises', as I termed them, were necessary for him to take part in the programme. The Press started to be interested and asked me whether he had been banned from the programme as a result of the incidents at Basingstoke.

In the event, he did not appear in the programme again until after I had ceased to be the producer.

One result of the publicity over the Basingstoke affair was to deter me from taking the programme to Northern Ireland again. We hadn't been there since November 1969 when, although the troubles had started, there hadn't been much danger of the programme being interrupted, and I had been under pressure for some time to return there, but had resisted on two main grounds.

First, it seemed rash to announce in advance precisely where we were going and to invite applications for tickets from all and sundry; yet if we didn't do this, and broadcast almost surreptitiously from the BBC Belfast studio with a hand-picked audience, it would hardly serve the purpose of our going, namely to demonstrate that life in the Province was much more normal than the rest of the UK believed. Second, the team. If we reflected the four main political/religious strands in the Province we should end up with a team, inexperienced in *Any Questions?* terms, which would be primarily geared to discuss a question about Northern Ireland. On the other hand, if we imported a team from England, we could get a normal *Any Questions?* but not one which could adequately reflect the Northern Ireland scene, and if we weren't able to do that, what was the point of going? I further cited the attitude of one or two well-known broadcasters who were reluctant to go to Northern Ireland, even for recorded programmes in unannounced places, and I thought it might be difficult to assemble a strong enough team of visitors.

However, the pressure intensified, and on 29 April 1977, we went to the new university at Coleraine. We didn't make any advance announcement about it; David didn't draw attention to it the previous week. An audience was assembled without much publicity. There were security checks, a search for bombs beforehand, but the broadcast itself, and indeed the whole visit, was little more alarming than a visit to Cornwall. The team, in the end, were all brought over from England, though one of them, John Cole, was an Ulsterman, and the others were all familiar with the situation in Northern Ireland.

Our visit coincided with the large-scale Protestant strike directed against the power-sharing agreement. It was the leading item on the news that evening – we could hardly have gone at a time when Northern Ireland was more in the centre of attention, and I had no hesitation in selecting a question on the subject to open the programme. It seemed to me that it would have been unrealistic to have begun, instead, with a question on the by-election results in England. If there is one absolutely obvious question it always seems to me better to get into it right away otherwise the team's and the listeners' thoughts are only half with the topic under discussion, while they wait impatiently for the expected one to appear. There was criticism afterwards. It is an arguable matter, like which card you lead at bridge. I am always ready to admit I am wrong, but I don't think I was on this occasion.

(DJ: *I disagree. I have never thought you should lead with the obvious. You should have it number three. Don't get into a fixed pattern, but there should be a little time for the team to get warmed up, and I don't think they are ready for the big stuff until about question number 3.*)

I noticed with some interest that when, on a recent visit to Northern Ireland, there was a very topical question on the hunger strike by Bobby Sands, my successor placed it first.

(DJ: *This time we wanted to get it out of the way; it was such an explosive issue, we couldn't relax until it had been dealt with.*)

As well as picking a suitable date for our Northern Ireland broadcast, I was very much on form during the 1976/77 series in the way of having the right man in the team in the right week. We had David Steel with us just at the time when the Lib-Lab pact was under discussion and beginning to hit the headlines – in fact, he told me that when the media were after him for a statement he simply told them to listen to *Any Questions?*. We had Donald Trelford, editor of the *Observer*, with us the week the paper was taken over by an American oil company, and Peter Jay the week his appointment as Ambassador to the United States was announced.

When David Steel was in the team and everyone was wondering whether or not there was going to be a Lib-Lab pact, the question was: 'Should other parties combine with the Conservatives in a vote of no confidence in the Government, thus bringing about a General Election?'

The Liberal Leader said: 'The one thing we cannot do as a country is stagger on with a lame duck government possibly being defeated on issue to issue because this undermines both national confidence and confidence internationally in us and therefore I think the question is not really one for the Liberal Party, it is one for the Government and it's one for the Labour Party. They have a clear option. They must either now decide that they will govern in the national interest, that they will not pretend that the Labour Party Manifesto for which only 28 per cent of the electorate voted in 1974 is the Bible and everything must depend on that; that they will not pretend that the all-powerful organs of opinion in this country are the Labour Party National Executive or indeed a Labour Party Conference or the leaders of the TUC, but that what matters is what is parliamentary opinion according to the wishes of the people. Now if they take that view I believe it is possible to construct a programme which will enable the Government to continue in office, not on the Labour programme but on a programme in the national interest. If they are not willing to accept that, then let them say so clearly and let the people have an opportunity to elect a House of Commons which may make them change their mind.'

In June, the Queen's Silver Jubilee was celebrated, and we had a question about it on two consecutive weeks. A somewhat jaundiced note was sounded the second week when we were at Ilkley in Yorkshire; the team included Michael Parkinson, the writer, Fay Weldon, and Lord Willis.

PARKINSON: I don't think a lot of it was about bowing to, or celebrating Royalty or anything like that. It was just people letting their hair down and having a good time.

WELDON: It was a fairly empty celebration, really. It was the echo of something past, of majesty and empire and the times when a procession went down the Mall because we'd conquered some wretched nation which was going to make us richer.

WILLIS: I was bowled over by it. I felt that for the first time after ten, fifteen dreary years, in which we've been knocking ourselves silly in self-criticism, a kind of self-destructive spirit seemed to have swept over the British people; for the first time we lifted our heads above this morass and saw ourselves as a whole nation once again. Whether it had anything to do with Royalty, I don't know. But if I had had a Union Jack last Monday, I would have put it out – not necessarily for the Queen, but for the nation.

I couldn't help feeling that it had been rather inept not to have assembled a more fervently pro-monarchy team for this particular week.

My morale was not lifted by the fact that Ted Willis criticized the choice of one of the questions, in which the panel were asked how they would achieve the safe release of the hostages then being held by South Moluccans in Holland. Ted said, 'I don't think that this is a question that we should deal with at such a meeting. If you'll forgive my saying so, I think it's an irresponsible question. I don't see there's any way in which we can sit up here as a panel and advise the Dutch Government. Just imagine that this programme, now going out live, could possibly be heard by the hostages on that train and by the teachers in that school. There they have been, penned up on that train in impossible sanitary conditions, with tommy guns pointed at them all the time, wondering whether they're ever going to join their wives and so on. How would they feel if they heard that somewhere up in Yorkshire, a panel of distinguished or undistinguished people and an audience of nice people were discussing their problem in this way? I know that if I were one of them, I'd go beserk!'

I think Ted was right. One can have a purely general discussion about how to combat the taking of hostages by terrorists, as we have done on several occasions, but not a specific question while a group of hostages are actually under threat, and nobody knows whether they will still be alive by the time the programme is repeated.

A few months later I was also criticized, probably justifiably, for accepting a question arising out of a tragic case in which a young girl, dreadfully injured in an assault, had only been kept alive by a life-support machine which had finally been switched off after tests for the existence of life had proved negative.

(DJ: *I totally disagree on both points. I feel that* Any Questions? *has a duty to discuss topical issues, no matter how sensitive they may be. There was no reason, in my view, why Ted Willis should have complained, but if he thought as he did, he was entitled to his own opinion. When else are we going to discuss such questions? We aren't likely to discuss life-support machines unless they happen to be in the news. Every story can be harmful to someone, and of course one must bear listeners' reactions in mind. When we discussed euthanasia, for example, I tried to put old people's minds at rest by making it clear that there were no proposals to bring in new legislation about it.*)

The 1976/77 series seems to me now to have been up to standard. But I had the impression that the new Controller of Radio 4, Ian McIntyre, who had taken over in 1976 when I was away in America, did not have quite the same feeling for *Any Questions?* that Tony Whitby had had. At any rate, he removed the Monday morning second repeat of *Any Questions?* and the Friday afternoon repeat of *Any Answers*. But I never hesitated to seek his advice. In April 1977, Dr A.L. Rowse had quoted Ernest Bevin's comment 'The buggers won't work' and bearing in mind Tony Whitby's views on the words uttered by Marghanita Laski, I rang Ian on Saturday morning to see if he thought this ought to be cut out of the repeat. But times had changed. 'Leave it in,' he said firmly.

Autumn 1977

I began the 1977/78 series with no premonition. If I thought about it at all, I assumed that I would continue producing *Any Questions?* until I retired from the BBC in August 1980, at the statutory retiring age of sixty.

However, on 11 October a casual hint was dropped to me over coffee in the canteen that there was a feeling in London that I had been producing *Any Questions?* too long. I didn't argue. And precisely seventeen days later I produced *Any Questions?* for the last time. But at no stage did it occur to me that my departure was the one magic ingredient which guaranteed an improvement in the programme. And had I known then that I should be retiring prematurely from the BBC in eighteen months' time, I think I might have tried to hang on.

It is, after all, the pleasantest job in the BBC.